BOUTELL'S HERALDRY

PLATE I

THE ROYAL ARMS

*(Reproduced by permission of
The Controller, Her Majesty's Stationery Office)*

Boutell's
HERALDRY

Revised by
J. P. BROOKE-LITTLE, M.V.O., M.A., F.S.A., F.H.S.
Norroy and Ulster King of Arms

With 28 Plates in Colour
and numerous text figures

FREDERICK WARNE
LONDON AND NEW YORK

FIRST PUBLISHED 1950
REVISED EDITIONS 1954, 1958, 1963, 1966, 1970, 1973, 1978, 1983
REVISED EDITION 1983 PUBLISHED BY
FREDERICK WARNE (PUBLISHERS) LTD, LONDON
COPYRIGHT © 1983 FREDERICK WARNE (PUBLISHERS) LTD
LIBRARY OF CONGRESS CATALOGUE CARD NO. 73–75030

This edition is dedicated to the memory of
Wilfrid Scott-Giles
Fitzalan Pursuivant of Arms Extraordinary
Sometime editor of this work

An elegant and prolific writer; a diverting
and inspired versifier; a competent artist
and an urbane speaker; but above all a
dear and generous friend, companion and host.

ISBN 0 7232 3093 5

PRINTED IN GREAT BRITAIN BY
BUTLER & TANNER LTD, FROME AND LONDON

0129·583

FOREWORD TO 1970 EDITION

IT IS sad to reflect that even today there is still a tendency to regard the study of coats of arms, popularly known as heraldry, as a fascinating but dead science.

In fact, it is very much a living thing, constantly changing and ever reflecting the social habits and artistic canons of the age. It has always been the aim of the various editors of *Boutell* to try and keep the book up to date and so present heraldry as it really is, alive, diverse and frequently capricious. Perhaps that is why the publishers constantly and gratifyingly demand new and revised editions at shorter and shorter intervals.

The first paragraph of the first edition of *The Manual of Heraldry* by the Reverend Charles Boutell, published in 1863, states: "It is the aim of this Volume to enquire into the true character and right office of Heraldry, and to describe and illustrate its general condition as it is in use amongst ourselves." Subsequent editors of Boutell's work have tried to live up to this excellent criterion which was epitomized in the new title given to the second edition of of the *Manual*, namely *Heraldry, Historical and Popular*. Indeed, the first edition proved so popular that in the preface to the second edition, Boutell wrote with obvious pleasure: "My surprise . . . has been as great as my gratification, at having found myself called upon by my publishers, before my First Edition had been published two months, to prepare for them a Second Edition with all possible speed." The third edition appeared in 1864. The present editor can vouch for the fact that to produce three editions, with fairly copious amendments, within two years is no mean task.

The other book on heraldry, for which Boutell is noted, is his *English Heraldry*. Compared with his first book, this one is, in the author's words, "a much shorter essay, more decidedly elementary in its aim and character and yet as far as possible within its limits complete." The first edition was published by Cassell, Petter and Galpin in 1867, followed by another edition in 1871. It was revised in 1892 by the Reverend S. T. Aveling and again in 1907 by A. C. Fox-Davies, this edition being published by Reeves and Turner.

Although, in his preface to the tenth edition, Fox-Davies was careful to disassociate himself from some of Boutell's opinions, he did not intrude his own, rather forceful sentiments. As he explained in his preface: "I hold that it is no part of an editor's duty to air his own opinions under the protection or repute of another's name, and herein I have inserted nothing for which my own opinion is the only authority."

In 1931 V. Wheeler-Holohan produced a book entitled *Boutell's Manual of Heraldry* for which he drew on both of Boutell's books, but virtually rewrote *Boutell* stressing the popular rather than the historical. He also re-illustrated the book discarding most of the original illustrations, the best of which were wood engravings by B. R. Utting. He also added thirty-two colour plates.

It was in the year 1950 that the present publishers, who also published Wheeler-Holohan's edition, produced *Boutell's Heraldry* edited by C. W. Scott-Giles, now Fitzalan Pursuivant Extraordinary. Scott-Giles faced the task of re-editing *Boutell* realistically. He took the best of the many editions of *Boutell* and produced a text-book on heraldry which reflected not the romantic, neo-medieval approach of Boutell, but the emancipated approach of the post-war generation of armorists. Boutell, along with Nicholas, Courthope, Seton, Planché, and others, was one of the pioneers of the new scholarly, romantic school of heraldic thought, which, as in most of the other arts, revitalized the second half of the 19th century.

But, to be of lasting value, the ideas of these worthy Victorians needed to be applied to the rapidly changing social scene; people had to be educated to see heraldry in its true context and not as that "most degenerate substitute for a noble Science" that so distressed Boutell. Fortunately, the 20th century has not lacked good heralds, artists and writers, so that today heraldry has probably never been more widely used and enjoyed.

Amongst those who have popularized (in the best sense of that word) heraldry, the name of Wilfred Scott-Giles is pre-eminent, and his editions of *Boutell's Heraldry* have been remarkably successful. Not only did he augment the illustrations with his own very competent drawings, but he gave to *Boutell* a new unity and cohesion. Three editions appeared under his editorship, before he invited me, with the publishers' approval, to join him in producing a further revised edition. Together, we produced the 1963 and 1966 editions, in each case revising the text where revision was needed, expanding certain sections and keeping the book up to date. It had always been understood between us that my position was that of a coadjutor with right of succession and, after the 1966 edition, Scott-Giles said that he wished to hand over the editorship to me. So, with the trepidation that is becoming to one who has inherited so august a mantle, I offer this new and revised edition.

In his foreword to the 1950 edition, Scott-Giles referred to the medley of styles in the illustrations. Some are reproductions of Utting's original wood cuts, many are Wheeler-Holohan's, others are Scott-Giles's. To these has been added work by Geoffrey Mussett, a Herald Painter at the College of Arms, and in this edition there are half a dozen new drawings by Alison Urwick, made under the direction of Norman Manwaring, also a Herald Painter at the College. I agree with Scott-Giles that the resultant diversity of style is itself interesting and it will be my policy, in the happy event of being invited to edit any further editions, to ask other noted heraldic artists to contribute to the *pot-pourri*.

Also in his foreword, Scott-Giles acknowledged his indebtedness to the late Sir John Heaton-Armstrong, Clarenceux King of Arms, and to Sir Anthony Wagner, Garter King of Arms. I should like this acknowledgement to stand because it was through his friends at the College of Arms that Scott-Giles was able to check so much of the text of *Boutell* against the official records.   I myself, being free of the College records, have, naturally, referred to them in the cause of accuracy, but I must make it clear that, whilst I sincerely hope that this edition is accurate, it is not authoritative in any official sense.

In conclusion, I should like to thank fellow members of The Heraldry Society who have assisted me with their observations and so enabled me to make many valuable alterations.   I hope that they will continue to aid me in this way, so that *Boutell's Heraldry* may continue to be a valued friend and guide to students of armory.

Heyford House, 1970   J. P. Brooke-Little
                                                     Richmond

FOREWORD TO REVISED EDITION

THIS FOREWORD supersedes that to the 1978 edition, but I have retained that to the 1970 edition, as it gives the bibliographical history of this book.

In the often quoted words of Chief Justice Crewe "Time hath his revolutions; there must be a period and an end to all temporal things, *finis rerum*". Since the last edition time has claimed my old friend and co-editor of two editions of *Boutell*, Wilfrid Scott-Giles, Fitzalan Pursuivant Extraordinary, who died in February 1982. The world, and particularly the world of armory, will be the poorer for his passing. Probably no one person has ever done so much to popularise the study of heraldry. As with everything he undertook, his approach to the subject he loved was scholarly, precise, urbane, flecked with humour and intellectually honest.

Mention is made in Chapter XX of the effects of the Local Government Act 1972. In the main the text of the book has not been altered to show whether arms depicted or quoted as belonging to a local authority refer to a pre- or post-1972 authority. To do this would involve rewriting considerable portions of this book to no real purpose, as the arms of obsolete authorities are historic and still make interesting heraldic examples. The same is true of the arms of certain colonies and Commonwealth countries.

As in previous editions certain minor alterations have been made; wherever possible the text has been brought up to date; new developments are detailed in Chapter XXVI and the critical bibliography has been augmented.

Finally, a new Chapter (XXV) on "How to Use Arms" has been added to help answer questions frequently put to me and also, I am sure, to my brother officers.

Heyford House, 1982   J. P. Brooke-Little
                                           Norroy and Ulster

LIST OF COLOUR PLATES

CONTENTS

ix

1. Arms attributed to EDWARD THE CONFESSOR,
in Westminster Abbey

CHAPTER I

THE BEGINNING AND GROWTH OF HERALDRY

STRANGE to the modern mind is the sentiment which Sir Walter Scott put into the mouth of Di Vernon: "What! Is it possible? not know the figures of Heraldry! Of what could your father be thinking?" In an age when education is directed to subjects of more obvious utility, the "gentle science" cannot expect to find a place, unless some enlightened art- or history-master shall introduce it to likely students as something worth attention in a leisure hour. Yet heraldry remains decidedly popular. Of those who are tempted to dip into it, enough are captivated by its interest and charm to form a small band of serious students, while many acquire a sufficient knowledge to understand and appreciate the armorial insignia they see around them. Furthermore, thousands of people who have never opened a book on heraldry can none the less enjoy its decorative display, and are genuinely interested when its meaning and history are pointed out.

In its widest sense, heraldry means all the duties of a herald. In the Middle Ages, these included the proclamation and conduct of tournaments, the carrying of messages between princes and armies, and the marshalling of ceremonies. To perform these functions, the herald had to be able to recognize men by the devices on their shields and pennons—their cognizances. He became the acknowledged authority on such insignia, and its hereditary character led him into the field of genealogy. Changing times robbed the heralds of their original duties, except for occasional assistance at state ceremonies, but their armorial and genealogical functions remained, and these are today their chief activities. Thus heraldry has acquired a limited meaning as the art and technique of insignia associated with defensive armour, especially the shield. This art is also called armory, and its insignia are known as armorial bearings.

Armory, or heraldry, was in its inception mainly a practical matter. It originated in the devices used to distinguish the armoured warriors in tournament and war, and also placed on seals as marks of identity. From the first, there was a symbolic and decorative element in many of these devices, but the utilitarian motive predominated. In the course of centuries this position has been reversed. Modern heraldry is primarily symbolic and decorative, and although it is still used on seals and in other ways, it is seldom solely relied upon to express identity.

While the forms of heraldry are associated with the age of chivalry, its spirit has proved to be capable of change to suit the needs of successive centuries. Heraldry has therefore survived, long after its original purpose has passed, into an age when the shields and helms of ancient knighthood have become museum pieces. Not only to different times, but also to different people it appeals in various ways. The scholar values it for its historical and antiquarian interest; the artist and architect for its decorative qualities; the man of ancient family for the tradition it enshrines; the new-made armiger for the attainment it represents. Its appeal is not limited to those who themselves possess armorial bearings. We have all a share in national insignia, and in the arms of our county, city or town; and many of us hold in esteem the shield of some college, school or society. Thus heraldry symbolizes many loyalties which interlock to form the social structure. It has long since ceased to be the prerogative of a class, and only in its debased periods was it a matter of snobbery. And here let me correct the influence of Gray's line about " the boast of heraldry." True heraldry does not boast—it aspires. For some, indeed, it possesses a spiritual value.

In various ways, therefore, heraldry appeals to the mind. To some extent it must always have done so. Those princes and knights who, in the 12th century, adopted devices for the purposes of distinction, were not always content with a mere meaningless arrangement of form and colour (though many shields of this character are found); they often showed imagination in their choice. Some took a lion or other beast characterizing strength or valour; some took a religious symbol; and many placed on their shields figures forming a play on their names. Symbolism of a rudimentary kind was present in early heraldry, and in this respect there is a link between it and the insignia which appeared on shields and banners in previous periods of history.

At pre-heraldic insignia we need only glance. At all times, and in all parts of the world, men have used symbols to focus ideas and senti-ment and express them in visual form. Warriors, and particularly leaders, have been accustomed to display such symbols on shields and standards. We have the evidence of their art that the Ancient Greeks bore on their round shields a wide variety of figures, such as lions, horses, dogs, boars, fish, birds, and objects of many kinds. Aeschylus (500 B.C.) records the emblems on the shields of the warriors who attacked Thebes. The legions and cohorts of Rome had their insignia. Virgil speaks of *insigne paternum* on the shield of Aventinus. There are traces of devices—probably tribal rather than personal—among the Teutonic peoples. Finally, there is the famous Bayeux Tapestry, with its record of shields and banners of both Normans and Saxons, decorated with beasts, birds, crosses and other forms.

These insignia of antiquity are to be regarded as the predecessors and not as the ancestors of medieval heraldry. Attempts have been made to establish a link between them. It is true that some of the emblems found in ancient symbolism have survived to take their place as devices in heraldry. For example, the British tribal emblem of a dragon became a supporter of the Royal Arms in Tudor times and is still the badge of Wales; and the fleur-de-lis was a symbol of royalty in France long before the heraldic shield of the French kings was evolved. But continuity in certain devices does not imply the lineal descent of heraldry as a whole from the symbolism of earlier times. The heraldry which began to appear in the early part of the 12th century, while possessing something in common with earlier insignia, so far differed from them in purpose and practice as to form a new system. In more remote times personal insignia may sometimes have been used to establish identity, and may sometimes have passed from father to son. In the 12th century it became purposefully distinctive and consistently hereditary. There came into being a system, where formerly there had been haphazard (though symbolic) decoration, and it is from the emergence of this system that we date the beginning of heraldry.

A modern herald has defined " true heraldry . . . as the systematic use of hereditary devices centred on the shield." [1]　The earliest known decorated shield which satisfies this definition is that which Henry I of England gave his son-in-law, Geoffrey of Anjou, when he knighted him in 1127. This was described by John of Marmoutier, Geoffrey's biographer, as *clipeus leunculos aureos ymaginarios habens*—a shield figured with little gold lions ; and an enamelled plate, formerly on Geoffrey's tomb, depicts him with a blue shield bearing gold lions, and another lion on his conical blue cap (2). The shield is curved, and little more than half of it is visible ; this portion contains four lions, and we may assume that two (or perhaps three) more appeared on the hidden part of the shield. Six gold lions on blue became the arms of Geoffrey's grandson, William Longespée, Earl of Salisbury (illegitimate son of Henry II), and his descendants (3).

Thus, so far as our records show, true heraldry began in the second quarter of the 12th century. It appeared almost simultaneously in several countries of western Europe. It is a reasonable conjecture that the rapid spread of the new idea was due to some exceptional opportunity for intercourse between warriors of different lands, and writers on heraldry have naturally seen this in the gathering together of the knighthood of many countries in the Crusades. But the earliest known instance of an heraldic shield occurs more than 25 years after the First Crusade, and several others are found before the resumption of military operations in the Second Crusade (1147–49). For example, the chevrons of De Clare (7) appear on a seal of Gilbert, Earl of Hertford, in use between 1138 and 1146.

[1] A. R. Wagner, Richmond Herald : *Heralds and Heraldry in the Middle Ages.*

Plate II

SOME ANCIENT SHIELDS OF ARMS

1. SCROPE. Azure, a bend or. (*p.* 106)

2. MONTAGU (or Argent, three lozenges cojoined in fess
   MONTACUTE). gules.

3. BARDOLF. Azure, three cinquefoils or. (*p.* 133)

4. BERKELEY. Gules, semé of crosslets formy, a chevron
   argent. (*p.* 110)

5. WILLOUGHBY. Or, fretty azure.

6. LE STRANGE. Argent, two lions passant in pale gules.
   (*p.* 109)

7. DE LA RIVER. Azure, two bars dancetty or. (*p.* 9)

8. PAULET. Sable, three swords pilewise proper, pomels
   and hilts gold. (Swords of St. Paul, in
   allusion to the name.)

9. NEVILLE. Gules, a saltire argent. (*p.* 116)

10. COURTENAY. Or, three torteaux, a label of three points
    azure. (*p.* 114)

11. THE MARSHAL Per pale or and vert, a lion rampant gules.
    OF ENGLAND
    (*ancient arms*).

12. CLIFFORD. Checky or and azure, a fess gules.

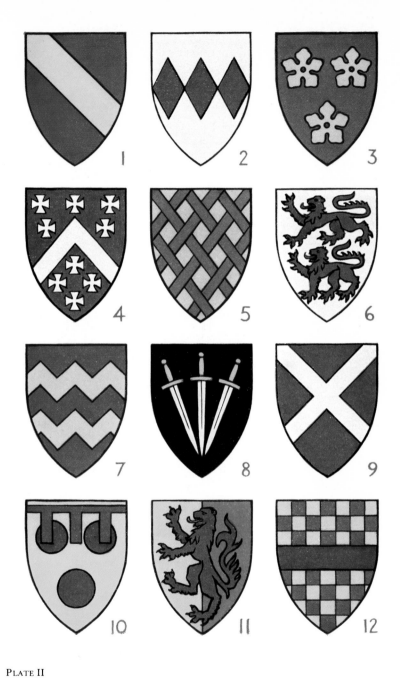

Plate II

SOME ANCIENT SHIELDS OF ARMS

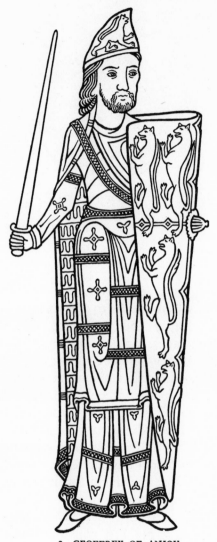

2. GEOFFREY OF ANJOU

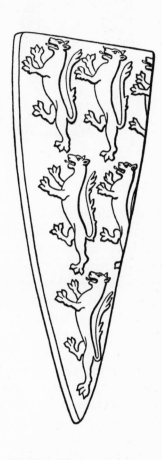

3. Shield of WILLIAM LONGESPÉE,
EARL OF SALISBURY

However great was the impulse the Crusades must have given to
the development of heraldry, we must consider whether there was not
some other factor to account for its inception. And there were, in
fact, other military assemblies which drew together knights from
various countries, and were popular in the first half of the 12th century,

5. Seal of THURSTAN

4. Seal of MAUGER LE VAVASSOUR

namely tournaments. These, equally with actual warfare, may be supposed to have provided conditions favourable to the origin of heraldry. They were occasions for display and pageantry, and it would be natural for leaders of opposed parties, and also for individual participants, in these sporting events, to adopt some device for the occasion, and thereafter consistently to use insignia which their prowess in the lists had made well-known. The fashion of personal devices, originating in tournaments, would naturally spread through the gathering of knights in the Holy Wars. It may have received a further impetus from the introduction of the closed helm, which rendered a fully-armed man recognizable only by something distinctive about his accoutrements, so that a device painted on the shield for decorative effect became of practical value as a " cognizance."

It was a matter of natural sentiment for a man to use, in campaign and tourney, the shield-device which his father had worthily borne, and perhaps made famous. This tendency towards the hereditary character of such cognizances was strongly reinforced by another factor. As the 12th century advanced, it became a growing custom for a man of the knightly class to display on his seal a little equestrian figure of himself in full armour, and naturally the cognizance he actually used was reproduced on the shield (and sometimes on the lance-pennon) borne by the figure in the seal. Often the shield alone, with its distinctive device, appeared on the seal which a man used for his civil transactions (4 and 5); in effect, his heraldic shield became his signature. Apart from sentiment, therefore, it was a matter of practical convenience for a son, on inheriting his father's lands and responsibilities, to continue to use the seal-device which men had learned to associate with the particular lordship or fief which he held. Thus, through both civil and military usage, personal insignia became hereditary

6. Seal of THOMAS DE BEAUCHAMP, 3rd EARL OF WARWICK, 1344 (see no. 425)

and truly heraldic, and also closely associated with feudal tenure and the class that held the land by military service.

Effigies on seals reflected the development of heraldry; for example, that of the third Beauchamp Earl of Warwick (6) shows his arms on shield, surcoat and horse bardings.

By the end of the 12th century heraldry was firmly established as a system, and in the 13th century it became so general and well-developed that it acquired the rules and terminology which are the basis of its present laws and language. Professional heralds who,

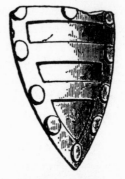

7. DE CLARE   8. Shield at Whitworth   9. GREY

through the conduct of tournaments, became specialists in armorial matters, now began the compilation of the Rolls of Arms which give us much information about early heraldry.

Shields of arms were at first very simple. A few consisted merely of some characteristic treatment of the entire surface, such as the ermine shield of Brittany. Some were parti-coloured, like the silver and red shield of Waldegrave (59a), and an ancient banner of the Earl of Leicester, also silver and red but with an indented line dividing the two halves. Clearly the number of separate and distinct shields of arms which could be produced in this way was very limited.

Some early heraldic shields were simply painted with one or more bands of colour—vertical, horizontal or diagonal—for example the arms of Grey, barry silver and blue (9). In some cases these may have resulted from bands of metal laid across or bordering the shield to strengthen it : when painted a different colour from the wooden surface, these bands would constitute simple arms of a geometrical pattern. But we need not assume that such arms were in all cases produced under the influence of the shield's structural formation. A man wishing to make his shield distinctive would readily think of painting a band of colour across it, without there necessarily being some metal clamp to suggest the idea to him. These bands of colour were later termed ordinaries, and as heraldry developed they were variously treated, and were used in conjunction with other figures.

Some shields had a central boss with decorative metal-work radiating from it, and this gave rise to the figure termed an escarbuncle (225), and possibly also to some forms of the heraldic cross.

Very soon, representations of beasts, birds, fishes, flowers, and common objects of various kinds began to make their appearance as devices on shields. As we have seen, the lion, which was probably associated with royalty in England before the emergence of true heraldry, is the earliest device known to have appeared on a shield of arms. It is found in the arms of several persons descended from or connected by marriage with the Plantagenet kings, but it was not exclusively a royal emblem, and at an early date it appeared on the shields of men not apparently connected with the royal house.

In the choice of arms, men followed their own fancies, and in many cases we have no clue to what led to the adoption of a particular device, but it is clear that the figures in very many early shields were selected because they illustrated, or played upon, the name of the bearer, thus indicating his identity in a way which would be easily understood and remembered. So in the time of Henry III we find De Lucy bearing three lucies (the fish now called pike—198); Corbett, two *corbeaux*; and De Swyneburne, *trois testes de senglier*—three swines' heads. This practice was so common that, in considering the origin of an ancient shield of arms, the possibility of its being allusive to the name (or sometimes to the office or fief) of its bearer should always be examined. The connection is often difficult to trace, because on the one hand the name may have changed its form, and on the other, the word for the device, on which the allusive quality of the arms depended, may have become obsolete. For example, the allusion in the arms of Burdon, *Gules, three pilgrims staves argent* (440), is apparent only when we recall that a pilgrim's stave was termed a bourdon. Some imagination is needed to see the connection between name and arms in the case of De la River, *Azure, two bars dancetty or* (suggesting sunlight on rippling water—Plate II, 7); and the ploughshares of Leversedge, which lever the sedge.

Since arms were primarily a means of identification, they necessarily aimed at being absolutely distinctive. At the same time there was a natural tendency for men allied by blood or feudal ties to bear similar arms, though with sufficient difference to prevent confusion between them. Furthermore, in the early days of heraldry, there was a likelihood of too close a similarity occurring between the arms of men in no way connected, due merely to the fact that a comparatively few devices and figures were in frequent use. " Differencing " of arms therefore became necessary not only to distinguish the shield of a cadet from that of the head of the family, and of a vassal from that of his feudal chief, but also to prevent identity between the arms of strangers who happened to have selected the same simple combination of form and colour. This differencing led to the introduction of new forms, devices, and treatment of line and colour, and heraldry was rapidly enriched through the practical necessity of its own development. By the marshalling of two or more coats of arms on one shield, men indicated their marriage alliances, or the acquisition of more than one lordship, and in some cases arms thus combined became hereditary.

Heraldic arms were personal to their owner. As a rule, he alone displayed them on his shield and lance-pennon, and later on his surcoat and banner. His followers did not bear his arms, but to meet the need for a device which they could use as a sign of their allegiance, badges came into extensive use in the 14th and 15th centuries. In addition to the " household badge " worn by his retainers, a man might have one or more badges which he reserved for his own personal use. The display of such personal badges on helms (probably more frequent in tourneys than in war) was one of the practices which gave rise to the heraldic crest. Later, the crest became a usual adjunct to arms.

In the 16th century, with the change in the character of armour, heraldry ceased to be a means of recognition in the field, and it lost the restraint and simplicity which its practical purpose had enforced. Arms became more elaborate. The marshalling of two or more coats of arms on one shield was carried far beyond the original principle of denoting a union of lordships, and complex shields of many quarterings were produced. These are interesting as an heraldic accompaniment and guide to the family tree, but they lack the practical simplicity and artistic merit of the unquartered paternal shield. Many crests took a form suitable only for painting " in the flat," and impossible ever to have been modelled for use on a helm.

While still associated with the knightly shield, helm and banner, heraldry was no longer a practical ancillary to the warrior's equipment, but became rather a decorative art, suited to the chimney-pieces and tapestries of the manor-house and to the ancestral monuments in the parish church. This loss of contact with reality was shown also in the imaginings of the heralds, who began to weave a mystery about their craft, deliberately complicating its nomenclature and language, and

Plate III

ARMS OF SOME SCOTTISH FAMILIES

(Showing the original or "undifferenced" coats)

1. BRUCE.   Or, a saltire and chief gules. (*p.* 105)
2. CAMPBELL.   Gyronny of eight, or and sable. (*p.* 34)
3. DOUGLAS.   Argent, a human heart gules, ensigned with an imperial crown gold, on a chief azure three molets argent. (*pp.* 63, 187)
4. FORBES.   Azure, three bears' heads couped argent, muzzled gules. (*p.* 71)
5. FRASER.   Azure, three fraises (strawberry-flowers) argent. (*p.* 85)
6. GORDON.   Azure, three boars' heads couped or.
7. GRAHAM.   Or, on a chief sable three escallops gold.
8. GRANT.   Gules, three antique crowns or. (*p.* 189)
9. HAY.   Argent, three escutcheons gules.
10. LESLIE.   Argent, on a bend azure three buckles or.
11. MACKENZIE.   Azure, a stag's head cabossed or.
12. MENZIES.   Argent, a chief gules. (*p.* 39)

PLATE III

ARMS OF SOME SCOTTISH FAMILIES
(showing the original or "undifferenced" coats)

introducing unnecessary rules and conventions. To this period belong such absurdities as

" gravely discoursing, in early heraldic language, upon the imaginary heraldry of the patriarchal and antediluvian worthies ; making a true coat of arms of Joseph's ' coat of many colours ' ; giving armorial ensigns to David and Gideon, to Samson and Joshua, to ' that worthy gentilman Japheth,' to Jubal and Tubal Cain ; and crowning the whole by declaring that our common progenitor, Adam, bore on his own red shield Eve's shield of silver, after the medieval fashion that would denote his wife to have been an heiress ! " [1]

Nevertheless, the heralds of the 16th and 17th centuries did a useful work in their periodical visitations for the purpose of recording arms and regulating their use, because in the process they compiled genealogical records of permanent value.

The progressive degeneration of heraldry eventually produced pictorial shields of arms like Lord Nelson's battle-scene (295), incongruous devices like Sir William Herschel's 40-foot reflecting telescope, which was granted to his son Sir John in 1818, in allusion to his father's invention, and absurdities like the Tetlow crest of " a silver penny on which is written the Lord's Prayer," with a dove holding in its beak the crow-quill with which the grantee accomplished this feat of penmanship.

With the renewed study of medieval heraldry, which began during the romanticism of the Victorian Age and has led to valuable research during the present century, there came a reaction against the follies and extravagance of the debased period. Lovers of armory—some truly scholarly, others knowledgeable in a more popular way—have turned to original sources, and examples of the art at its best, for inspiration in the development of a heraldry worthy of the old but suited to modern times. Something of the medieval spirit has been recaptured. Modern grants of arms give us fewer instances of overloaded shields and impracticable crests. Attempts have been made to simplify heraldic language and where possible awkward conventions, unknown to medieval armory, are avoided. Whilst new objects enter the heraldic field daily, and old objects take on new meanings, the tendency is to continue to draw upon the time-honoured symbols, thus preserving continuity and retaining the simplicity, vigour and grace which characterised early armory.

[1] *English Heraldry.*

Heraldry today has a new purpose. Although it has always been decorative, at its inception it was mainly practical; then, in Tudor times, it was very much a status symbol, and has remained such to some extent until the present century, when its popularity can be attributed more and more to a spirit of rebellion. Rebellion against uniformity, against the impersonal, against the transient and against the new " spirit of the age " where parental responsibility has decreased as divorce has increased. Heraldry is individual, personal, perpetual, a symbol of the unity of the family and the obligations and duties of those who comprise this basic unit of society.

Corporate heraldry, too, has grown, both in Great Britain and in Commonwealth countries. Here again it is partly a rebellion against centralization, impersonality and bureaucracy, partly a symbol on which the loyalty of members and servants of a corporation can be centered and partly, and particularly, in the Commonwealth, a grant of arms is a direct link with the motherland and with the Queen, the head of the Commonwealth, whose arms adorn every new grant.

CHAPTER II

DEFINITIONS, HERALDIC LANGUAGE, AND BLAZONING

MANY people apply the words " arms," " crest," or " badge " indiscriminately to any insignia of heraldic appearance. These, and other terms of heraldry, have each a distinct meaning, and it is necessary for the student at the outset to know the names of the various parts of an heraldic composition.

As a man bore a shield, so he was said to bear the devices thereon, and such devices are accordingly called armorial bearings. This term now embraces not only arms, which are normally displayed on a shield or banner, but also crests, supporters, badges, etc. To rank as true armorial bearings, insignia must be properly borne according to the Laws of Arms.

The Act 32 and 33 Victoria cap. 14 defined armorial bearings to mean and include " any Armorial Bearing, Crest, or Ensign, by whatever name the same shall be called, and whether such Armorial Bearing, Crest, or Ensign shall be registered in the College of Arms or not." This definition was framed to prevent the evasion of taxation by persons using bogus heraldry, and notwithstanding its scope, the fact remains that devices used without the authority of the Kings of Arms do not observe the Laws of Arms, and are not true armorial bearings, even though they may have an heraldic form and appearance.

A complete display of armorial bearings is termed an " achievement of arms," or " achievement." Its components are :

The ARMS, or SHIELD OF ARMS (often termed COAT OF ARMS because in the days of chivalry the arms were commonly displayed on the surcoat as well as the shield) : this is the essential feature, and may constitute the whole of the bearings ; though most personal arms have a crest associated with them.

The CREST : a device displayed on the helm (not used by women).

SUPPORTERS : figures which flank and uphold the shield in the case of peers, certain other dignitaries, and some corporations.

BADGES : supplementary devices which may be displayed alone or in association with arms, but not an integral part of them.

The MOTTO, CORONET, INSIGNIA OF ORDERS, etc., if any.

All heraldic figures and devices, whether placed upon shields or displayed in any other manner, are termed charges, and every shield or other object is said to be charged with any device placed upon it.

It is not always convenient to present or record insignia pictorially. From the inception of heraldry it has often been necessary to describe a man's arms in words. Such a verbal description is termed a blazon, and the armorist must be versed in the complementary processes of visualizing or drawing arms from a blazon, and blazoning (i.e. describing) arms which he sees depicted. The word blazoning is sometimes applied to painting arms in colours, but in view of the technical meaning of this word, it is better to use " emblazoning " and " blazonry " when referring to painted heraldry.

It is, of course, necessary to blazon so exactly (and at the same time concisely) that arms can be correctly and completely visualized or drawn from the verbal description. Blazoning has therefore given rise to an heraldic language. This has sometimes proved to be an obstacle to those attracted to the study of heraldry, who are apt to regard its " jargon " as artificial and unnecessary. Nevertheless, much of the nomenclature is worth retaining, partly because it is traditional, and also because it has an exact meaning and is therefore economical in words. It is clearly easier to speak of a lion passant, or a lion rampant, than to describe the lion's attitude in great detail every time you mention him. In the matter of style, however, heraldic language has become unduly complicated.

Nothing could be simpler or more direct than the language of ancient heraldry. The early heralds described shields and banners in the Anglo-French of their day, with a minimum of technical expressions. To them, the Earl of Leicester's shield was *de gules ove un leon blank la cowe furchée*—red, with a white lion, the tail forked ; Sir Anketyn Salveyn's was *d'argent ove j cheveroun de goules iii testes de sengler de goules* —silver, with a red chevron and three red boars' heads ; and *Munsire Nich' Malemeyns l'escu de gules a treis meyns d'argent*—red with three white hands. Certain words were used with a definite heraldic meaning, for example, those applied to the various parts of the shield ; but for the most part early blazon was straightforward description in the ordinary language of the period.

As shields of arms became more elaborate, greater care was needed to describe them without ambiguity, and the language of heraldry grew more complicated. It became mixed, as English words and construction were introduced, partially replacing the Anglo-French. A syntax was developed, whereby the various charges, with their tinctures, position and other details, were mentioned in such an order that there could be no doubt as to their arrangement in the shield and in relation to one another. So far the growth of heraldic language was the result of practical needs. Unfortunately the armorists did not leave it there; in their mistaken enthusiasm, they introduced unnecessary refinements in descriptive terms, and also adopted a style whereby they sought to avoid repetition of words by cumbersome expressions. It is at this point that the student may well become impatient of what he will regard as "jargon," [1] but in a book in which people may expect to find guidance in deciphering technical descriptions of arms, the rules with regard to style cannot be omitted.

In blazoning, the features of a shield of arms are described in the following order:

1. The surface, or field, of the shield; whether of one tincture party of two tinctures, varied, or scattered with small charges
2. The principal charge, or group of charges, resting immediately on the surface of the shield, and normally occupying the central and most commanding position.
3. Any secondary charges resting on the surface of the shield.
4. Objects placed on one of the charges already mentioned.
5. Important charges resting on the surface of the shield, but not occupying a central position, e.g. a chief, canton, or bordure.
6. Objects placed on the charges mentioned in No. 5.
7. Marks of cadency, if any.

In blazoning any charge, its name, type or position, tincture and other characteristics are first specified, and then such details and accessories as it may be necessary to mention; e.g. *a bull statant argent pied*

---

[1] These opinions as to the value of "style" in heraldic language are my own. Boutell wrote at a time when the customary style was unquestioned, and he habitually observed it.—C. W. S.-G.

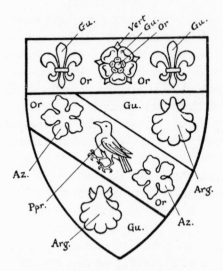

10. Trick of the arms of PETRE

sable, collared and chained, the chain reflexed over the back, gold—crest of Neville, Marquess of Abergavenny.

Taking as a specific instance the fairly complicated shield of a branch of the family of Petre (here " tricked " or sketched—10), the steps in blazoning are as follows :

1. The field of the shield	*Gules* (red)
2. The principal charge resting on the field and holding a central position, i.e. the diagonal band, termed " bend "	*a bend or* (gold)
3. Secondary charges resting on the field of the shield, i.e. the scallop shells . . .	*two escallops argent* (silver)
4. Objects resting on the charges already mentioned, i.e. on the bend . . .	*a Cornish chough proper* (i.e. in natural colours) *between two cinquefoils azure* (blue)
5. Important charges resting on the field of the shield but not in a central position, i.e. the horizontal band at the top, termed " chief "	*a chief or* (gold)
6. Charges on No. 5	*a rose gules seeded or and barbed vert* (green) *between two fleurs-de-lis gules.*

We have now the components from which we can compile the following : *Gules, a bend or and two escallops argent, with a Cornish chough proper between two cinquefoils azure on the bend ; and a chief or charged with a rose gules seeded or and barbed vert between two fleurs-de-lis gules.*

While the foregoing is correct as regards heraldic nomenclature and syntax, it has yet to be considered from the point of view of style. It will be seen that the tinctures gules and or, and the number two, are all mentioned three times, and the bend is mentioned twice. Repetitions of this sort, though common in medieval blazoning, later came to be considered as inelegant, and to be avoided. The methods of doing so were as follow :

If a tincture or number occurs more than once in the same sentence of a blazon, it is indicated by reference to the words already used, and not by repeating them. Thus, should a charge be of the same tincture as the field of the shield, it is said to be " of the field," or (as the field is always first specified) " of the first."

Similarly, any charge is said to be " of the second," " of the third," " of the last," etc., if its tincture is the same as the second, third, or last-mentioned tincture in the blazon. In the case of the metal gold, the word gold may itself be used as an alternative to " or."

The tincture is placed after the charge to which it refers, and a tincture refers back to all charges mentioned since the preceding tincture.

The words " as many " are used to avoid a repetition of a number.

The prepositions " on," " between " (or sometimes " inter "), and " within " are employed, and the clauses so arranged, to shorten the blazon as much as possible.

Applying these methods to the foregoing blazon we get : *Gules, on a bend or between two escallops argent a Cornish chough proper between as many cinquefoils azure ; and on a chief of the second a rose of the first seeded gold and barbed vert between two fleurs-de-lis of the field* : for Petre.

When one charge is several times repeated in the same composition, the objects are generally arranged in rows, and the number in each row is stated, e.g. " six cross-crosslets, 3, 2, 1," to indicate three in the top row, two in the second, and one in the third. Similarly, 4, 4, 1, or 3 and 1, etc., can be used. In the case of three like charges, however, it is unnecessary to specify 2, 1, as this is the normal arrangement of three objects, and they will be placed in this position unless some other is stated in the blazon.

When a charge of small size is many times repeated, whether arranged in some orderly manner or at random, the field is said to be semé, i.e. strewn or scattered, with such a charge, e.g. semé-de-lis (in the case of fleurs-de-lis), semé of cinquefoils, etc. The term poudré, or powdered, may be used if the charges are very small and numerous.

These, then, are the rules and style of blazon, based upon the earlier editions of Boutell's books. The student should be familiar with them so as to be able to read a blazon which follows them, but he should not regard them as canonical. So long as he is correct in nomenclature and descriptive terms, and clear and concise in construction, he may do as he pleases in the matter of style. A study of blazons in grants of arms will soon convince the student of the truth of this observation. Individual Kings of Arms have their own preferences as to style, punctuation and orthography, as indeed do heraldic authors. In this book clumsy repetition has been avoided and commas introduced to make blazons more intelligible. Boutell's insistence in his original books on (for example) " three leopard's faces " had been abandoned for the more usual " three leopards' faces." Where possible words ending -é or -ée have been anglicized: thus cheqée becomes checky. This also helps get over the difficulty posed by trying to make a French adjective, such as paté, which has only masculine and feminine endings, qualify an English neuter noun such as " cross."

However, the student should know the style of blazon currently favoured by the Kings of Arms, which is briefly as follows. Blazons are unpunctuated. The names of charges and tinctures begin with a capital letter. It is usual to repeat the name of a tincture, sometimes prefaced by the word "also"; "gold" is frequently used to avoid repeating "or" but "silver" to replace "argent" is not so popular. With regard to orthography the ending -y is preferred to é or ée, giving affronty, bezanty, gutty and semy. Fess is used rather than fesse, guardant than gardant, courant than current and sejant than sejeant.

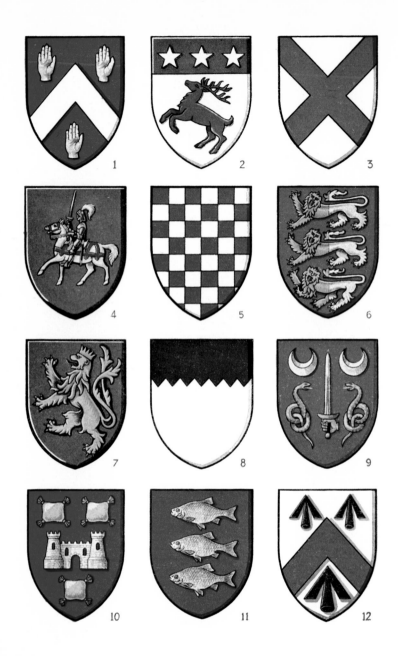

Plate IV

ARMS OF SOME IRISH FAMILIES

Plate IV

ARMS OF SOME IRISH FAMILIES

(Showing the original or " undifferenced " coats)

1. BYRNE.   Gules, a chevron between three dexter hands appaumé couped at the wrist and erect argent. (*p.* 62)

2. DOGHERTY.   Argent, a stag springing gules ; on a chief vert three molets argent. (*p.* 69)

3. FITZGERALD.   Argent, a saltire gules.

4. MAGUIRE.   Vert, a horse argent, caparisoned gules, thereon a knight in complete armour, on his helm a plume of ostrich feathers and in his dexter hand a sword erect, all proper. (*p.* 62)

5. MOONEY.   Checky gules and argent.

6. O'BRIEN.   Gules, three lions passant guardant in pale, per pale or and argent.

7. O'CONNOR.   Vert, a lion rampant, crowned and double-tailed or.

8. POWER.   Argent, a chief indented sable. (*p.* 44)

9. QUIN.   Gules, a hand couped at the wrist holding a sword erect all proper, between in base two serpents erect and respecting each other, tails nowed or, and in chief two crescents argent. (*p.* 80)

10. REDMOND.   Gules, a castle with two towers argent between three cushions or. (*p.* 94)

11. ROCHE.   Gules, three roaches naiant in pale argent. (*p.* 79)

12. WALSH.   Argent, a chevron gules between three broad arrow heads, points upwards, sable.

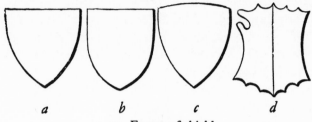

a   *b*   *c*   *d*

11. Forms of shield

CHAPTER III

THE SHIELD AND COAT OF ARMS

THE shield has always been the principal object for the display of armorial bearings, whether in war or tournament, or on seals and monuments. It has thus become closely associated with heraldry, and to this day, centuries after it ceased to be used as a means of defence, the shield continues as the figure on which arms usually appear.

The form of the shield has strongly influenced heraldic design; for example, the characteristic position of the lion rampant (the earliest attitude in which the lion is found), and the frequency of arms consisting of three charges placed " two and one," are both due to the shape of the shield.

Early heraldic shields vary very considerably in their forms, the simplest and most effective having the contour of an inverted equilateral arch, slightly stilted (11*a*). The shields actually used by the Normans in England were of the long and tapering form called " kite-shaped." To these succeeded short, almost triangular, " heater-shaped " shields, so called from the form's resemblance to a flat-iron. Examples abound in the monumental effigies of the 13th and 14th centuries. The equilateral form became prevalent early in the 14th century, when several modifications were introduced. Two of the more effective of these varieties are seen in 11*b* and *c*, drawn respectively from the Percy monument at Beverley (1350) and the monument of John of Eltham in Westminster Abbey (1336).

19

In the next century shields were shortened, and as it advanced their form was altogether changed and became somewhat square, the outlines being produced by a series of concave curves (11*d*). Shields of this class appear to have been introduced during the second half of the 14th century, but they did not become general until a later period. In these shields, a curved notch was cut in the dexter chief for the lance to pass through, and when thus pierced the shield was said to be *à bouche*, that is "with a mouth".

The shield is sometimes represented as bowed, or as having a slightly convex contour, and shields of the form of 11*d* often have a ridge or ridges dividing them down the centre.

At an early date, arms were sometimes displayed on lozenges and roundles for decorative purposes, as in the border of the late 13th-century Syon cope. The arms of men as well as of women occasionally took this form. The lozenge or oval shape is now used to display the arms of an unmarried woman or a widow. Otherwise the form of the shield is a matter of individual preference, and may be varied having regard to the design of the arms to be displayed therein. In the 19th century, shields of fantastic design outlined in scroll-work became fashionable. With the improved heraldic taste of our own times, the early and simple forms of shield have returned to favour.

In early architectural and monumental compositions, and also often upon seals, heraldic shields are represented as if suspended from the guige, or shield-belt. In some instances the long guige appears on each side of the shield and is passed over the corbels, as in one of the beautiful series of shields carved in the time of Henry III in the choir-aisles of Westminster Abbey (1). More usually the shield was represented as suspended from a single corbel, boss, or cluster of foliage. Occasionally, and more particularly on seals, the shield appears as if suspended by the sinister chief angle, and so hangs diagonally from the helm and crest (64). A shield in this position is said to be *couché*.

The heraldic shield, or shield of arms, may be entitled an escutcheon (from *scutum*, a shield; σκῦτος, a hide); and when a shield is itself borne as a charge on a shield of arms, it is called by this term. The entire surface of the shield is called the field.

The side of the shield which would cover the right side of the warrior holding it in front of him is known as the dexter side, and that which would cover his left side is the sinister side. It follows that from the point of view of the observer, the dexter and siniſter sides of an heraldic composition are respectively the left- and right-hand sides. This use of the terms dexter and siniſter is also applied to the supporters and other components of an achievement of arms.

The different parts and points of an heraldic shield are diſtinguished and entitled as follow :

A	Dexter side	H	Dexter base
B	Siniſter side	J	Siniſter base
C	Chief	K	Middle base
D	Base	L	Honour point
E	Dexter chief	M	Fess point
F	Siniſter chief	N	Nombril or Navel point
G	Middle chief		

12

The same terms that denote the parts and points of a shield are also applicable to a flag, or to any figure that may be charged with heraldic arms. In flags, the depth from chief to base is entitled the hoiſt, and the length from the point of suspension to the fore extremity is diſtinguished as the fly.

The term " coat of arms " is frequently used as synonymous with achievement, embracing not only the shield but also the creſt, supporters (if any) and other accessories. Strictly, however, it applies only to the heraldic insignia now normally displayed on the shield. A coat of arms was in fact a coat, or tunic, which a man wore over his armour, and on which were painted or embroidered the same devices as appeared on the wearer's shield.

The original surcoat was a long, loose, flowing garment, probably of white linen (though rich materials may have been used on occasion), with the double purpose of protecting the armoured man from the sun's heat, and the armour from damp and consequent ruſt. The fashion of displaying heraldic arms on the surcoat began in the 13th century. The monumental brass to Sir Robert de Setvans (c. 1305) at Chartham, Kent, shows seven winnowing fans (six visible) on his

13. SIR ROBERT DE SETVANS,
C. 1305

14. HENRY, DUKE OF LANCASTER,
1347

surcoat and ailettes—*sept vans*, allusive to his name—and three similar
fans on his shield (13). About 1325, the surcoat began to be superseded by the cyclas, which hung to the knees at the back but was
much shorter in front. Later this was shortened at the back, and a

Plate V

ROYAL HERALDRY

(See Chapter XIX)

THE ROYAL ARMS OF ENGLAND

From Richard I to Edward III the royal arms were *Gules, three lions passant guardant in pale gold*—anciently blazoned as leopards.

Edward III quartered the arms of France in token of his claim to the French throne. Henry IV reduced the number of fleurs-de-lis in the French quarters to three, and *France and England quarterly* remained the royal arms until the end of Elizabeth's reign.

With the accession of the Stuarts, the arms of Scotland and Ireland were introduced. William III added on an inescutcheon his paternal arms of Nassau.

At the union of England and Scotland, the arms of the two countries were impaled in the first quarter, and the accession of the Hanoverians led to the arms of Hanover being placed in the fourth quarter. The arms of France were omitted in 1801, and those of Hanover when Queen Victoria came to the throne, the royal arms then assuming their present form: Quarterly, 1 and 4 England, 2 Scotland, 3 Ireland.

THE ARMS OF H.R.H. ALBERT EDWARD, PRINCE OF WALES, AFTERWARDS KING EDWARD VII

The royal arms differenced with the label of the eldest son, with his paternal arms of Saxony on an inescutcheon.

THE ARMS OF H.R.H. EDWARD, PRINCE OF WALES, AFTERWARDS KING EDWARD VIII, THEN DUKE OF WINDSOR

The royal arms differenced with the label of the eldest son, with the arms of Wales on an inescutcheon ensigned with the coronet of the Prince of Wales. These arms are also borne by H.R.H. Charles, Prince of Wales. For the full achievement see Plate XV.

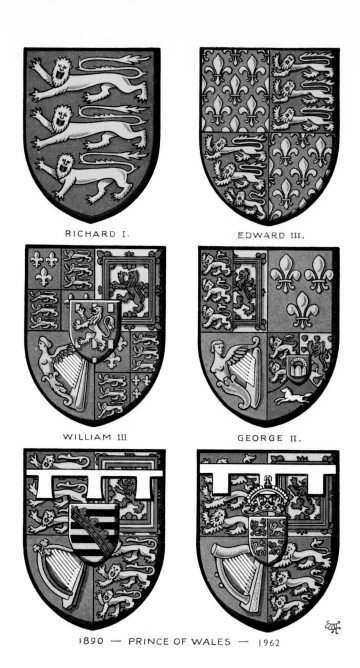

RICHARD I.   EDWARD III.

WILLIAM III   GEORGE II.

1890 — PRINCE OF WALES — 1962

Plate V

ROYAL HERALDRY

15. THOMAS BEAUCHAMP, 4th EARL
OF WARWICK, 1406

16. JOICE, LADY TIPTOFT, 1446

transitional garment between the cyclas and the jupon was produced. This appears in the effigy of Henry, Duke of Lancaster, on the Hastings brass at Elsyng, Norfolk, 1347 (14).

The jupon, which came into fashion about 1360, was a short, sleeveless and closely-fitting tunic, usually of leather, though no doubt rich material was sometimes used. Its lower edge was scalloped or fringed. Fine examples exiſt in the effigies of the Black Prince at Canterbury, and Thomas Beauchamp, fourth Earl of Warwick, at St. Mary's, Warwick (15).

The jupon ceased to be worn early in the 15th century, and during the period of complete plate-armour—itself often richly decorated—its splendid panoply was not as a rule covered by any garment, until in the latter part of the century the tabard was introduced. This only became general in the reigns of Henry VII and Henry VIII. The

17. Tabard of JOHN FELD, 1477

tabard hung half-way down the thighs, had broad sleeves to the elbow, and was open at the sides. Early examples are waiſted, as in the brass to John Feld, at Standon, Herts., 1477 (17); later ones fall ſtraight from the shoulder. The tabard was essentially an heraldic garment. The arms of its wearer were displayed on both front and back, and also on the sleeves; and in some monumental effigies, e.g. that of Sir Roger Le Strange, at Hunſtanton, 1506, the tabard bears the various quarterings to which the wearer was entitled. It went out of fashion about the middle of the 16th century. It remains in use as the official habit of heralds.

Another garment probably devised to proteƈt an armoured man from the sun was the mantling or lambrequin, which hung from the helm. Equally it is possible that the principal purpose of the mantling was to deflect sword blows aimed at the back of the neck. This has become a decorative accessory to arms, and is dealt with in connection with crests.

The mantle was a long cloak falling from shoulder to foot, worn ceremonially over armour or clothing, and used by both men and women. The brass to Henry Bourchier, Earl of Essex, and his wife Isabel, aunt of Edward IV, at Little Easton, 1483, shows both figures in mantles, the Earl having the badge of the Garter on the shoulder (361). Ladies' mantles were sometimes heraldic, for example that of Lady Tiptoft at Enfield, 1446. She was the daughter of Edward Cherlton, Lord Powys, and Eleanor Holland, and her mantle bears the arms of her father and mother impaled (16). The mantle survives as the peer's robe of estate and parliamentary robe, and also as part of the insignia of Orders of Chivalry.

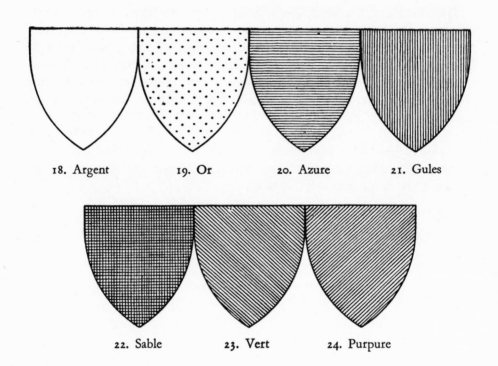

18. Argent   19. Or   20. Azure   21. Gules

22. Sable   23. Vert   24. Purpure

CHAPTER IV

TINCTURES, LINES, AND FIELDS

HERALDIC arms, in their simplest form, consist of a combination of tincture and line. If you take a shield and divide it by a straight line into two halves, then colour each half differently, you produce a shield of arms consisting merely of a party field. There is a number of tinctures, several variations of line, and various ways in which lines may be placed so as to divide and subdivide the shield. Consequently a number of different shields of arms may be produced merely by a combination of these elements of design.

TINCTURES

The tinctures of heraldry comprise two metals, seven colours, and various furs. The following are the tinctures, with their heraldic names and the abbreviations permissible in blazon :

	Heraldic Name	Abbr.	
METALS			
Gold	Or, or *Gold*	Or	In painting, gold may be represented by yellow.
Silver	*Argent*	*Arg.*	Usually represented by white.
COLOURS			
Blue	*Azure*	B.	Sometimes *Az.* but this can be confused with *Arg.*
Red	*Gules*	Gu.	
Black	*Sable*	Sa.	
Green	*Vert*	Vt.	Known as *Sinople* in French heraldry.
Purple	*Purpure*	Purp.	
Orange or Tawny	*Tenné*	(none)	Sometimes known as the " stains " these are rarely found, though they have increased in popularity in recent years.
Blood red	*Sanguine*	(none)	
Purply red (mulberry colour)	*Murrey*	(none)	

FURS
       Heraldic Name

Ermine pattern, consisting of " spots "

Black spots on white	. . . . . .	*Ermine*
White spots on black	. . . . . .	*Ermines*
Black spots on gold	. . . . . .	*Erminois*
Gold spots on black	. . . . . .	*Pean*

Vair pattern, consisting of alternate white and blue pieces variously shaped and arranged   . . . . *Vair*

     Counter-vair
     Potent
     Counter-potent

In the ermine group of furs, the spots represent tails. These take various forms, two of which are shown in 25 and 26. In the vair group, the white and blue pieces represent alternately placed belly and back skins of the grey squirrel. In vair the pieces may be rounded (27) or angular (28). Vair is the original form, the other furs in the group being variants which have gained recognition as separate forms

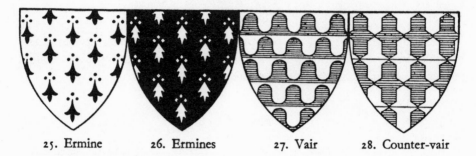

25. Ermine   26. Ermines   27. Vair   28. Counter-vair

and have been given distinct names.   Potent is so called because the
pieces are shaped like crutch-heads (*potence*, a crutch).   The furs in
the vair group are all represented by white and blue pieces unless
other tinctures are specified in the blazon.   In the case of vair-pattern
otherwise tinctured, the word vairy may be used, e.g. *Vairy ermine
and gules*—Gresley.   Apart from counter-vair (28), there are other
little-used arrangements of vair, one of which, called vair en point,
is shown (29).

Objects and figures represented in heraldry in their natural or normal
colours are described as proper, abbreviated ppr.

While the colours of heraldry are usually rich, they may vary as to
shade within reasonable limits.   No exact meaning attaches to the
words gules, azure, etc.   When necessary, the heralds of today are
prepared to abandon them in favour of words expressing a particular
shade.   Thus the arms of the Borough of Barnes, containing emblems
of the University Boat Race, are blazoned, *Azure, on a saltire or between
four ostrich feathers argent, two oars in saltire proper, the blade of that to the
dexter dark blue and that to the sinister light blue* (333).

In uncoloured representations of arms, the metals and colours may

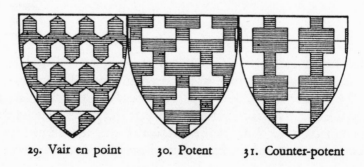

29. Vair en point   30. Potent   31. Counter-potent

be indicated by a system of dots and hatching introduced in the 17th century (18–24). The use of this indication of tinctures is optional, and is now less common than in the past, present-day artists often preferring to leave uncoloured drawings in outline, though sometimes putting in sable as solid black. (In this book, hatching lines are generally omitted except where they are needed for clarity.) More convenient for record purposes is the method known as tricking, in which arms are drawn in outline, repeated charges being indicated by numbers, and the tinctures noted on the sketch by abbreviations.[1] No. 32 shows a trick of the arms of Shovel : *Gules, a chevron between in chief two crescents argent and in base a fleur-de-lis or.*

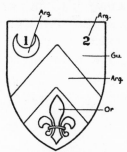

32. Trick of the arms of SHOVEL

As a general rule of heraldry, a metal object may not be laid upon a metal field, nor a coloured one upon colour. This originated in the utilitarian purpose of heraldry to distinguish warriors in the field and lists, where arms of contrasting tinctures would be more clearly visible than (say) gold charges on silver, or blue on green. To this rule there are exceptions. Where a field is varied of a metal and a colour, a charge of either metal or colour may be laid on it, provided it rests on the field as a whole, and not only on one of the tinctures of the field. The rule is likewise relaxed in the case of bordures and chiefs, and of a charge surmounting both the field and another charge. The rule does not apply to furs, or to charges blazoned as proper.

A very few shields of arms consist of a single tincture. The ermine shield of Brittany has already been mentioned. Another instance is the vair shield borne by Hugh de Ferrers, temp. Henry III.

One of the fancies introduced in the 16th century was that in the arms of Sovereigns, tinctures should be represented by heavenly bodies (Sol for gold, Saturn for black, etc.), and that in the arms of nobles, the names of precious stones should be used for tinctures. For purposes of reference, these terms are included in the Glossary.

---

[1] These are not always the abbreviations used in blazon, which may be too long for the purpose. Contractions found in tricking include : O for *or*; A or Ar for *argent*; G for *gules*; B for *azure* (because Az might be confused with Ar); S for *sable*; and V or Vt for *vert*.

LINES

Lines used in dividing the shield into parts, or in outlining the figures placed in the shield, may be plain or ornamental. It is assumed that a line is plain unless the contrary is stated in the blazon. If a line is other than plain, its precise form must be specified. In early heraldry there were relatively few variations of line, and the terms applied to them had a less exact meaning than they have since acquired. Thus the words engrailed and indented were both used for a series of either angular notches or curved incisions. Indented was applied equally with dancetty to a bold "zig-zag" line. Here we are concerned with the precise meanings attached to these terms by later armorists, and also with forms of line (such as dovetailed) which are modern developments.

The following are now the various forms of line:

Engrailed [1] . . .	∿∿∿∿∿∿
Invected [1] . . .	∿∿∿∿∿
Wavy [2] or *Undy* . . {	∿∿∿∿∿
Nebuly . . . {	ʊʊʊʊʊʊ
	ϽϽϽϽϽ
Indented	ᐯᐯᐯᐯᐯᐯ
Dancetty	⋀⋀⋀
Embattled . . .	⊓⊔⊓⊔⊓⊔
Raguly	⊿⊿⊿⊿
Dovetailed . . .	⧖⧖⧖⧖⧖
Potenty	⊐⊏⊐⊏⊐⊏

33a

[1] An engrailed figure has the points outwards (34a); an invected figure has the convex curves outwards (34b).

[2] *Wavy crested* is a new form in which the waves are in the semblance of breakers.

a   34   *b*

To the foregoing, given in the former editions of this book, the following should be added for completeness, though some of them are seldom found :

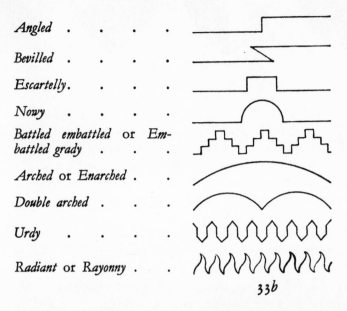

Angled	
Bevilled	
Escartelly. . . .	
Nowy	
Battled embattled or *Embattled grady* . . .	
Arched or *Enarched* . .	
Double arched . . .	
Urdy	
Radiant or *Rayonny* . .	

33b

A further variation consists in the introduction of the fleur-de-lis form, e.g. at the points of dancetty ; this is termed *floretty*. An example of *dancetty floretty* is given in no. 110.

FIELDS

The field of a shield, or of any charge thereon, may be simply divided by a line or lines into two, three or four parts in the ways indicated in nos. 35–42, the parts being differently tinctured.   Such fields are said to be party or parted, and the direction of the partition lines (i.e. whether horizontal, vertical, diagonal, or a combination of these) is indicated by terms which are related to the corresponding ordinaries (Chapter V). Thus, a horizontal band across the middle of the shield being a fess, a shield divided by a horizontal central line is party per fess, or parted fesswise, this phrase being followed by the tinctures of the two parts. The other divisions are party per pale (or palewise), per bend (or

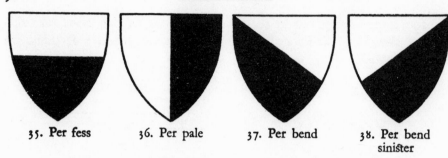

35. Per fess   36. Per pale   37. Per bend   38. Per bend
sinister

bendwise), per bend sinister, per chevron (or chevronwise), per pall (or tierced in pairle), per saltire (or saltirewise), and per cross (or quarterly) (35–42). In blazon, the word party is often omitted. A party field may itself constitute simple heraldic arms, e.g. *Per pale argent and gules*—Waldegrave (59a). The number of different arms which can be produced by such simple combinations of line and tincture is obviously limited, and party fields therefore generally form the ground on which ordinaries or other charges are laid.

Quarterly is the more usual term than per cross. When necessary to the blazon, the quarters may be distinguished by numbers, i.e. the dexter chief is the first quarter, the sinister chief the second, the dexter base the third, and the sinister base the fourth. In quartering a shield for the purpose of including in it more than one coat of arms, by the system known as marshalling (Chapter XII), one or more quarters may be subdivided, or the shield may be quarterly of six, eight or more pieces, each being termed a quartering. These more complex forms of quarterly are dealt with later.

In early heraldry the word party, used alone, implied a palewise division, other directions of the dividing lines being specified.

In all party fields the partition lines may be ornamental.

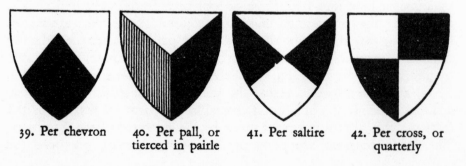

39. Per chevron   40. Per pall, or   41. Per saltire   42. Per cross, or
                 tierced in pairle   quarterly

| 43. Barry | 44. Bendy | 45. Bendy-sinister | 46. Paly |

Fields of a rather more complex character, termed varied fields, may be produced by further division, e.g. three, five or some other *odd* number of palewise lines produce paly ; a similar number of fesswise lines produce barry (called barruly, or burulé, if the divisions are numerous—say ten or more) ; and bendy, bendy-sinister, and chevronny result from similar subdivision of the field (43–47). It will be noted that these fields always consist of an even number of pieces.

Again slightly more complex are varied fields produced by crossing lines. These are checky (a combination of paly and barry), lozengy or fusily (resulting from crossing diagonals, the latter term generally implying rather narrower diamond-shaped pieces than the former), barry-bendy and paly-bendy (which explain themselves) and their sinister equivalents (48–54).

A single row of chequers, as shown in no. 49, is termed compony or gobony, and a double row is termed counter-compony or counter-gobony (50).

Gyronny is a field divided into a number of gyrons, or triangular pieces, radiating from a middle point (55). A combination of per cross and per saltire produces gyronny of eight pieces, e.g. *Gyronny*

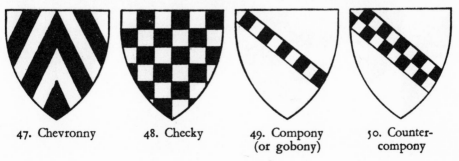

| 47. Chevronny | 48. Checky | 49. Compony (or gobony) | 50. Counter-compony |

51. Lozengy　　52. Fusily　　53. Barry-bendy　　54. Paly-bendy

of eight gold and sable—Campbell (Plate III, 2). Gyronny may also consist of six, ten or twelve pieces, produced by three, five or six partition lines crossing at the centre of the shield.

Fields may be a combination of party and varied, e.g. party per pale and barry counterchanged (56). Variations of line may also be applied to the simpler varied fields, e.g. barry dancetty (57) and paly wavy (58) but not to checky, lozengy, etc.

In blazoning party and varied fields, the tincture first mentioned is, in the case of

per fess, bend, chevron, saltire, and
  barry . . . . . . that of the chief, or top of the shield
per pale and paly . . . . that in the dexter
per cross and checky . . . that in the dexter chief corner
bendy . . . . . . that in the sinister chief
bendy sinister . . . . . that in the dexter chief
gyronny . . . . . . that in the sinister chief half of the
                   first quarter

per pall . . . . . . the tinctures are mentioned in the
                   order: chief, dexter, sinister.

55. Gyronny　　56. Per pale　　57. Barry　　58. Paly wavy
　　　　　　　　　and barry　　dancetty

Party and varied fields are deemed to have a perfectly plane surface. Neither tincture constituting such a field is laid upon or raised above the other; consequently, in relief no ridge should appear between the divisions, and in painting there should be no shading to suggest one part to be at a different level from the other.

A charge placed on a party or varied field is said to be counter-changed, or countercoloured, when there is a reciprocal exchange of the tincture, e.g. *Per pale argent and gules, a bend counterchanged*—Chaucer (59*b*); here the bend is gules where it lies on the argent half of the shield, and argent where it lies on the gules. In early blazoning, a charge which was counterchanged was described as *de l'un en l'autre*.

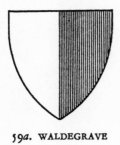

59*a*. WALDEGRAVE   59*b*. CHAUCER

A field is said to be semé, poudré, or powdered, when a charge is many times repeated in it so as to form a pattern. Such a field is often treated as though cut out of a larger surface, some of the charges on the edges being incomplete. Certain special terms are used for the commonest forms of powdered fields. A field powdered with fleurs-de-lis is semé-de-lis, fleury, or floretty, e.g. *Azure, semé-de-lis or* (211*a*), are the ancient arms of France. A field semé of billets is billety; of crosslets, crusily; of bezants, bezanty, and so on. Where there is no special term, the phrase semé of, or powdered with, escallops, cinque-foils, etc., is used.

A field scattered with drops of liquid, termed gouttes, is described as goutté or gutty (59*c*), the tincture of the drops being added, e.g. *goutté gules*. Although there is no obligation to use them, fanciful terms have been invented for fields spattered with drops of various tinctures, viz.:

gold	.	.	.	*goutté d'or*
argent	.	.	.	*goutté d'eau*
azure	.	.	.	*goutté de larmes*
gules	.	.	.	*goutté de sang*
sable	.	.	.	*goutté de poix* (pitch)
vert .	.	.	.	*goutté d'olive* or *d'huile*

59c

DIAPER

To increase the vividness of a field, whether of the shield or a charge, decorative design known as diaper may be introduced. This is only an ornamental accessory, and great care must be taken to keep it in

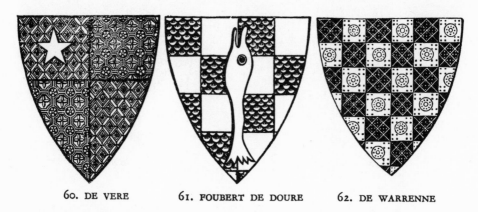

60. DE VERE   61. FOUBERT DE DOURE   62. DE WARRENNE

subordination to the devices forming the arms. It is particularly necessary to avoid any form of diapering which might be mistaken for a powdered field.

Diaper may be executed in any metal or colour, and need not conform to the law of tinctures. It must not be so pronounced as to predominate over or compete with the heraldic tincture of the field so treated. A very effective diaper is produced by executing the decorative accessory in a different tint of the same tincture as the field, or in black. Gold and silver diapers may be placed upon fields of any of the colours. Every variety of charge may be diapered.

The examples of diaper given in the illustrations are:

No. 60: the shield of Robert de Vere, Earl of Oxford, 1298, at Hatfield Broadoak, Essex. Here the diaper is in relief.

No. 61 : the shield of Foubert de Doure, c. 1180, copied from *Archaeologia Cantiana*. The arms are *Checky, a luce hauriant* ; and the alternate squares are appropriately decorated with fish-scales.

No. 62: diaper on a shield of De Warenne, *Checky or and azure*, at Castleacre Priory, Norfolk, c. 1300.

No. 63 : diaper (enlarged) from the seal of Thomas (Plantagenet), Duke of Gloucester. Here the diaper consists of badges. This form of diaper is permissible on the groundwork of a seal, but could not be used on a shield of arms because the swans and feathers would constitute heraldic charges on the shield, and not merely decoration without significance.

Occasionally diaper is allusive to the bearer's name. The seal of William de Filgeriis, 1200, contains a shield with a bend on a field diapered with fern (*fougère*).

63

64. Arms and crest of HUMPHREY, EARL OF STAFFORD,
from his Garter stall-plate, c. 1429

CHAPTER V

SIMPLE FORMS OF HERALDRY: THE ORDINARIES

IN the early practice of painting a band or bands of colour across the
shield for the purpose of distinction certain simple forms originated,
and on account of their common usage these have come to be called
ordinaries. (Other simple figures are termed subordinaries, and are
dealt with in Chapter VII.)   The classification of ordinaries is arbitrary,
and writers on heraldry vary in what they include in it.   Here it is
taken to embrace : the chief, fess, bar, pale, bend and bend sinister,
chevron, pile, pall, saltire and cross.   In ancient heraldry these varied
considerably in width according to the design as a whole and the fancy
of the artist, and later the narrower forms came to be regarded as

PLATE VI

THE ARMS OF SCOTLAND

Plate VI

THE ARMS OF SCOTLAND

(*See Chapter XIX*)

THE ROYAL ARMS AS USED IN SCOTLAND

By comparison with the frontispiece, it will be seen that in this version of the royal arms precedence is given to the Scottish components. The Scottish arms occupy the first and fourth quarters of the shield, those of England being placed in the second quarter. The crest of Scotland is used. The Scottish unicorn forms the dexter supporter, and is crowned; it maintains a banner of St. Andrew, while the English lion, on the sinister side, bears that of St. George. The shield is encircled with the collar and pendant of the Order of the Thistle. Thistles (and in some representations roses and shamrock also) spring from the ground on which the supporters stand.

THE ARMS OF SCOTLAND

The shield bears the famous arms, *Gold, a lion rampant gules armed and langued azure, within a double tressure flory counter-flory gules*. The crest is the lion sejant affronté on a royal crown, holding a sword and a sceptre. The supporters are unicorns with antique crowns about their necks and royal crowns on their heads, one bearing a banner of Scotland and the other of St. Andrew. The collar and pendant of the Order of the Thistle surround the shield, and thistles grow from the ground forming the compartment. The Scottish royal motto appears above the crest, and the motto of the Order of the Thistle below the shield.

diminutives of the broader ones and were given distinctive names. The ordinaries with their diminutives (if any) are as follows :

Ordinary	*Diminutives*
Chief	
Fess	
Bar	Closet, Barrulet, Bars gemelles
Pale	Pallet, Endorse
Bend and	
Bend sinister . . .	Bendlet, Bendlet sinister or Scarp, Cotise
Chevron	Chevronel, Couple-close
Pile	
Pall	
Saltire	
Cross	

Some writers have assigned definite proportions to the ordinaries and their diminutives. The chief, fess and pale are each said to occupy one-third (or rather less) of the shield ; the bend, saltire and cross one-third if charged and one-fifth if uncharged ; and the bar and chevron one-fifth of the shield. The closet is said to be half, and the barrulet a quarter the width of the bar ; and the pallet, bendlet and chevronel are said to be half the width, and the endorse and cotise one-quarter the width of their respective ordinaries. In fact, however, heraldic art is not bound by such exactitude and these proportions should be taken as a general guide rather than as an absolute rule.

An ordinary is often the predominant charge, and may be the sole object in the shield. It may be accompanied by or charged with other devices. More than one ordinary may be found in the same arms, though in practice some ordinaries are incompatible ; for example, the chief and fess are rarely found together. All the ordinaries and their diminutives may be ornamentally treated by engrailing, indenting, etc. They do not lie in one plane with the field of the shield, but are superimposed on it, and this is shown in relief and shaded paintings.

THE CHIEF

The chief is formed by a horizontal line containing the uppermost part of the shield (65 and Plate III, 12). While usually classed as an ordinary, it is a development of " party per fess " (35), and consequently instances are found of a metal chief on a metal field, or a

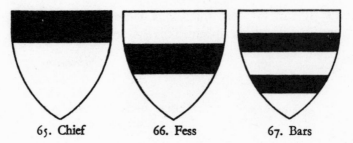

65. Chief　　　　　66. Fess　　　　　67. Bars

coloured chief on colour, e.g. in the arms of Leeds (p. 236). Though in my view permissible, some do not regard this as good heraldry.

The Fess and Bar

The fess is formed by two horizontal lines containing the central part of the shield (66).

The bar, which is normally narrower than the fess (of which some writers regard it as the diminutive), is seldom found singly unless in conjunction with some other ordinary. It is never placed along the top edge of the shield, because in this position it would simply be a narrow chief. Two, three or more bars frequently occur together (67, 68). A group of bars must be placed so that the field shows above and below as well as between them; thus two bars will show three strips of field, and three bars four strips. In this respect, bars must be distinguished from the varied field known as barry (43).

Of the diminutives of the bar, the closet is held to be deeper than the barrulet, but the latter word is now generally used to denote a narrow bar regardless of precise depth.

When barrulets are placed together in couples, each couple is termed bars gemelles, i.e. twin bars (69).

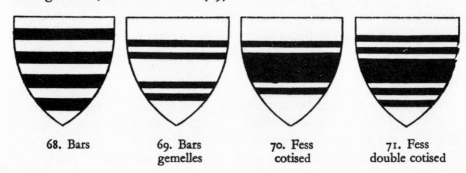

68. Bars　　　　69. Bars　　　　70. Fess　　　　71. Fess
　　　　　　　　gemelles　　　　cotised　　　　double cotised

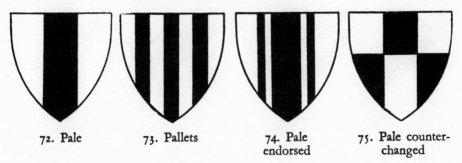

72. Pale   73. Pallets   74. Pale endorsed   75. Pale counter-changed

When a closet or barrulet is placed on either side of a fess, the fess is said to be closeted or cotised, the latter term being the more usual (70). When there are two barrulets on each side, the fess is double cotised (71).

THE PALE

The pale is formed by two vertical lines containing the central part of the shield (72). Two or more palewise stripes are termed pallets (73). (These must be distinguished from paly as bars are from barry.) The endorse, deemed to be narrower than a pallet, is usually found in pairs enclosing other charges ; thus, a pale may be endorsed (74).

A field may be parted twice per pale and once per fess ; in ancient heraldry this was simply described as a shield of six pieces, but later it was blazoned and regarded as party per fess with a pale counterchanged (75). In view of the blazon, this is not a plane surface as party or varied fields are, but in relief and shaded paintings the pale is shown standing out from the field of the shield. This arrangement is applicable only to a single and impartible coat of arms. It must be distinguished from quarterly of six, used when it is desired to marshal six separate coats on one shield (see Chapter XII).

THE BEND AND BEND SINISTER

The bend is formed by two diagonal lines from dexter chief to sinister base (76). Two or more bends may be borne on one shield (77), and if there are three or more they may be termed bendlets. These must be distinguished from bendy. The cotise is held to be narrower than the bendlet. A bend between cotises is termed a bend cotised (78), or double cotised if there are two on each side.

A single cotise, used as an ancient mark of difference, was called

76. Bend   77. Bendlets   78. Bend cotised   79. Baton

a baston or riband. The term baton is now applied to a bendlet couped, i.e. cut short at the ends and not extending to the edge of the shield (79).

The bend sinister extends from the sinister chief to the dexter base (80). It has similar diminutives to the bend, but the bendlet sinister is sometimes known as a scarp or escarp.

Charges placed on a bend or bend sinister slope with it unless the contrary is specified in the blazon (81).

THE CHEVRON

A chevron (82) has its point in chief unless blazoned as reversed. Two or more chevrons may be borne in one shield, and if there are three or more they may be termed chevronels (83). They are placed one above the other unless some other arrangement is specified, e.g. three chevronels interlaced, or braced (84).

Like the fess and bend, the chevron may be cotised (85) or double cotised. In the case of the chevron, an alternative term to cotise is couple-close, this figure ranking as narrower than a chevronel.

Charges on a chevron are placed erect and do not usually follow the direction of the chevron, although there are ancient examples of this (86).

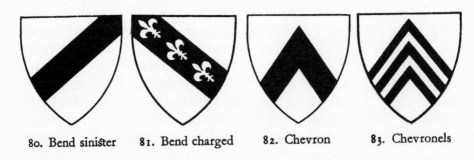

80. Bend sinister   81. Bend charged   82. Chevron   83. Chevronels

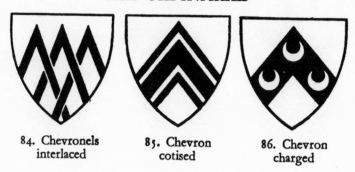

84. Chevronels
interlaced

85. Chevron
cotised

86. Chevron
charged

THE PILE

The pile is a wedge-shaped figure (87). More than one pile may appear in the same composition (88), or a field may be divided pily. Piles normally issue from the chief, but they may issue from the side or base of the shield.

THE PALL

The pall is a figure resembling the letter Y, its three limbs extending to the edge of the shield (89). When the limbs are cut short, the figure is termed a shakefork (90). While derived from the pallium, the ordinary must be distinguished from the true ecclesiastical pall found in the arms of the Province of Canterbury, which is argent edged with gold and charged with crosses paty fitchy sable, the lower portion terminating in a fringe and not reaching the point of the shield (384).

THE SALTIRE

The saltire (91) is a diagonal cross; the "crosses" of St. Andrew and St. Patrick in the Union Flag are saltires. Charges set on a saltire are placed erect unless otherwise blazoned (92).

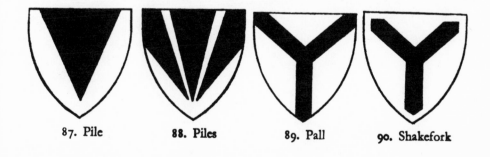

87. Pile

88. Piles

89. Pall

90. Shakefork

91. Saltire   92. Saltire charged   93. Cross

THE CROSS

The cross (93) has so many varieties of form, decoration and arrangement that it is the subject of a separate chapter.

In their simplest form, the ordinaries have straight border-lines, but the ornamental lines shown in no. 33 are frequently used to vary them. In the case of the chief, which lies along the top of the shield, the ornamental treatment can obviously be carried out only on its lower edge, e.g. *Arg. a chief indented sable*—Power (Plate IV, 8). In other cases, engrailing, indenting, etc., is carried out on both sides of the figure unless the blazon limits the treatment to one side. There is, however, an exception in the case of embattlement. A fess, bend or chevron blazoned as embattled is so treated only on the upper side. If the embattlement is carried out on both sides, these ordinaries are blazoned as embattled counter-embattled, or (shortly) counter-embattled.

A charge so placed on a shield as to occupy the position of a fess, pale or bend may be described as fesswise, palewise or bendwise. Two or more charges placed horizontally and parallel may be described as barwise. Charges forming a group so arranged as to follow the line of one of the ordinaries are said to be in chief, in fess, in pale, in bend, in chevron, in pile, in saltire, or in cross (94–101). The distinction

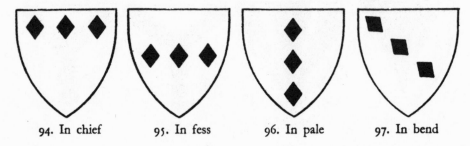

94. In chief   95. In fess   96. In pale   97. In bend

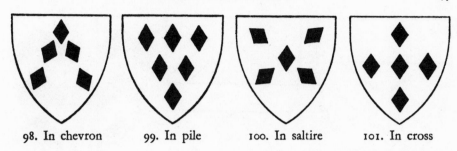

98. In chevron   99. In pile   100. In saltire   101. In cross

between, on the one hand, fesswise, palewise and bendwise, and on the other, in fess, in pale and in bend, must be carefully noted. Thus in the arms of Bowes (218) the three bows placed erect and side by side are *palewise in fess*; but three bows placed horizontally one above the other would be *fesswise in pale*.[1] The lions of England, while individually fesswise, are collectively in pale.

The following are examples of arms composed of ordinaries, or ordinaries and diminutives, in some cases with party fields :

Or, a chief and a saltire gules—Bruce (102).
Or, a fess between two chevrons gules—FitzWalter (103).
Argent, three bars dancetty sable, over all a pale ermine—Enderbie (104).
Argent, two bendlets sable, the under one engrailed—Lever (105).
Argent, three bendlets enhanced gules—Byron (106).
Gules, a bend or and three bendlets sinister argent interlaced, the centre bendlet sinister surmounting the bend—Allwright (107).
Gules, on a chevron argent three bars gemelles sable—Throckmorton (108).
Argent, a pile sable and a chevron counterchanged—Alwell (109).
Per fess dancetty argent and sable, a fess dancetty floretty at the points counterchanged—Woodmerton (110).

The arms of Allwright, above quoted, illustrate the relaxation of the law of tinctures where one charge surmounts another without being charged wholly upon it ; one bendlet sinister argent crosses the bend or, and the latter crosses two of the bendlets sinister argent, without violation of the rule against placing metal on metal.

---

[1] They may alternatively be described as *barwise*.

102. BRUCE

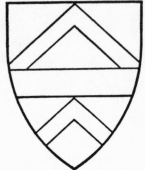

103. FITZWALTER

104. ENDERBIE

105. LEVER

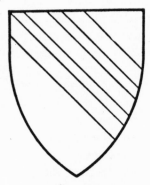

106. BYRON

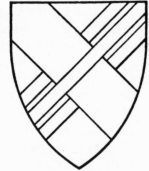

107. ALLWRIGHT

108. THROCKMORTON

109. ALWELL

110. WOODMERTON

III. WESTON

CHAPTER VI

THE HERALDRY OF THE CROSS

THE cross is of outstanding importance among the ordinaries because, besides being a simple form well suited to the purpose of heraldry, it has special significance as a religious emblem. It occurs frequently in the ancient Rolls of Arms in both plain and ornamental forms. A few terms originally did duty to describe the various forms of cross. Thus a cross patté or paty (paw-shaped) might have limbs splayed out broadly into three points, or its limbs might be straight for the greater part of their length, and be shaped at the ends like the head of a fleur-de-lis. In due course different names were given to the variants, the former being termed patonce, and the latter flory, while paty came to be applied to a cross with splayed limbs cut straight across the ends (also called formy). Again, the terms moline and recercelé are now used to describe variants of what was originally the same form of cross.

Some students of ancient heraldry have deplored the multiplicity of terms and types of cross introduced in later times, but these must be

47

112. Cross   113. CREVEQUER   114. GENTLE   115. SCOTT-GILES
fimbriated

set out in a book which aims at being a guide to modern no less than to ancient heraldry.

The term Cross, without any qualification, implies the plain straight-sided figure placed erect in the centre and extending to the sides of the shield, or of any division of the shield in which it stands (93). In early Rolls of Arms this is sometimes found blazoned as a " cross passant." If the border-lines are treated in any of the ways shown in no. 33, the figure is a cross engrailed, cross embattled, cross indented, etc.

The plain cross, and its varieties produced by ornamental treatment of the border-lines, may be further varied in the manner shown in the following instances :

FIMBRIATED : having a narrow border of a different tincture ; *Sable, a cross gules fimbriated argent* (112). The fimbriation lies in the same plane with the rest of the cross.

VOIDED : having the central area entirely removed ; *Or, a cross voided gules*—Crevequer (113). The voided portion lies in the same plane as the rest of the field of the shield. In a flat and unshaded representation, this might be taken for a cross surmounted by another. Unless the contrary is indicated, it may be blazoned as a cross voided where the central portion is the same tincture as the field of the shield, and as a cross surmounted by another where the central portion is of a different tincture from the field.

QUARTER-PIERCED : having the centre square removed ; *Or, a cross quarter-pierced sable*—Gentle (114).

PARTED AND FRETTY : the cross is parted into two endorses and two barrulets and they are fretted at the centre ; *Ermine, a cross double-parted and fretty gules, an annulet gold interlaced*—Scott-Giles (115). Where each

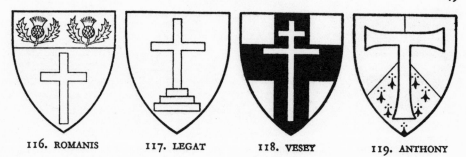

116. ROMANIS   117. LEGAT   118. VESEY   119. ANTHONY

limb is split into three parts, the figure is termed a cross tripartite and fretty.[1]

The foregoing types are all crosses which normally extend to the edges of the shield. Such a cross may be further varied by having its limbs cut short, in which case it is termed *couped*.

There is a wide variety of crosses whose limbs do not extend to the edges of the shield. Some of these have squared ends to the limbs; others are distinguished by the decorative treatment of the ends of the limbs. They may be borne singly or in groups.

The LATIN CROSS, LONG CROSS or PASSION CROSS has a shaft considerably longer than the other limbs. This was the normal plain cross when shields were of the long, tapering form, but the shortening of shields resulted in the plain cross having limbs of nearly equal length, so that the long cross became a special form. Romanis (116); *Azure, a passion cross or, on a chief of the last two thistles slipped proper.*

The CALVARY CROSS is a long cross placed on steps, degrees or grieces, the number of which must be stated in the blazon; *Argent, a Calvary cross on three degrees gules*—Legat (117); *Argent, a cross Calvary mounted on three degrees gules, on a chief azure five bezants*—granted to Stephen Weston, Bishop of Exeter, 1725 (111).

The PATRIARCHAL CROSS has the upper limb crossed; *Or, on a cross*

[1] Skirlaw, Bishop of Durham (d. 1406), the son of a basket weaver, bore, "silver, a cross of three upright wattles sable, crossed and interwoven by three more" (Oswald Barron, article on Heraldry in *Encyclopaedia Britannica*). This blazon of the cross tripartite and fretty preserves the reference to the bearer's origin.

120. GRAVELEY   121. LEXINGTON   122. MOLINEUX   123. DE UVEDALE

sable, a Patriarchal cross of the field—Vesey (118). This cross may also
be placed on degrees.

The TAU, TAU CROSS or CROSS OF ST. ANTHONY has no upper limb,
and the others are usually slightly splayed ; *Tierced in pairle reversed,
or, gules and ermine, over all a tau cross azure*—Anthony (119).

POINTED : having the ends of the limbs so treated ; *Sable, a cross
pointed, in the dexter chief a molet argent*—Graveley (120). If the ends
are slightly splayed as well as pointed, this form may be termed *cleché*
or *urdé* (455).

FOURCHÉ : having the ends forked ; *Argent, a cross fourché azure*
—Lexington (121).

MOLINE : *Azure, a cross moline argent*—Molineux (122). As a mark
of cadency, the cross moline represents the eighth son.

CERCELÉ or RECERCELÉ : *Argent, a cross recercelé gules*—De Uvedale
(123).

The cross moline is said to have derived its name and form from
the iron at the centre of a mill-stone, and the charge termed a mill-iron,
mill-rind or fer-de-moline, is sometimes represented as a cross moline
pierced at the centre. The cross recercelé is a variant of the cross
moline. The cross ancré, or anchory, so called because its ends resemble
the flukes of an anchor, is an alternative term for the cross moline
rather than a separate form.

PATONCE : having the ends splayed into three points ; *Argent, a cross
patonce gules*—Colvile (124).

FLORY : having the limbs ending in fleurs-de-lis ; *Argent, a cross flory
sable*—Swinnerton (125).

FLORETTY : a variant of flory, with the fleur-de-lis heads sprouting
from a knop, or from the squared ends of the limbs ; *Azure, a cross*

124. COLVILE   125. SWINNERTON   126. WARD   127. STEWARD

floretty or—Ward (126); *Sable, a cross paty floretty argent*—Steward (127).

POMMÉ: having the limbs ending in roundels; *Argent, a cross pommé between four plain crosslets or*—Crusader Kings of Jerusalem (early form —128).

POTENT: having crutch-shaped ends; *Argent, a cross potent between four plain crosslets or*—Crusader Kings of Jerusalem (later form—129).

The last two indicate the process of the development of one form of cross from another. The arms are a violation of the law that metal may not be laid upon metal, perhaps done deliberately to confer distinction on the arms of the King of Jerusalem. *Azure, a cross potent engrailed or*—Brenchley (130), illustrates that these special forms of cross are susceptible to ornamental treatment of border-lines. No. 131 shows a *cross potent rebated*, also termed a *cross gammadion*, or a *fylfot*.

CROSSLET: having each limb crossed; *Or, a cross crosslet gules*—Howorth, of Herefordshire. (132).

BOTONNY or TREFLÉ: having each limb ending in three knobs; *Gules, a cross botonny or*—Bokyngham (133).

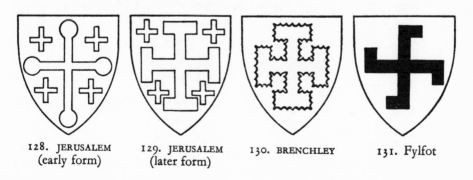

128. JERUSALEM   129. JERUSALEM   130. BRENCHLEY   131. Fylfot
(early form)   (later form)

132. HOWORTH   133. BOKYNGHAM   134. GOLDEAR   135. Maltese cross

The cross botonny is a modification of the cross crosslet. A field covered with small crosslets of either of these types is said to be *crusily*; or *crusily botonny* may be specified in the latter case. A cross crosslet placed diagonally is known as the cross of St. Julian.

FORMY or PATY: having the limbs splayed, with straight ends; *Gules, a cross formy or*—Goldear (134). This cross is sometimes found carried to the edges of the shield, when it is described as *a cross formy throughout*. Another treatment of this type is dealt with above under *Floretty*.

The MALTESE CROSS, or CROSS OF EIGHT POINTS (135). This is used as a badge by the Hospitallers, or Knights of St. John.

When the shaft of any cross tapers to a point, the cross is described as *fitchy*, i.e. "fixable" in the ground—*Sable, a cross formy fitchy or*, granted to Francis Colier of Staffordshire in 1629 (136). The term *fitchy at the foot* is used in the case of a cross formy when the point is merely an appendage to the lower limb—*Or, a cross formy fitchy at the foot gules*, the ancient coat of Scudamore of Kenchurch (137).

Any form of cross is termed *quadrate* when the limbs project from a squared centre.

The cross avellane, representing four filberts placed together in cross-

136. COLIER   137. SCUDAMORE

form, and the cross gringolé, which has limbs ending in snakes' heads, are examples of a number of forms too rarely encountered to need detailed reference. Some of them are included in the Glossary.

A very narrow cross is termed a fillet cross. This is sometimes added to a quartered shield containing separate coats of arms so as to difference and unify it, making it an impartible or indivisible coat. An instance is found in the arms of Tonbridge School (Plate XXIII).

138. NEVILL

CHAPTER VII

SIMPLE FORMS OF HERALDRY: THE SUBORDINARIES

A NUMBER of secondary devices of a simple character are classed as subordinaries. This is an arbitrary classification and opinions vary as to the figures it should include.

The BORDURE, or border (139), was in medieval heraldry usually borne as a difference, but is now frequently found as a principal charge. It may be plain, or formed by one of the ornamental lines (33), and it may be parted, varied, and charged with other figures. Examples are found in nos. 156, 183, 227 and 285.

The ESCUTCHEON (140) is borne singly or in groups, and is often charged. When one escutcheon is borne on a shield, it should be appreciably smaller than the space enclosed by a border, otherwise difficulty may be met in distinguishing between (for example) *Argent, a bordure sable*, and *Sable, an escutcheon argent*. The escutcheon of pretence used to display the arms of an heiress wife in her husband's shield, is dealt with in Chapter XII; this is usually smaller than a single escutcheon borne as a charge.

The ORLE (141) was blazoned by early heralds as a " false escutcheon " or an " escutcheon voided "; it is in form an escutcheon with the centre cut away leaving only a narrow border. Charges placed

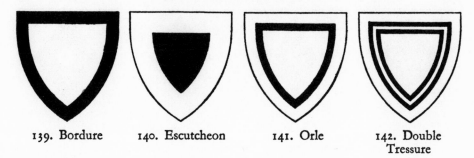

139. Bordure   140. Escutcheon   141. Orle   142. Double
                                                                    Tressure

along the line an orle would occupy (143) are said to be " in orle," or
the term " an orle of " such charges may be used.   De Valence bore
Barruly argent and azure, an orle of martlets gules (263*b*).

A TRESSURE is a narrow border inset from the edges of the shield.
It is usually found double (142) and enriched with fleurs-de-lis (158).
It occurs in the Royal Arms of Scotland as a double tressure flory
counter-flory, i.e. the heads of the fleurs-de-lis point alternately outwards
and inwards, but the fleurs-de-lis are broken at the centre, the space
between the two concentric parts of the double tressure being voided
throughout.

The CANTON (144) is a rectangle in the dexter chief, always occupying
less than a quarter and sometimes only one-ninth, or even less, of the
shield.   Its earlier form was the QUARTER.   It is often charged.   When
borne with a bordure to the shield, the canton is not contained by the
bordure but surmounts it, unless the bordure has been added later as
a difference.   A canton in the sinister is specified as a sinister canton.

The GYRON (145) is the lower half of a canton or quarter when
divided diagonally by a line from the dexter chief to the fess point.
A sinister gyron is also found.   Two gyrons occur in fig. 157.

FLANCHES OR FLAUNCHES (146), always borne in pairs, are formed by

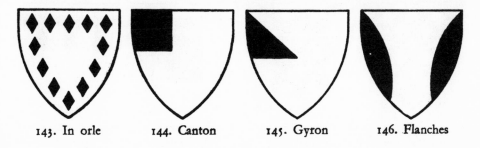

143. In orle   144. Canton   145. Gyron   146. Flanches

147. Lozenge   148. Fusil   149. Mascle   150. Rustre

curved lines from the top corners of the shield to the dexter and sinister base. They may be charged. Flanches formed by curves of greater radius, thus impinging less on the field of the shield, are sometimes termed flasques or voiders.

The LOZENGE (147) is a diamond-shaped figure, and the FUSIL (148) is of a similar shape but narrower. The MASCLE (149) is a voided lozenge (sometimes blazoned as *faux lozenge* in ancient heraldry), and the RUSTRE (150) is a lozenge pierced with a round hole. Lozenges and fusils are often found cojoined in fess, in bend and in cross (160, 161).

FRETTY consists of bendlets dexter and sinister interlaced and covering the field (151). The FRET is a modification of this, consisting of one bendlet and one bendlet sinister interlaced with a mascle (152). An early variant of fretty is trellis or treille, in which the pieces do not interlace, but all those in bend overlie those in bend sinister, and they are cloué, i.e. fastened with nails where they cross: *Argent, a trellis gules cloué or*—De Trussell or Tressell.

The BILLET is an oblong figure set upright (153). A field semé of billets is termed billetty.

The gyron, fret, lozenge, fusil, and billet are not found as single

151. Fretty   152. Fret   153. Billet   154. Label

charges in early heraldry. The heralds divided the fields of shields lozengy and gyronny, or made them billetty, masculy or fretty, the single charges being later derived from such treatment of the field.

The LABEL is a riband with several shorter ribands (usually three or five) pendent from it (154). The pendent pieces may be straight or slightly splayed, and are sometimes shown in dovetail form (155). The label is normally placed barwise in the upper part of the shield. In early heraldry it was usually a difference, and except where it has become a permanent charge in ancient arms, it is now used solely as a mark of cadency borne by the eldest son during his father's lifetime (except in Royal Heraldry—see Chapter XIX).

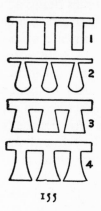

155

ROUNDELS (or roundles), as their name implies, are circular objects (156, 159). In ancient heraldry, roundels were variously termed bezants, torteaux, pelots, and gastells. Bezants, supposed to have been derived from Byzantine coins, were either gold or silver, their tincture being specified as *bezants d'or* or *d'argent*. The other terms were applied to roundels of the various colours, the particular tincture being named. Thus torteaux might be found either gules or azure. Later, roundels of various tinctures were given distinctive names: the word torteau became applicable only to a roundel gules, pelot to one sable, and so on. The names of the roundels are now as follows:

Tincture	*Name of Roundel*
Or	Bezant (from Byzantium)
Argent	Plate (from *plata*, silver)
Azure	Hurt (possibly from the hurtleberry)
Gules	Torteau (a cake ; the obsolete term gastell had the same meaning)
Sable	Pellet, Ogress, or Gunstone
Vert	Pomme, or Pomeis (an apple)
Purpure	Golpe (a wound)
Tenné	Orange (the fruit)
Sanguine	Guze (an eye-ball)

The last three are rarely found, but one of the badges granted to Wilkinson Sword Ltd. in 1970 contains a guze and an orange features in the arms of a family of Selley. As bezants and plates represent coins they tend to be treated artistically as discs. Other roundels are frequently shaded to suggest their spherical origin.

A roundel may be of one of the furs, in which case it is so described, e.g. a roundel ermine. A roundel may be parted, varied or charged, full details being given in the blazon.

A roundel barry wavy argent and azure is termed a fountain, sometimes designated as heraldic fountain to distinguish it from the natural fountain, which is also found as a charge. This roundel is sometimes termed a syke (well), and by this name appears in the arms of Sykes.

A field scattered with roundels may be termed semé of torteaux, semé of hurts, etc., or in appropriate cases the terms bezanty, platy, hurty or pellety may be used. An animal semé of roundels may be described as spotted with them.

An ANNULET is a plain ring, sometimes blazoned as a false roundel. It is found singly or in groups (437). Two or three annulets may be interlaced and these are sometimes termed gemel (or gimmel) rings (i.e. twin rings). In cadency, the annulet is the mark of the fifth son. The following arms give examples of the subordinaries:

Per fess gules and argent, a bordure gold charged with eight torteaux, over all a canton ermine—Woodfield (156).

Or, three bars azure, on a chief gold three pallets between two gyrons azure (or of the second), over all an inescutcheon argent—Mortimer (157). (This coat is also found with two pallets on the chief. See no. 306, p. 137.)

Or, a fess checky azure and argent within a double tressure flory counterflory gules—Stuart (158).

Sable platy, two flaunches argent—Spelman (159).

Gules, five lozenges conjoined in bend argent—Raleigh (160). Sir Walter Raleigh bore this with a martlet, for difference.

Azure, five fusils conjoined in fess or—Percy (161).

Gules, seven mascles conjoined 3, 3, 1, or—Ferrers (162).

Quarterly argent and gules fretty or, over all a bend sable—Le Despencer (163).

Or, ten billets sable, in chief a label of five points gules—Geffrey (164).

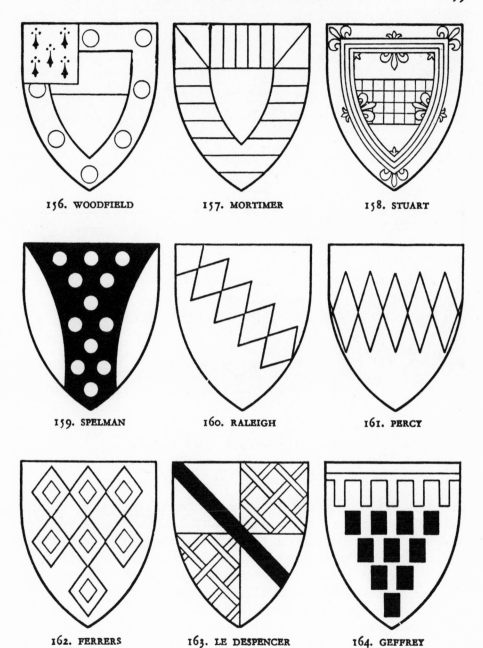

156. WOODFIELD   157. MORTIMER   158. STUART

159. SPELMAN   160. RALEIGH   161. PERCY

162. FERRERS   163. LE DESPENCER   164. GEFFREY

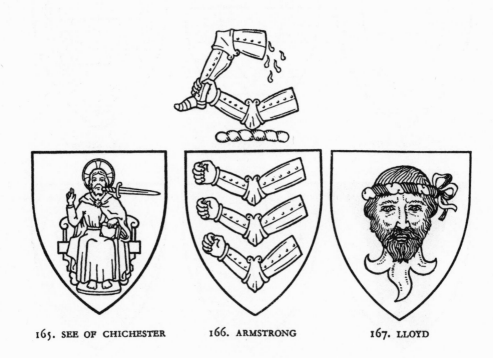

165. SEE OF CHICHESTER 166. ARMSTRONG 167. LLOYD

CHAPTER VIII

HERALDIC CHARGES

ANYTHING which is capable of being depicted or symbolized in form and tincture may be a charge in heraldry. So immense is the store on which heralds have drawn, that it is possible to refer here only to the principal classes of charges, and to deal in some detail with those of most frequent occurrence, and especially those which (like the lion) have acquired a distinctive heraldic character and special descriptive terms. Some other charges will be found listed in the Glossary.

For convenience, charges are here considered under the headings : Divine and human beings, the lion, deer, other creatures, monsters, natural objects, and inanimate objects.

DIVINE BEINGS

The Almighty is represented in the arms of the See of Chichester (165). The blazon is, *Azure, our Lord vested argent and with a glory about His head, His sinister hand resting upon a book or, and His dexter hand raised in benediction, seated upon a throne of gold, and issuant from His mouth a sword argent, pommel and hilt also gold.* Possibly in error, but more probably to avoid any suspicion of idolatry, this was formerly blazoned as " Prester John sitting on a tombstone."

Gules, our Lord upon the cross proper, forms the arms of the Burgh of Inverness.

The See of Salisbury bears, *Azure, the Virgin and Child or*; and the Madonna also figures in some other ecclesiastical arms, and as the crest of the Borough of St. Marylebone.

Figures of the Apostles and Saints sometimes appear in civic heraldry. St. Peter and St. Paul stand under a canopy in the shield of the Borough of Wisbech; St. Andrew with his saltire is the crest of Holborn; St. Martin dividing his cloak with the Beggar forms the arms of Dover; and St. Pancras is the crest of the London borough that bears his name.

Sacred Persons are more usually represented by the emblems associated with them, e.g. roses and lilies for the Virgin, the winged bull for St. Luke, the winged lion for St. Mark, the Holy Lamb for St. John the Baptist, the sword for St. Paul, and the keys for St. Peter.

Angels rarely occur as charges, but sometimes as supporters. A cherub is found in the arms of the Borough of Taunton.

HUMAN BEINGS

When human beings appear in armorial bearings, the blazon should clearly describe their attitude, costume, action, etc. They occur frequently as supporters, less frequently in arms and crests. Parts of the human body are more often found in arms than the whole figure.

The arms of Dalzell, Earl of Carnwath, are *Sable, a naked man, his arms extended proper*. Three naked savage men of the wood, each bearing a club and a shield, occur in the arms of Wood, Earl of Halifax. The savage, or wild man, is usually wreathed about the loins, and often also about the temples.

Men in armour are found occasionally in arms, and are common as crests and supporters. Armour is usually depicted as plate unless another form is specified. The arms of Maguire (Plate IV, 4) provide an instance of a knight on horseback.

Three demi-ladies affronté, arrayed and veiled argent and crowned or, occur in the arms of the See of Oxford.

Men in naval and military uniform and other distinctive dress are frequently found as supporters, and are dealt with later.

The human head, arm, hand and leg, when they appear as charges, must be so blazoned as to describe their position and other details, and in the case of the head the type must be given, e.g. Englishman's, Saxon's, Savage's, Blackamoor's or Negro's, Saracen's or Moor's, maiden's, child's, etc. A head will be in profile or affronté, couped or erased at the neck or shoulders, and may be wreathed about the temples, or helmed. When it is necessary to specify the tincture of the hair, the head is said to be crined of such tincture.

An arm may be couped or erased at the elbow or shoulder, or embowed (bent at the elbow), and it may be vambraced (in armour), habited or vested and cuffed, the tincture of the armour, sleeve or cuff being mentioned.

The hand should be specified as either dexter or sinister; appaumé (open and showing the palm) or closed, or grasping some object; and as erect or fesswise, etc.

Legs may be couped or erased at the knee or thigh, and flexed (bent at the knee).

The following arms provide instances :

Gules, a Saracen's head affronté erased at the neck proper, wreathed about the temples argent and sable—Lloyd (167).

Gules, three dexter arms vambraced and embowed argent, the hands closed proper. Crest: a dexter arm vambraced and embowed proper, the hand grasping an armed leg couped at the thigh and bleeding, also proper—Armstrong (166).

Gules, a chevron between three dexter hands appaumé couped at the wrist and erect argent—Byrne (Plate IV, 1).

Gules, three legs armed proper cojoined in the fess point at the upper part of the thighs, flexed in a triangle, garnished and spurred or—Isle of Man.

The badge of Ulster is a dexter hand open and erect, couped at the wrist, gules (410). The distinguishing badge of baronets (other than those of Nova Scotia) is a white shield or canton charged with a sinister hand appaumé, couped at the wrist and erect, gules, this being placed on the baronet's own shield of arms (Plate XXV).

The human heart, sometimes termed body-heart, represented in heraldry as on playing cards, is famous for its appearance in the Douglas arms : *Argent, a human heart gules ensigned with a royal crown proper, on a chief azure three molets of the field* (Plate III, 3). The royal heart was that of Robert Bruce, which " good Sir James Douglas " was carrying to the Holy Land, that he might bury it at Jerusalem, when he himself fell in battle with the Saracens of Andalusia, 1330. The crown is a comparatively modern addition to the heart added to the Douglas shield to commemorate this event.

Bones are occasionally found, e.g. *Sable, two shin bones in cross argent*, the canting arms of Baynes. A skeleton of human bones occurs in the arms of the city of Londonderry.

168. FITZALAN

THE LION

The king of beasts naturally occupies a pre-eminent position among the animals used in heraldry. From the dawn of armory, the lion has been borne on the shields of sovereigns, princes and nobles, and also of men of lesser rank. The Kings of England and Scotland have displayed lions in their arms since first they possessed any true armorial insignia. Lions also appear in the arms of the native Princes of Wales, the Kings of Leon, of Norway, and of Denmark, and the Counts of Holland, Hainault, Eu, etc. Among the great English baronial families to bear lions were Bohun, Longespée, FitzAlan (168), and Lacy.

From its first appearance in heraldry, the lion was represented conventionally rather than true to nature. The shield of Prince John of Eltham, younger brother of Edward III, finely sculptured in Westminster Abbey in 1336, gives us examples of lions of the best heraldic

168a. Types of Heraldic Lion

style; their frames, though attenuated, being perfect types of fierce elasticity (183). Later the heraldic characteristics of the lion became much exaggerated, as in no. 168a, and the 15th-century Garter-plate of Sir Simon de Felbrigge (324).

The heraldic lion was originally found in only one attitude, namely, erect with one hind paw on the ground, the other three paws being raised, the head facing forward and shown in profile and the tail erect. In early blazons, this is the attitude implied by the term lion without

| 169. Salient | 170. Passant | 171. Statant | 172. Sejant |

qualification. It is now known as the lion rampant. The Royal Arms of Scotland are, *Or, a lion rampant within a double tressure flory counter-flory gules* (Plate VI).

New attitudes were found for the lion so as to create different and distinctive arms incorporating this favourite beast, and it became necessary to give terms of blazon to the various forms. The early heralds considered a lion walking and looking about him to be behaving like a leopard, and they consequently blazoned him as a *lion-leopardé*, or merely as a leopard, though they always drew him as a stylized lion without spots or other leopard-like characteristics. So it is that the lions of England were sometimes blazoned as leopards. They are now termed lions passant guardant.

The lion is now classified, firstly by the attitude of the body, secondly by the position of the head, and thirdly by the type or position of the tail if other than normal. The various attitudes of the body are:

LION RAMPANT: erect, one hind paw on the ground, the other three paws raised, the beast looking forward and having the tail erect (168). A demi-lion rampant, often found in crests and sometimes as a charge in arms, is the upper half of the beast including the tufted end of the tail as it stands erect.

LION SALIENT: in the act of springing, both hind paws on the ground, both forepaws raised, tail erect (169). This was originally merely a variant of the lion rampant.

LION PASSANT: walking, three paws on the ground, the dexter forepaw being raised; the head looking forward, and the tail curved over the back (170).

LION STATANT: as passant, but with all four paws on the ground (171).

172*a*. Sejant affronté   173. Sejant erect   174. Couchant   175. Dormant

LION SEJANT : seated with forepaws on the ground, looking forward, tail passed between the hind legs and its end erect (172). A lion sejant affronté is shown in 172*a*.

LION SEJANT RAMPANT OR SEJANT ERECT: as sejant but with the forepaws raised (173). The Royal Crest of Scotland contains *a lion sejant erect affronté gules crowned or, in the dexter paw a sword and in the sinister a sceptre erect proper* (Plate VI).

LION COUCHANT : crouching, with legs and belly on the ground, looking forward, tail passed between the hind legs and its end erect (174).

LION DORMANT : as couchant but with the head lowered on the forepaws and the tail lying on the ground (175).

All the foregoing attitudes except dormant are subject to the secondary classifications according to the position of the head. These are :

Guardant : having the head turned so as to face the spectator (176). The dexter supporter of the Royal Arms is *a lion rampant guardant regally crowned*. The arms of England are *Gules, three lions passant guardant in pale or.* One such lion, gold upon gules, may be blazoned as " a lion of England " if specifically granted as such. A *lion statant guardant regally crowned* occurs in the Royal Crest (Plate I).

Reguardant : having the head turned so as to look backwards over the shoulder (177, 178, 179).

A lion is normally rampant, passant, etc., to the dexter, i.e. whatever the position of the head, the forepaws are on the dexter side of the shield. There is no need to specify the direction in the blazon unless it is to the sinister.

The lion's tail, if not in the normal position, may be extended (straight out behind it), coward (between the legs—182), or nowed (in a knot).

176. Rampant guardant

177. Rampant reguardant

178. Passant reguardant

179. Statant reguardant

A lion may be double-tailed or *queue fourché* (fork-tailed), and while in practice these are synonymous terms, careful armorists hold that in the former case the fork occurs close to the body (181), and in the latter halfway along the tail's length (180).

Two lions rampant facing one another as though in combat are lions combatant or counter-rampant (286).

Two lions rampant back to back are termed addorsed.

Two lions passant in pale, one to the dexter and the other to the sinister, are described as counter-passant.

Several lions, whether rampant or passant, may be charged on one shield. When more than four occur in the same composition, they may be termed lioncels (little lions), but this distinction is not generally observed in modern blazon. The shield of William Longespée, Earl of Salisbury (3), gives an instance of lioncels. The De Bohun Earls of Hereford bore, *Azure, a bend argent cotised between six lioncels or* (301).

Lions are normally armed and langued gules, i.e. having red claws and tongues, but if themselves gules or on a field of that tincture they

180. Queue fourché

181. HESSE

182. Double-headed and coward

are armed and langued azure or such other tincture as the blazon may specify.

The lion is frequently crowned, or he may be collared, and a chain may be attached to his collar; or he may be gorged (encircled about the throat) with a coronet; or his body may be charged with various devices; or he may be vorant (devouring his prey) or grasping some object in his mouth or paw; e.g. *Azure, a lion double-tailed barry of ten argent and gules crowned or, holding in the dexter paw a sword proper, pommel and hilt gold*—Hesse (181).

When an ordinary is placed across a lion, the lion is said to be

183. Shield of PRINCE JOHN
OF ELTHAM, 1336, in Westminster Abbey

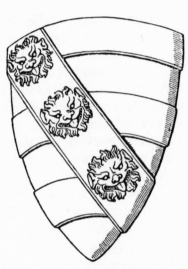

183a. PEMBRIDGE
shield at Clehongre

debruised by such ordinary; when a lion is represented as rising up out of a chief or fess or other charge, he is said to be issuant or naissant from it. (These terms also apply to other creatures.)

Varieties of lion rarely encountered are double-headed (182), bi-corporate (a lion's head affronté with two bodies in the combatant position), tri-corporate (a head affronté with three bodies attached), and dismembered, dechaussé or mutilé (having the head, paws and tail separated from the body by cuts). There are also the man-lion and the heraldic sea-lion, which belong to the class of monsters.

Parts of the lion used as charges include the lion's head consisting of the head and part of the neck in profile, either couped or erased; the lion's face (anciently blazoned as a leopard's face), always affronté, including the beard but not the neck (183*a*); the lion's jamb or gamb, i.e. the entire leg; the lion's paw, which is couped or erased at or below the middle joint; and the lion's tail. A lion's face is sometimes found with a fleur-de-lis thrust through the mouth and appearing at the top of the beast's head; it is then said to be jessant-de-lis (449).

184. Badge of RICHARD II, in Westminster Hall

DEER

Deer and kindred animals form an important group in heraldry, with special terms to indicate their attitude and parts. They include:

The STAG, or HART (which are the same for heraldic purposes), usually represented with a full head of antlers (184).

The BUCK, which differs from the stag only in having broad, flat antlers.

The HIND, which has no antlers.

The REINDEER, ELK, ANTELOPE, SPRINGBOK and other deer-like creatures (some of them recent introductions to heraldry), shown true to nature. These are more often found as supporters than as charges. (The "heraldic antelope" is quite different from the natural antelope here referred to, and is dealt with under the heading of monsters.)

Stags and other animals of the deer type may be rampant, but a more usual attitude is salient or springing, i.e. having both hind hoofs on the ground, the forelegs raised and bent at the knee, as in the arms of Dogherty (Plate IV, 2). A walking stag is termed trippant or tripping, and when it runs it is termed courant, or at speed, or in full chase. It may be statant, and if the head is turned so as to face out of the shield it is at gaze. When resting on the belly with legs bent under, it is lodged or couchant (184).

The head of a stag or similar beast is shown in profile and with part of the neck, couped or erased, unless it is blazoned as caboshed (or

cabossed), when it is full-face with no neck, e.g. *Sable, three bucks'*
heads caboshed argent—Cavendish (185).

The stag's antlers are called attires, and if they are of a different
tincture from the body the animal is said to be attired of such tincture.
The attires of a stag are sometimes found as a charge. Each prong
of the attires is a tyne. With respect to the hoofs, the stag is said to
be unguled.

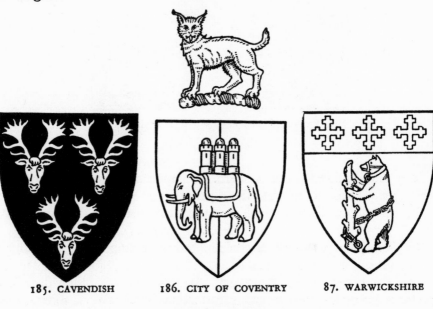

| 185. CAVENDISH | 186. CITY OF COVENTRY | 87. WARWICKSHIRE |

OTHER BEASTS

Any beast may be found in heraldry, and including those of in-
frequent appearance not only in arms but also in crests and supporters,
the variety of animals actually used is large. Only a few, however,
are common, and in some cases the head is a more frequent charge
than the whole animal. As will be seen from the examples in the
following list of common beasts, an allusion to the family name has
in many cases led to the adoption of a particular animal as a charge.

The terms descriptive of attitude (rampant, passant, statant, etc.)
already given in the section on lions, are applicable to other beasts
unless some special term is indicated ; and when it is necessary to specify
their various parts in the blazon, they are said to be langued (of the
tongue), armed (of horns, tusks and claws), and unguled or hoofed.

The LEOPARD, as has been shown, in ancient heraldry meant a lion passant guardant, but in modern heraldry it is found as a separate charge, and was true to nature as a supporter of Rhodesia and Nyasaland. The leopard's face, like the lion's face, is affronté, and may be jessant-de-lis (449). A leopard's head may be in profile or affronté; if the latter, it differs from the leopard's face because it shows part of the neck.

The TIGER, when drawn true to nature, is termed a Bengal tiger. This is to distinguish it from the heraldic tiger (sometimes spelt tyger), which is dealt with under " Monsters." Tasmanian tigers are the supporters of Tasmania (399).

The PANTHER also has heraldic characteristics which place it among the monsters.

The CAT is usually blazoned as a wild cat, mountain cat, or cat-a-mountain, and is usually depicted as tabby. It appears in the arms of Catt, Catton, Keats, and Tibbet. Care must be taken to distinguish from the general term " cat " those animals of the cat family which form separate charges in heraldry, e.g. the LYNX, borne by the family of Lynch and the crest of the City of Coventry (186).

The BEAR is common in heraldry, and is borne as a canting charge by FitzUrse, Beresford, Barnard, Barham, etc. If he is muzzled, or collared and chained, this must be noted in the blazon. The bear and ragged staff was famous as the badge of the Earls of Warwick, and is now a charge in the arms of the Warwickshire County Council : *Gules, a bear argent muzzled of the first, collared and chained or, supporting a ragged staff argent ; on a chief gold, three cross crosslets of the field* (187).

A bear's head, whether couped or erased, takes two forms ; in the English fashion the coup or erasure is carried out horizontally at the bottom of the neck, while in the Scottish fashion the head is couped or erased close, i.e. vertically immediately behind the ears, no portion of the neck being shown, e.g. *Azure, three bears' heads couped close argent, muzzled gules*—Forbes (Plate III, 4). Bears' legs and paws are occasionally found as charges.

The ELEPHANT may be found alone, e.g. *Gules, an elephant passant argent armed or*—Elphinston ; or with a castle on his back : *Per pale gules and vert, an elephant statant and on his back a castle triple-towered and domed, both or*—City of Coventry (186). Elephants' heads occur as charges, as in the arms of the Marquess Camden.

The CAMEL is an occasional charge, found naturally in the arms of the Camel family. He may be laden with bales, as in the crest of the Grocers' Company of London.

The BOAR, or SANGLIER, is borne by Bacon, MacSwynie, Swinhoe and others. Its bristles may be of a different tincture from the rest of the animal, in which case it is said to be crined or bristled of such tincture. The boar's head is borne as a charge by Pigg, Hogg, Swinburn, Swyneshead, etc. It may be couped or erased at the neck or close, according to the English or Scottish fashion (188, 189).

The WOLF and wolf's head are found as charges, the latter being borne by Wolfe and Lupton (*loup*), also attributed to Hugh Lupus, Earl of Chester, and forming the crest of Wolseley (191).

188. Boar's head couped at the neck

189. Boar's head couped close

The Fox, in addition to the usual attitudes, is found courant, and thus (with the motto "For'ard, for'ard") forms the crest of the Leicestershire County Council. Williams of Bodelwyddan bears two foxes counter-salient in saltire. Foxes' heads are borne by Fox and Todd.

The HORSE is found rampant, passant, and also trotting and courant. When rearing with both hind hooves on the ground he is termed forcené (enraged). He may be bridled, or if fully equipped with saddle, etc., is described as furnished or caparisoned. Families bearing the horse include Horsby, Coulthurst, and Trotter. Horses' heads, often termed nags' heads, are borne by Horsefall, Horsley, and Chevall, and occur in the arms of Pepys, as borne by the diarist (190).

HOUNDS common in heraldry are the talbot and greyhound. They are found in the usual attitudes, including courant as well as passant, and if shown chasing another animal they are termed in full chase, or in full course. The family of Talbot bears hounds of that name, and Dogget bears greyhounds. Wolseley also has a talbot (191). Hounds' heads frequently occur; when they are collared, this should be stated in the blazon, and the tincture mentioned.

The BULL and the CALF are often found in canting arms, e.g. Bull, Buller, Turnbull, Metcalfe, Laveale, etc. If ringed through the nose, this should be stated, and the tincture of the ring given. A bull's

190. PEPYS   191. WOLSELEY

head is normally in profile, but if blazoned as caboshed it is affronté and without neck.

The GOAT, when rampant, is sometimes blazoned as climant. Goats' heads are found couped or erased, and may be caboshed.

The RAM is borne by Ramsey, and the ram's head by Ram, Ramston and other families. The latter may be caboshed.

A SHEEP occurs in the arms of Sheepshanks. The fleece is found as a charge in the arms of Leeds, Bury (396), and other cities and towns connected with the woollen industry.

The LAMB is borne by Lambert. A variant of this charge is the Holy Lamb, Paschal Lamb, or *Agnus Dei*, i.e. a lamb passant with a nimbus about its head, supporting on the dexter shoulder a cross-staff from which flies a pennon argent charged with a cross gules.

The BADGER is sometimes blazoned as a brock, and is a canting charge in the arms of the Brock family : *Argent, three brocks proper*.

The BEAVER occurs in the arms of the Borough of Beverley, and supports the arms of Lord Beaverbrook.

The RABBIT, usually termed a coney, is found sejant in the canting arms of Coningsby, and courant in those of Cunliffe.

The SQUIRREL is usually sejant, and frequently shown holding a nut.

The HEDGEHOG, often blazoned as an urcheon, or urchin, is borne by the families of Herries, Harries and Harris, including the Earl of Malmesbury. Here again there is a punning reference to the surname, the hedgehog being in French *hérisson*.

Other beasts, found more frequently as supporters than as charges in arms, are dealt with in Chapter XVI.

192. Arms from the chantry of ABBOT RAMRYDGE (d. 1524), at St. Albans

BIRDS

Birds of many kinds are found in heraldry, some being usually represented in a stylized form while others are depicted according to nature. They have their own descriptive terms. Birds are said to be :

Close or *trussed* when standing on the ground with wings folded; and *perched* when standing on some object.

Rising or *rousant* when about to take wing; this has four varieties according to the position of the wings :

> *wings elevated and displayed*, when the bird has one wing spread on each side of the body, tips upwards ;
>
> *wings displayed and inverted*, when in the same position with wing-tips downwards ;
>
> *wings elevated and addorsed*, when the wings are spread and back to back, tips upwards ;
>
> *wings addorsed and inverted*, when in the same position with wing-tips downwards.

Soaring when flying upwards.

Volant when flying horizontally.

Displayed when the body is affronté with the head turned (usually to the dexter) and wings and legs spread out on each side, the wing-tips upwards ; and *displayed, wings inverted* when in the same position with the tips of the wings downwards.

Where beaks and legs are of a different tincture from the rest of the bird, it is said to be beaked and legged, or beaked and membered, of such tincture ; or, in the case of birds of prey, the word armed may be used.

The EAGLE, sometimes called erne, holds the predominant position among birds in heraldry that the lion has among beasts, and has likewise acquired a distinctive heraldic form. In arms, it is normally displayed, but may be in any of the other positions. An early instance of the eagle as the sole charge in arms is, *Or, an eagle displayed vert*—Monthermer ; while D'Ernford bore, *Sable, an erne displayed argent* as a canting device. More than one eagle may be borne in a shield, and when a number occur they are sometimes blazoned as eaglets, e.g. *Vert, six eaglets or*—Piers Gaveston. Eglesfield bore, *Argent, three eagles displayed gules, armed or*, and these arms, with the addition of *a molet of six points pierced or* charged on the first eagle, are borne by The Queen's College, Oxford, founded in 1340 by Robert de Eglesfield, chaplain to Philippa, Queen of Edward III.

Eagles may be crowned, gorged with a collar or coronet, or charged on the body or wings ; they may grasp any object in their talons ;

they may be shown preying or trussing on another creature.   An eagle preying on a child in swaddling clothes forms the arms of Culcheth.

As an imperial emblem, the eagle displayed was derived from the Roman eagle.   It was formerly depicted sometimes with one head and sometimes with two, but as the eagle became a common charge in heraldry the two-headed eagle was adopted as the distinctive emblem of the Holy Roman Empire, and its two heads came to be regarded as symbolic of dominion over the Eastern and Western Empires (193, 194).   Edmund, Earl of Cornwall, whose father (Richard, second son of King John) was elected King of the Romans in 1256, had on his seal his shield suspended from the beak of an eagle displayed, the wings

193. Imperial eagle from the tomb of William de Valence

194. Imperial eagle, at King's Langley

195. Earl of Cornwall

appearing on each side of the shield (195).   A Prince of the Holy Roman Empire may display his complete achievement of arms (including crest and supporters) on the breast and wings of an imperial eagle, his princely crown being placed above (but not on) the eagle's heads.   An instance of this in British heraldry is provided by the armorial bearings of the Duke of Marlborough.

In the early heraldry of Scotland, a shield is occasionally found displayed on the breast of an eagle, its head, wings and talons appearing from behind the shield.   This practice survives in the achievement of Lord Methuen.

An eagle displayed is sometimes blazoned as an alerion, and is thus usually depicted without beak or legs.

Eagles' heads, wings and legs are found as charges.   Heads may be either couped or erased. Wings may occur singly or in pairs; when two wings are cojoined with tips downwards they are said to be in lure; and when joined with tips upwards they are a vol. Legs are usually erased *à la cuisse*, i.e. at the thigh.

The FALCON and HAWK are in heraldry indistinguishable, and closely resemble the eagle, but while the eagle's head and neck are tufted, the falcon's are smooth. Unless otherwise blazoned, the falcon is represented as close. If rising or volant, the position of the wings must be defined. It may be shown preying. When represented with bells thonged to their legs, falcons are blazoned as belled and jessed; and when the thongs, or jesses, end in rings (vervels or varvels) the bird is described as vervelled. The head may be hooded, i.e. covered by the mask used when the bird is carried on the wrist.

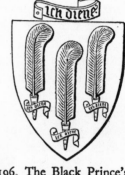

196. The Black Prince's "shield for peace"

The PELICAN, always depicted in a form more heraldic than natural, is generally shown standing above its nest and vulning, or wounding its breast with its beak to nourish its young with its blood. In this form it is blazoned as "a pelican in its piety" (292). In ecclesiastical heraldry it is a symbol of the Eucharist, and it is found in the arms of the Colleges of Corpus Christi at Oxford and Cambridge. The Pelham family bear the pelican as a canting charge.

The SWAN is a favourite device, both as a charge and a crest. A swan ducally gorged and chained was the famous badge of De Bohun, and was derived therefrom by Henry V (334). The bird is shown close unless otherwise blazoned, and when it is rising the wings may take the various forms indicated above. Swans' heads or swans' necks (each term implying both head and neck) are found as charges.

The OSTRICH is usually shown with a horseshoe or other metal object in its beak, apparently in exaggerated reference to its digestive powers. Ostrich feathers are used as charges, the famous instance being the Black Prince's "shield for peace": *Sable, three ostrich feathers, their quills passing through escrolls argent bearing the words Ich Dien* (196).

The CRANE frequently appears standing on one leg and holding a ſtone in the other. It is then said to be " in its vigilance," because if it falls asleep it will rouse itself by dropping the ſtone.

The HERON, STORK, SHELDRAKE, SHOVELLER and CORMORANT are among birds which are generally represented according to nature. The cormorant is termed a liver-bird in the arms of the City of Liverpool.

The RAVEN, ROOK and CROW are indiſtinguishable from one another in heraldry, and any of them may be termed a corbie, as in the canting arms of the family of Corbett. These birds are usually blazoned sable or proper, their legs being also black.

The CORNISH CHOUGH (or simply chough) only differs from the corbie in having red beak and legs (395).

The PEACOCK, sometimes termed pawne, may be found either in profile with its tail close, or affronté with its tail displayed. In the latter position it is blazoned as " a peacock in its pride."

The COCK is the farmyard rooſter, sometimes termed " dunghill cock " to diſtinguish it from other cocks—the gamecock, which has its comb cut and its spurs ſtrengthened for fighting ; and the moorcock or heathcock, which has the farmyard cock's head and body and a tail which may take any form charaſteriſtic of game birds. A cock should be blazoned as armed or spurred, and combed (or creſted) and jelopped, when specifying the tinſtures of beak, spurs, comb and wattles. Cocks' heads are found as charges in the arms of Alcock and others.

The PARROT is blazoned as a popinjay, and the DOVE may be termed a colomb.

The MARTLET is an heraldic form representing a swallow often without legs or feet, preserving the old belief that a swallow cannot perch on the ground. It is a common charge, and is also used as a mark of cadency denoting the fourth son.

Birds are often borne allusively to surnames, e.g. in the arms of Falconer, Hawker, Arundel (*hirondelles*), Swan, Cranſton, Heron, Starkie, Cockburn, etc. In a Roll of Arms temp. Edward II, the Sire Mounpynzon has a lion charged on the shoulder with a chaffinch (*pinson*).

197. Dolphin   198. DE LUCY   199. Escallop

FISH

Fish of many kinds are borne in arms. Sometimes the blazon simply states fish without specifying the variety. The following terms are used to denote position :

Naiant, swimming fesswise.

Urinant (or *uriant*), palewise with the head in base, i.e. diving.

Hauriant, palewise with the head upwards, as if rising to the surface for breathing.

The DOLPHIN has a characteristic heraldic form, and is usually embowed, i.e. bent in a curve (197). When blazoned as proper, it is shown green with scarlet fins and tongue. In the Roll of Arms of Henry III, it occurs in the arms of Giles de Fishbourn : *Gules, a dolphin naiant embowed argent.* While a common heraldic charge, it is particularly associated with the Dauphin, eldest son of the Kings of France, who bore *Or, a dolphin azure* marshalled with the French Royal Arms.

The PIKE, LUCE, or LUCY (borne gold on gules by De Lucy—198), and the SALMON, HERRING, ROACH, TROUT, EEL, etc., have no special heraldic characteristics and are shown according to nature. The ROACH occurs in the canting arms of Roche (Plate IV, 11).

The BARBEL, so named from the barbs attached to its mouth to assist in its search for food, was introduced into English heraldry by John, Count de Barre, who bore at Caerlaverock, 1300, *Azure, crusily-fitchy, two barbels hauriant embowed and addorsed or, within a bordure engrailed Gules* (200).

" As the symbol of a name, almost all Fish have been used in Heraldry ; and in many instances Fish have been assumed in arms in reference to the produce of tne estate, giving to the quaint device a two-fold interest." [1]

Of SHELLS found in heraldry, the commonest is the escallop (199), or cockle-shell, the emblem of St. James, formerly worn as a badge by pilgrims, of whom he was patron. An ancient example is, *Gules, three escallops argent*—Dacre (202). Instances of canting arms including shells are : *Per pale or and vert, a chevron between three whelk-shells, all counterchanged*—Wilkinson (201) ; *Sable, a fess engrailed between three whelk-shells or*—Shelley.

200. DE BARRE   201. WILKINSON   202. DACRE

REPTILES

The SERPENT, or SNAKE, may be nowed, i.e. knotted, as in the arms of Quin (Plate IV, 9), or it may be coiled, the head erect, or glissant, i.e. gliding. It is depicted with open mouth and projecting fangs.

The LIZARD is sometimes blazoned " scaly lizard."

Other reptiles are of rare appearance.

INSECTS

The BEE is a common charge, and in corporate heraldry appears as a symbol of industry. A bee and arrow occur in the arms of Barrow-in-Furness. The arms of Earl Beatty of the North Sea are, *Azure, a beehive beset by nine bees volant or, on a chief argent a cross of St. George gules* (440).

[1] Moule, *Heraldry of Fish*.

The GRASSHOPPER is well known as the crest of Gresham.

The STAG-BEETLE is an allusive charge in the arms of Dore.

Butterflies, scorpions, crickets, hornets, gadflies, ants, and spiders are occasionally found as charges.

MONSTERS

Heralds have drawn on classical and medieval mythology, and on their own creative imaginations, to add a number of monsters and hybrids to the animals of nature. The following occur in British heraldry, though some only rarely.

The DRAGON is a monster with a horny head and forked tongue, a scaly back and rolls like armour on chest and belly, bat-like wings, four legs ending in talons, and a pointed tail. It is found rampant, passant and statant, and (rarely) displayed. A dragon gules occurs in the royal badge for Wales (see page 218), and is a common charge in the civic heraldry of the Principality, while dragons' heads occur in the arms of several Welsh families. A dragon sans wings, or sea-dragon, is found in the arms of Easton.

The WYVERN, or WIVERN, is a species of dragon with only two legs. When blazoned proper it has a green head, back and legs, and red chest, belly, and insides of wings. A forerunner of the wyvern appears on the Bayeux Tapestry as the dragon of Wessex, the standard of the English. A legless wyvern argent, vulned gules, is the crest of the City of Leicester.

A COCKATRICE is a wyvern with a cock's head, comb and wattles.

The GRIFFIN, or GRYPHON, has the head, breast, foreclaws and wings of an eagle, and the hindquarters and tail of a lion. It has ears. When rampant it is frequently termed segreant, and it is also found passant. An early example is, *Azure, a griffin segreant or*—Montagu (ancient arms). When wingless, this monster is termed a male griffin, and in this form it sometimes has horns and a spiky hide.

The OPINICUS has a griffin's head, neck and wings, a lion's body and a bear's tail. It is the crest of the Barber-Surgeons' Company of London.

The UNICORN, famous as the Scottish royal supporter, resembles the horse in the head and body, and has one long horn projecting from the forehead, cloven hoofs, a lion's tail, tufted hocks, and a beard.

Unicorns' heads are found as charges, e.g. *Argent, gutty de sang three unicorns' heads erased sable, armed and crined or, langued azure*—Brooke-Little.

The PEGASUS, the winged horse of classical mythology, is sometimes found as a supporter, and in some recent civic heraldry has been used as an emblem of air-transport.

The ENFIELD has a fox's head and ears, a wolf's body, hind legs and tail, while eagle's shanks and talons form its forelegs. It is the crest of the Irish family of Kelly, and the principal charge in the arms granted in 1946 to Enfield Urban District Council.

The HERALDIC TIGER (sometimes spelt tyger), believed to have resulted from the medieval heralds' ignorance of the natural tiger, resembles the lion but has a down-curving tusk on the end of its nose.

The HERALDIC ANTELOPE or IBEX has a head and body like the heraldic tiger's, with serrated horns and deer's legs. It was a badge of Henry V, and in Plate XXI is seen as a supporter and in the crest of Lord Byng of Vimy.

The HERALDIC PANTHER generally resembles the panther of nature, but is " incensed," i.e. it has flames issuing from the mouth and ears. It was a badge of Henry IV and Henry VI, and is now found as a supporter of the Duke of Beaufort's arms.

The SALAMANDER is generally represented as a lizard-like creature amid flames, but sometimes as a fire-breathing dog with a lion's tail.

The PHOENIX in flames is found as a crest, and was a badge of Queen Elizabeth I.

The MERMAID was a badge of the Berkeleys, and Sir Walter Scott's dexter supporter. She figures, with the customary mirror and comb, in the arms of Birmingham University as an emblem of the Mason family. MERMEN, or TRITONS, also occur in heraldry.

The HERALDIC SEA-LION is a lion terminating in a fish's tail. It is found as a supporter of Lloyd's Corporation (Plate XXIV, 2) and the Port of London Authority. It must not be confused with the natural sea-lion, which is also found as a charge.

The CAMELOPARD is a hybrid only in name, being no other than the giraffe, but believed by early heralds to be a cross between a camel and a leopard.

Some other heraldic monsters which are rarely found are listed in the Glossary.

203. DE LA HAYE   204. DRAKE   205. LEESON

CELESTIAL OBJECTS

The SUN in heraldry is represented by a disc, sometimes with a human face, environed with rays which may be alternately straight and wavy, symbolic of both light and heat (203). The sun may be blazoned as " in his splendour " or " in his glory." The number of rays is variable and need not be specified. In an early instance of this charge, *Argent, the sun in glory gules*—De la Haye, 12, 16 and 24 rays are shown in various drawings. In some cases, always to be specified, the sun appears as shining from behind a cloud, or as rising or setting, or a ray of the sun may be borne alone : *Azure, a ray of the sun issuing from the dexter corner bendwise proper*—Aldam.

Several rays of the sun issuing from a cloud are termed a sunburst. This was a badge of Edward III and Richard II (329) and, surmounted by a crown, is the badge of Windsor Herald. A charge placed on the sun so that the rays appear all round it is said to be *en soleil*. A white rose en soleil was a badge of the House of York, and is now part of the badge of York Herald.

The MOON, when full, may be blazoned " in her complement " or " in plenitude." It may be represented with a human face. The moon is crescent when the horns point towards the chief, increscent (or in increment) when they point to the dexter, and decrescent when they point to the sinister. (The crescent as a separate charge is dealt with later.)

The stars of heaven are blazoned as ESTOILES, and have six (or sometimes more) wavy rays. The estoile must be distinguished from the star-shaped figure called a molet, or mullet, which has straight rays and may be pierced (see Inanimate Objects). In Scotland the term star applies to an unpierced molet.

Sir Francis Drake bore, in allusion to his course round the world between the poles, *Sable, a fess wavy between two estoiles argent* (204). A representation of the Southern Cross occurs in the arms of Birdwood of Anzac, Bart.; and Caird bears: *Per fess wavy azure and argent, in chief eight molets or forming a representation of the North Star and the constellation Ursa Major, and in base two bars wavy of the first.*

CLOUDS appear as charges, e.g. *Gules, a chief argent on the lower part thereof a cloud, rays of the sun issuing therefrom downwards proper*—Leeson (205). Clouds are sometimes represented conventionally by a nebuly line. Raining clouds are shown symbolically in the arms of the Metropolitan Water Board: *Argent, on a pile vert a dexter hand gold issuing from a cloud in chief proper and scattering eight gouttes d'eau; in base three bars wavy azure; on a chief nebuly argent a cross of St. George charged with a lion of England.*

A RAINBOW occurs in the crest of Hope.

The THUNDERBOLT is represented by a twisted column of flame between two cojoined wings, with four jagged darts of lightning in saltire. It has come to be an emblem of electrical power and as such appears in the crest of the B.B.C. (Plate XXIV).

206. CARLOS

207. Planta genista

208. ORANGE FREE STATE

TREES AND PLANTS

While trees and plants are found in heraldry in great variety, only a few kinds are common. A tree may be depicted growing naturally from the ground, when it is blazoned as on, growing on, or issuing from, a mount. If uprooted it is described as eradicated ; or it may be couped at the trunk. A tree bearing fruit is termed fruted, or in the case of an oak, acorned. Some little-used terms applied to trees will be found in the Glossary.

Several trees growing from one mount are a hurst of trees. A hurst of elms is the crest of Elmhirst.

Of trees found in British heraldry, the oak is the commonest. A famous example is, *Or, on a mount in base vert an oak-tree proper fruted gold, surmounted by a fess gules charged with three royal crowns proper*— Carlos (206). These arms were granted to Colonel Carlos, who shared Charles II's refuge in the oak at Boscobel after the Battle of Worcester.

Trunks and stumps or stocks of trees are found as charges, and often in crests. The stock of a tree, couped and eradicated, was a royal badge in Plantagenet times in allusion to the Manor of Woodstock.

Branches, sprigs and leaves of trees and plants are also found. When a sprig or leaf has the stem which attached it to the branch, it is termed slipped.

Famous among plants in heraldry is the *Planta genista*, or broom-plant, the badge from which the Plantagenets derived their name (207). The pods with their seeds, as well as leaves and flowers, are represented on the effigy of Richard II in Westminster Abbey.

The trefoil is a conventional leaf with three lobes, usually slipped. A trefoil slipped vert, representing shamrock, is a badge of Ireland. The maple-leaf stands for Canada and wattle (mimosa) for Australia.

Like other charges, trees and plants frequently make allusion to the names of their bearers. Thus the arms of the Orange Free State consist of an orange tree (208); Leman bears a lemon-tree; Aikenhead, acorns; Aikman and Okstead, oak branches; Hazlerigg, hazel leaves; and Fraser, strawberry flowers (*fraises*—Plate III, 5).

Fruits of various kinds are found as charges, apart from the trees on which they grow, e.g. *Argent, three apples slipped gules*—Applegarth *Gules, three pears or*—Perrott.

Wheat, barley and other grain is found sometimes as ears or clusters of ears, e.g. *Gules a chevron between three clusters of wheat each containing three ears or*—John de Wheathamstede, Abbot of St. Albans (temp. Henry VI) ; but grain is commonly in the form of a sheaf, termed a garb. A garb should be treated as wheat unless some other grain is specified or clearly intended, e.g. garbs in the arms of Barley should

209. EARLS OF CHESTER   210. CITY OF LEICESTER

have the characteristic barley ears. *Azure, three garbs or*, are the arms of the Earldom of Chester (209). When the band which ties a garb is of a different tincture from the rest, the garb is said to be banded of such tincture.

211. Forms of Fleur-de-lis

FLOWERS

Chief among the many flowers and floral forms used in heraldry is the fleur-de-lis, the ancient cognizance of France and also from an early date found as a general charge in arms.

As the French emblem, the FLEUR-DE-LIS, or *fleur-de-luce*, may be a rebus signifying "flower of Louis." It was first borne on a royal seal by Louis VII of France (1137–80). Edward III of England quartered the French arms, *Azure, semé-de-lis or* (367), on his Great Seal in 1340, and in or about 1405 Henry IV reduced the number of fleurs-de-lis to three, following the reduction made in the French seal by Charles V (1364–80). The fleurs-de-lis of France were removed from the Royal Arms of Great Britain in 1801, but as adornments of the Scottish tressure fleurs-de-lis are still found in our Royal Arms.

Plate VII

AN EARLY ROLL OF ARMS

THE DERING ROLL

These shields are taken from a facsimile of the Dering Roll which
was probably compiled c. 1270–80. The facsimile is one of the
Hatton-Dugdale facsimiles painted c. 1640 and now in the
possession of the Society of Antiquaries. It should be noted
that in the colours of the facsimile, although far clearer than in
the original roll, there is occasional confusion between green
and blue.

le connte de P

le connte de Penenas

le connte de Anegos

le connte de carriby

le Connte de Asseles

le Connte de Patenes

le connte de mantefte

le connte de Ffyf

Johan Wake

Genenill

Hastyng

Robert de Offord

Johan de mounfort

Robt le fiz Wauter

Johan de sant Johan

Thomas de chalbord

PLATE VII

AN EARLY ROLL OF ARMS
THE DERING ROLL

In general heraldry, the fleur-de-lis may be borne as the sole charge in arms, e.g. *Azure, a fleur-de-lis argent*—Digby; sometimes varied: *Azure, a fleur-de-lis gold fimbriated ermine*—City of Wakefield. It is frequently borne in groups of three or more, in bend, cross, saltire, etc., and in conjunction with ordinaries and other charges. It may be used to ornament other forms, e.g. the tressure and the fess dancetty floretty already noted. As a mark of cadency, the fleur-de-lis is the difference of the sixth son. The fanciful elaboration of the boss apparently gave rise to the lion's or leopard's face jessant-de-lis (449). A variation on the traditional fleur-de-lis was devised shortly after World War II and is described as burgeonee, that is, "bursting forth", and it is shown as being in bud but with the outer petals just parting (211*a*).

211*a*. Fleur-de-lis burgeonee

The LILY of nature is found as a charge distinct from the fleur-de-lis, e.g. *Sable, three lilies argent, on a chief per pale azure and gules a fleur-de-lis on the dexter and a lion passant guardant on the sinister side, both gold*— Eton College (Plate XXIII, 1),   Here the lilies stand for St. Mary the Virgin, to whom the College is dedicated; the fleur-de-lis is also an emblem of the Virgin.

212. Forms of Heraldic Rose

The ROSE is represented in heraldry by a stylized form of the dog-rose, being normally a flower of five petals, though a cluster of five others may form an inner ring round the seeded centre. The tips of the sepals appear between the petals. The tincture of the flower must be blazoned, since no one colour is "proper" to the rose. A rose of any tincture may be barbed and seeded proper, when the sepals will be green and the centre gold; or it may be barbed and seeded of some other tinctures. Only the flower is shown unless the blazon states that it is leaved and slipped, or stalked. On the rare occasions when a natural rose is shown, the name of the rose is included if it is not of an heraldic tincture. Such a rose has sometimes been blazoned "proper", but this gives no indication of what colour it should be.

It is said that a golden rose was a badge of Edward I, and that his descendants differenced its tincture, the House of York bearing a white rose and the House of Lancaster a red one as badges. The white and red roses were united by Henry VII in the Tudor rose which took various forms, i.e. quarterly argent and gules, or gules and argent; or more frequently, a rose argent charged upon another gules, or vice versa. The royal badge for England is still the red and white rose united, slipped and leaved proper.

Apart from its national significance, the rose is found as a common charge in heraldry. As a mark of cadency, it is the difference of the seventh son.

The THISTLE, slipped and leaved proper, is the floral emblem of Scotland, and is borne by a number of Scottish families, sometimes as an augmentation, as in the arms of Keith, Earl of Kintore (294).

The QUATREFOIL, CINQUEFOIL or QUINTFOIL, SIXFOIL and OCTOFOIL (or double quatrefoil) are conventional floral forms consisting of as many petals as their names imply. They may be slipped if so described in the blazon, and if they have a hole in the centre they are blazoned as pierced. In cadency, the octofoil is the mark of the ninth son. The City of Leicester bears *Gules, a cinquefoil pierced ermine* (210). In early heraldry, no clear distinction was drawn between the rose, the cinquefoil and the sixfoil.

The GARLAND or WREATH (not to be confused with the crest-wreath) consists of sprays of leaves, or leaves and flowers, twined into a circle. The blazon should state the kind of leaves and flowers composing the garland, but if it does not, any conventional form may be depicted. The garland is sometimes termed a chaplet.

213. CHAPPELL   214. M'ADAM   215. OLDMIXON   216. GERVAYS

INANIMATE OBJECTS

The objects which appear as charges in heraldry are very numerous, and many of them are rarely found. In this section only a few objects, or classes of objects, are selected for mention, on account of their frequency or special heraldic form, or the terms applied to them in blazon. Some others are listed in the Glossary.

ANCHOR : drawn without rope or chain unless blazoned as cabled, when the cable is shown twisted round the beam (or cross-bar) and stock. An anchor is borne fesswise gold on a flag gules by the British Admiralty (436). An anchor is placed palewise unless otherwise blazoned. The points or barbs are termed flukes. *Or, an anchor erect sable*—Chappell (213).

ARROW : placed palewise unless otherwise blazoned; the position of the points should be stated, e.g. *Vert, three arrows points downwards argent*—M'Adam (214). When it is necessary to specify the tinctures of the point and feathers, the arrow is said to be armed or barbed, and feathered or flighted, of such tincture. A sheaf or bundle of arrows consists of three, unless more are specified, one erect and the others crossing in saltire, all tied at the centre; the term banded is used in describing the tie. The arms of the City of Sheffield and Sheffield University contain a sheaf of eight arrows in saltire banded argent. The broad arrow, a form of arrow-head, is dealt with under Pheon.

AXE : several kinds occur, viz. :

The battle-axe or broad axe has a curved edge and a spike on the back of the blade, which is mounted on a straight haft with a spike at the top. *Azure, a battle-axe palewise or, headed argent*—Oldmixon (215). These arms were granted in 1573.

The Danish axe is similar but has a curved haft.

The Lochaber axe has a straight haft with a hook at the top.

The pole-axe has a long haft.

Axes are placed erect with their heads in chief, edge to the dexter, unless otherwise blazoned. If the blade and haft are of different tinctures, this must be noted in the blazon. The axe should be distinguished from the bill and the halberd (*qq.v.*).

BEACON : an iron cage containing material in flames set on the top of a pole with a ladder against it. It was a badge of Henry V, and appears on his monument at Westminster. It is frequently blazoned as fired, or flammant proper. *Azure, three beacons with ladders or fired gules*—Gervays (216).

BELLS are of two kinds : the church bell (sometimes called war bell) and the hawk's bell. The former is understood unless the latter is blazoned. *Sable, three bells argent*—Porter (220) ; *Sable, three hawk-bells or*—Bellchamber (221).

BILL, BILL-HOOK, or WOOD-BILL : a weapon or instrument with a hooked blade on a long shaft.

BIRD-BOLT : a blunt or ball-headed arrow, also termed *boson*.

BOMB or GRENADE : shown as a ball with flames issuing from a hole in the top. The arms of Lord Nelson include three bombs fired proper (295).

BOOK : a common charge among educational bodies. The blazon should show whether the book is open or shut, and, as regards tinctures, how it is clasped, edged, and bound or leathered ; also any inscription it bears. *Azure, between three open crowns or an open book proper, leathered gules, garnished and having on the dexter side seven seals gold, and inscribed with the words* DOMINUS ILLUMINATIO MEA— University of Oxford (217 ; see also the University of Cambridge, 386).

Bow : the long-bow is shown unless the cross-bow is specified. The bow is shown bent and strung unless otherwise blazoned. If the cord is of a different tincture, the bow is blazoned as stringed of that tincture ; *Ermine, three bows bent and stringed palewise in fess proper*—Bowes (218), quartered by H.M. Queen Elizabeth the Queen Mother. *Ermine, a cross-bow (or arbalest) palewise gules*—Arblaster (219).

217. UNIVERSITY OF OXFORD   218. BOWES   219. ARBLASTER

BRIDGE: the number of arches should be stated; also if the bridge is towered or embattled.

BUCKLE: the shape should be indicated, i.e. whether lozenge, oval, round, square, etc. An "arming buckle" is lozenge-shaped. The position of the tongue, whether pendent, point in chief, or fesswise with point in dexter or sinister, should be noted. A buckle is sometimes termed a *fermail* (plural *fermaux*). *Azure, three round buckles or, tongues pendent*—Rosselyne (222).

BUGLE-HORN or HUNTING-HORN: a curved horn, usually shown suspended by ribbons or strings tied in a knot, and so blazoned as stringed, the tincture of the strings or ribbons being mentioned if different from that of the horn. When the horn is decorated with bands of a different tincture, it is described as garnished or viroled of that tincture. *Argent, a bugle-horn sable, garnished or, stringed gules*—Forrester (223).

CALTRAP or CHEVAL-TRAP: a contrivance consisting of four co-

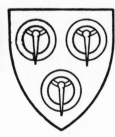

220. PORTER   221. BELLCHAMBER   222. ROSSELYNE   223. FORRESTER

224. Caltraps

joined spikes so arranged that when it lies on the ground one spike is always upwards (224). It was used in war to maim horses, and figured particularly at the battle of Bannockburn, in reference to which it occurs in the arms of Stirling County Council (397).

CAP OF ESTATE or MAINTENANCE, or CHAPEAU: a cap usually of crimson velvet, lined and guarded with ermine, sometimes forming the basis of a crest (325, 442).

CARBUNCLE, ESCARBUNCLE, or CHARBOCLE: an ornamental boss with sceptre-like rays (usually eight in number) sometimes joined by cross-pieces (225). This charge probably originated in decorative treatment of radiating bands of metal used to strengthen the shield. In early heraldry it was found in the centre of the shield, but it has now become a charge which may be found in any position.

CASTLE: unless otherwise described, the castle is depicted as consisting of two round towers connected by a wall containing a port, or archway, in which a portcullis may be shown (226). If a central tower rises from the connecting wall, the castle is blazoned as triple-towered. Triangular and quadrangular castles also occur, consisting of three and four towers respectively, with connecting walls, shown in perspective. The towers of a castle are battlemented, and usually flat-topped, but they may have domes or conical caps. The port and windows, or

225. Carbuncle

226. Castle

227. SCOTT

228. ROOKE
(Chessrooks)

arrow-slits, may be of a different tincture from the rest.   A castle is said to be masoned of a particular tincture when the cement pointing is of a different tincture from the stones.   A castle must be distinguished from a tower and a gateway (*qq.v.*).

CATHERINE WHEEL : a wheel, usually of six or eight spokes, with a number of short, curved blades along the rim; the emblem of St. Catherine's martyrdom. *Argent, three catherine wheels sable, within a bordure engrailed gules*—Scott of Scott's Hall, Kent (227).

CHESSROOK or COCKE : represented heraldically by two wing-like projections on the base of a chess-piece, because the actual rook or castle of chess would be confused with the heraldic tower.   *Sable, three chessrooks argent*—Rooke (228).

CLARION, CLARICORD, or SUFFLUE : a wind-instrument of doubtful form, but possibly consisting of pan-pipes or a mouth-organ with a handle.   It is shown in various forms (229), sometimes with upright

229. Forms of Clarion or Sufflue

pipes and sometimes with a flat top pierced with holes.   It has been confused with a lance-rest (a bracket for holding lances, found as a charge), and is sometimes blazoned as a rest, and even as an organ-rest, a term which makes confusion worse confounded.   The clarion was the rebus-badge of the De Clares, and occurs in the arms of Granville *Gules, three clarions or* (229a).

CRESCENT : a form which probably originated in the crescent moon, but has acquired a distinct existence as a separate charge.   It is normally shown with the points upwards.   When the points are to the dexter it is an increscent, and when they are to the sinister it is decrescent. In cadency, the crescent is the mark of the second son. *Azure, three crescents or*—De Rythre (230).

CROWNS and CORONETS of various types are frequent as charges in arms, and are dealt with in Chapter XVII.

CROZIER, CROSIER or PASTORAL STAFF : the official staff of a bishop

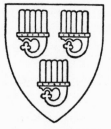

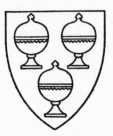

229a. GRANVILLE　　230. DE RYTHRE　　231. BUTLER　　232. Fetterlock

or abbot, having a crook-head (*crocia*, a crook). It is a frequent charge in ecclesiastical and civic heraldry (383).

CUP : depicted as a goblet with stem and foot, and sometimes termed a standing cup or chalice. If it has handles, this should be stated in the blazon. When the cup is provided with a dome-shaped cover, it is termed a covered cup : *Azure, three covered cups or*—Le Botiler, Butler (231).

CUSHION, OREILLER, or PILLOW : usually square or lozenge-shaped with a tassel at each corner (260 and Plate IV, 10).

FETTERLOCK : a shackle and padlock (232). It was borne as a badge, sometimes encircling a falcon, by Edmund Langley, fifth son of Edward III, and his successors as Plantagenet Dukes of York, including Edward IV.

FIRE-BALL : a ball with four flames bursting from it cross-wise ; to be distinguished from a bomb.

FOUNTAIN : a roundle barry wavy argent and azure. A natural fountain must be blazoned accordingly.

GALLEY or LYMPHAD : an ancient ship with a single mast (unless blazoned as a three-masted galley) which may be in full sail (233), or sail furled and oars in action. Particulars and tinctures of sails, flags and pennants should be given in the blazon, e.g. *Argent, a galley, or lymphad, sable, sails furled, flag and pennants flying, and oars in action proper*—Lordship of Lorne (quartered by the Duke of Argyll).

233. Galley

GATE : the ordinary five-barred gate is shown unless otherwise blazoned.

GATEWAY or GATEHOUSE : a towered and embattled portway, differing little from a castle except that the port is much larger in proportion to the rest of the structure. Instances are found in civic heraldry.

GAUNTLET and GLOVE : the blazon should state whether such a charge is dexter or sinister, appaumé, open or clenched, erect or fesswise, etc., as in the case of a hand. Hawking gloves and falconers' gloves have pendent tassels, the tincture of which should be stated.

GEM RING : a ring with a gem set in it, blazoned as gemmed azure, or gules, etc.

GLOBE, TERRESTRIAL GLOBE or SPHERE : depicted as a sphere with the lines of latitude and longitude marked on it, and sometimes mounted on a stand. The continents may be shown, and indeed in some cases are necessary to the blazon, e.g. the arms of Captain James Cook (1728–79) : *Azure, between two pole stars gold a sphere on the plane of the Meridian, North Pole elevated, circles of latitude for every ten degrees and of longitude for fifteen, showing the Pacific Ocean between sixty and two hundred and forty west, bounded on one side by America and on the other by Asia and New Holland, in Memory of his having explored and made Discoveries in that Ocean, so very far beyond all former Navigators : his Track thereon marked with red lines* (234).

GORGE, GURGES or WHIRLPOOL : this is represented by a spiral or a number of concentric rings covering the whole field (246). *Argent, a gorge azure*—Rafe de Gorges (Roll of Henry III).

HALBERD : a weapon consisting of a combination of spear and axe on a long pole. In its later and ceremonial form it is decorative and has a fringe under the head.

HAMMER, MALLET or MARTEL : if the haft is of a different tincture from the head, this should be stated in the blazon. Care should be taken in accurate representation if the blazon indicates that the implement is one associated with a particular craft.

HARP : the tincture of the strings must be mentioned if different from that of the frame : e.g. *Azure, a harp or stringed argent*—Ireland (235). The decorative treatment of the frame is a matter of taste. The Irish harp has commonly been shown in the Royal Arms with the frame in the form of a winged woman, but the modern practice is to adopt a Celtic form associated with Brian Boru.

HAWK'S LURE : a decoy used by falconers to entice the hawk back after chasing its prey. It consisted of two wings, tips downwards, joined by a line and ring.

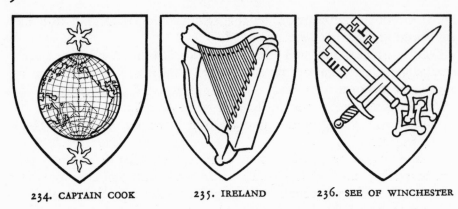

234. CAPTAIN COOK   235. IRELAND   236. SEE OF WINCHESTER

HELM, HEAUME, HELMET: types of helms occurring as charges in arms include knight's, esquire's, antique, and barred, as well as the morion or steel cap. The blazon should state whether a helm is close, or has the beaver or vizor up; and whether in profile or affronté; and if it is garnished and plumed the tinctures should be given. (Types of helm are dealt with in Chapter XIII.)

HORSESHOES are shown with the toes upwards unless blazoned as reversed. They are sometimes termed *ferrs*.

KEY: the blazon should state whether the ward is upwards or downwards, and to the dexter or the sinister. Keys in saltire usually have the wards upwards and outwards. In ecclesiastical heraldry the keys " of binding and loosing " (St. Matthew xvi, 19) are the emblem of St. Peter: *Gules, two keys addorsed bendwise, the uppermost argent and the other or, and between them a sword bendwise sinister, blade silver, pommel and hilt gold*—See of Winchester (236).

KNIFE: if the handle is of a different tincture from the blade, the knife is termed hafted of such tincture. Particular types of knives are sometimes found, e.g. shoemaker's, tanner's, etc.

MAUNCH or MANCH: a sleeve having a long lappet pendent from the cuff, worn by ladies in the time of Henry I (237). It was probably as a lady's favour that it became a charge in heraldry. It was borne at a very early date by De Hastings: *Or, a maunch gules* (238).

MILL-RIND, MILL-IRON, or FER-DE-MOLINE: The iron retaining piece fixed at the centre of a millstone (242). It is a canting charge in the arms of Mills and Molineux. (Refer to cross moline, page 50.)

MOLET or MULLET: derived from *molette*, a spur-rowel, and distinct

237. Forms of Maunch

in origin and in form from the estoile. The molet has straight rays, and normally five of them, unless a greater number be specified, e.g. a molet of six (or more) points. If it has a hole in the middle, it is a molet pierced. In Scottish blazonry, the term molet (or spur-rowel) is applied only to the pierced molet, the unpierced form being termed a star. No. 243 shows two St. John shields, viz. *Argent on a chief gules two molets of six points or;* and *checky or and azure, on a chief gules two molets of six points gold pierced of the field.*

PHEON : the barbed head of an arrow, engrailed on the inner edges of the barbs. When not so engrailed, it is sometimes termed a broad arrow. The pheon is borne point downwards unless a different position is indicated in the blazon. *Or, a pheon azure*—Sidney (239).

PORTCULLIS : a defence for a gateway formed of transverse bars bolted together, the vertical bars being pointed at the foot. It is usually represented as having rings at its uppermost angles from which depend the chains by which it was raised and lowered (240). It was a badge of the Beauforts, and was derived from them by Henry VII and Henry VIII (Plate XII, 8). It is a charge in the arms of the City of Westminster, and is frequently found in both personal and corporate heraldry.

SEAX : a Saxon sword, having a broad, curved blade with a notch

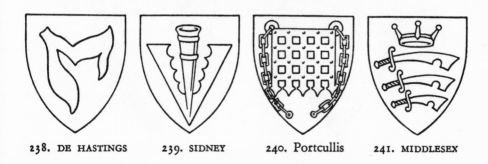

238. DE HASTINGS   239. SIDNEY   240. Portcullis   241. MIDDLESEX

242. Forms of Mill-rind

in its back. *Gules, three seaxes barwise proper, hilts to the dexter, in chief a Saxon crown gold*—Middlesex County Council (241).

SHIP : as well as the heraldic galley, or lymphad, already noticed, ships of many kinds and periods appear in heraldry. An ancient ship has one mast and sail, and a high prow and stern, which may be castellated, but differs from the galley in having no oars. A Viking ship or a Dragon ship is sometimes found. A ship in full sail is usually depicted as a square-rigged three-masted vessel, but regard should be paid to the date of the grant of arms, and a vessel of appropriate period should be shown, e.g. in the case of Sir Francis Drake's crest of a ship in full sail on a terrestrial globe, round which it is being drawn by a hand appearing from clouds, the ship should obviously be a representation of Drake's "Golden Hind." Steamships also appear as charges, e.g. a paddle-wheel steamship under steam and canvas in the arms of Barrow-in-Furness. Sometimes a particular vessel is blazoned, as in the case of *H.M.S. La Lutine in full sail*, the crest of the Corporation of Lloyd's (Plate XXIV, 2). Details should be blazoned of flags, pennons, etc., and any devices on the sails.

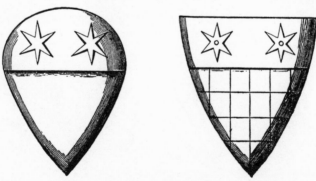

243. ST. JOHN family

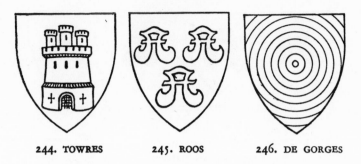

244. TOWRES   245. ROOS   246. DE GORGES

SPEAR : usually a lance or tilting-spear; *Or, on a bend sable a spear gold, the point steeled proper*—William Shakespeare (424).

SPUR : before the reign of Edward II the spur consisted of a single goad-like point, and was known as the prick-spur. About 1320 the spur with a wheel began to supersede the earlier form, and shortly after the true rouelle spur, having the wheel spiked, made its appearance. The last type is normally shown when the spur appears as a charge in heraldry. (For spur-rowel, see molet.)

SWORD : this is represented as straight in the blade and cross-hilted, and is unsheathed unless otherwise blazoned (236). The hilt includes the grip and quillons, and the pommel is the knob at the end of the grip. When these are of a different tincture from the blade, the sword is described as pommelled and hilted of such tincture, although some pedants insist on the blazon, "the pommel, hilt and quillons etc".

TORCH or FLAMBEAU : blazoned as fired, or inflamed.

TOWER : this differs from a castle, as it consists of a single tower, battlemented at the top and having a portway in the base. It may have three turrets rising above the battlements, when it is a tower triple-towered, or triple-turreted; *Sable, a tower triple-turreted or*—Towres (244). It may be masoned of a particular tincture, as in the case of a castle.

TRIDENT : the pronged spear associated with Neptune, derived from (and sometimes blazoned as) a salmon-spear or fishing-spear.

WATER-BOUGET : a vessel used for carrying water, consisting of two conjoined skins, or bags, with a wooden cross-piece by which they were carried over the shoulder: *Gules, three water-bougets argent*—Roos (245). It takes various forms (247).

WHEEL : usually depicted as a wagon-wheel, sometimes with decorative spokes, unless some particular form is specified, e.g. cog-wheel.

247. Forms of Water-bouget

Cycle wheels are found in the arms of Bowden. Winged wheels occur
in arms, often as emblems of engineering and transport.

WHIRLPOOL (246), see GORGE.

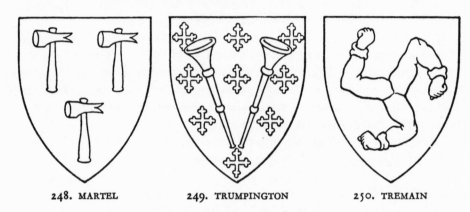

248. MARTEL   249. TRUMPINGTON   250. TREMAIN

CANTING ARMS AND REBUSES

In the foregoing notes on charges, attention has been drawn to
several which have obvious reference to the name of the bearer of
the arms. Allusive or canting arms (termed also *armes parlantes*) abound
in early heraldry, and if it were possible to trace every ancient shield
and every surname to its origin, it would probably be found that an
allusive connection between name and arms was much more prevalent
than is now apparent. The original allusions are now often difficult
to trace, partly because some names have changed their form, and partly
because some devices have lost the old terms which constituted the play
on the name. In some cases, too, the play appears to have been on
the Christian name of the original bearer of the arms. In the Walford
Roll (c. 1280), Garin de Bassingbourne bears *geroune (gyronny) d'or et
d'azure* ; and Eschelard de Monsyrolle, *d'argent un bend gulez engrele six
scallops d'azure.*

Instances of ancient canting arms (in addition to those already given) are: Martel, *Or, three martels gules* (248); De Trumpington, *Azure, crusily, two trumpets pileways or* (249); De Ferrers, horseshoes (*ferrs*); Tremain, *Gules, three dexter arms cojoined and flexed in triangle or, hands clenched proper* (250); De Hertley, a hart; Ramsey, rams; Rossel, three roses; Leveson, three laurel leaves; Arundel, swallows (*hirondelles*); Wingfield, wings; De Eschales, escallops; and Pigot, pics (pick-axes).

In blazoning, where possible a term should be used which preserves the allusion to the name; e.g. for Corbett, three corbies rather than three ravens.

251. Rebus of
ABBOT RAMRYDGE

252. Rebus of
BISHOP OLDHAM

Canting figures are found not only in arms but also in devices termed *rebuses* because they speak *non verbis sed rebus*. This was a favourite practice in the Middle Ages. For instance, the monument of Abbot Ramrydge at St. Albans bears figures of rams, each with the word *rydge* on its collar (251). An ash-tree growing out of a tun for the name Ashton, at St. John's, Cambridge, is another example of a numerous series. The tun to represent the termination " ton " was in great favour; thus at Winchester, in the chantry of Bishop Langton (1500) a musical note called a " long " is inserted into a tun for Langton; a vine and a tun for his See, Winton, and a hen sitting on a tun for his prior, Hunton. In the chantry of Bishop Oldham at Exeter, an owl with a label in its beak charged with the letters *dom* (252) expresses his name in the dialect which still prevails in Lancashire, where the Borough of Oldham bears arms (granted in 1894) containing three owls.

Other instances are, a hart lying in water for Bishop Walter Lyhart (Norwich Cathedral); peaches, each charged with a letter *e*, for Sir John Peché (253); a human eye and a slip of a tree, and a man in the act of falling from a tree ("I slip!") for Abbot Islip (Westminster Abbey). The practice extends to mottoes, as will be noted later.

253. Arms and rebus of
SIR JOHN PECHÉ

CHURCHILL

HOWARD

LANE

SHOVEL

TREVES

WELLESLEY

Plate VIII

AUGMENTATIONS OF HONOUR

Plate VIII

AUGMENTATIONS OF HONOUR

(See Chapter XI)

CHURCHILL : Quarterly Churchill and Spencer, showing (i) the canton of St. George added to the arms of Sir Winston Churchill in the reign of Charles II ; and (ii), the escutcheon of St. George charged with the arms of France, commemorating the victories of John Churchill, Duke of Marlborough. (*p.* 127)

HOWARD, with the escutcheon of augmentation for Flodden. (*p.* 125)

LANE, with the canton of England granted by Charles II. (*p.* 126)

SHOVEL, alluding to the victories of Sir Cloudesley Shovel. (*p.* 127)

TREVES, with the lion of England in chief granted to Sir Frederick Treves, Bt., Surgeon to King Edward VII.

WELLESLEY, with the inescutcheon charged with the Union device granted to the first Duke of Wellington. (*p.* 127)

CHAPTER IX

DIFFERENCING

THE early Rolls of Arms, compiled when the number of persons using heraldic insignia in any realm was small, show that distinction was attained by ringing the changes on relatively few forms, emblems and tinctures. We find many shields simply parted or varied, or charged with an ordinary or other geometrical form; a fair number with a lion; some with an eagle or other bird; a few with fish; while fleurs-de-lis, cinquefoils or roses, molets, garbs, crescents, escallops and boars' heads complete the list of charges occurring with any frequency.

As heraldry developed, it was enriched by the elaboration of some of its early forms, and the introduction of new emblems. This was, no doubt, partly due to a growing realization of its decorative and symbolic possibilities, but heraldic inventiveness was also stimulated by necessity. The number of men using armorial insignia steadily increased. To create new arms while avoiding duplication, the ordinaries and other common charges of early heraldry had to be supplemented.

Two converse tendencies are found in the development of heraldry. On the one hand there was the practical motive of individual distinction, based on the purpose of armorial bearings to identify their owner; and on the other there was a factor of sentiment which led a man to adopt arms bearing some resemblance to those of a feudal superior or ally. This latter tendency to assimilate arms under feudal influence made it the more necessary to preserve sufficient distinction between shields thus related.

The measures taken to secure distinctiveness between the arms of persons feudally connected, and also between those of persons in no way associated but by chance using a similar combination of form and tincture, are known as differencing.

Differencing was also employed to secure distinction between the arms of members of one family who, by inheritance, used the same predominant design or charge. This differencing for cadency is dealt with in the next chapter.

254. LUTERELL　　　　　255. DE WADSLEY　　　　256. DE WORTLEY

The following instances show the various ways in which feudal differencing was effected.

On his seal, Randulph de Blundevill, Earl of Chester (d. 1232), bore three garbs or wheatsheaves, and Rolls of Arms of the time of Henry III show the shield of the Earl of Chester as *Azure, three garbs or* (209). In token of feudal alliance, many Cheshire families bear one or more garbs; e.g. since about 1390 the arms of Grosvenor have been, *Azure, a garb or.*

A cinquefoil was the device of Robert FitzParnel, Earl of Leicester, who is said to have borne it on a red shield. Accordingly as early as the 13th century the cinquefoil appears in token of feudal connection on the shields of many families in Leicestershire. A Berkeley of Leicestershire substituted ten cinquefoils for the ten crosses paty of the Berkeley shield, themselves originally a difference for cadency.

Many a red chevron or chevronel, with other devices, charged on a gold field, or a gold chevron on red, is a sign of feudal alliance with the great house of De Clare, who bore *Or, three chevronels gules* (7). For example, the FitzRalphs, near neighbours of the Clares in Suffolk, differenced their arms by charging three fleurs-de-lis argent on each chevronel. Again, by a change of tinctures without affecting the charges, the arms of L'Ercedeckne (Archdeacon) are, *Argent, three chevronels sable.*

At Caerlaverock, the brothers De Hastings bore *Or, a maunch gules* (238), the younger differencing them for cadency with a label of five points sable; and their friend and comrade, John Paignel, bore, *Vert, a maunch or.*

The Luterell arms, *Or, a bend between six martlets sable* (254), were differenced by other families to mark their feudal alliance. Thus the

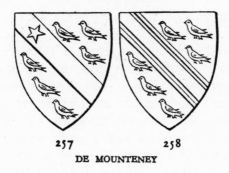

257   258
DE MOUNTENEY

De Furnivals, who held their lands by feudal tenure under the Luterells bore, *Argent, a bend between six martlets gules* ; and families dependent on the De Furnivals further differenced the arms, e.g. De Ecclesall, *Sable, a bend between six martlets or* ; De Wadsley, *Argent, on a bend between six martlets gules three escallops or* (255) ; De Wortley, *Argent, on a bend between six martlets gules three bezants* (256) ; De Mounteney, *Gules, a bend between six martlets or*. The De Mounteneys further differenced their arms for cadency : Sir Ernauf changed the tincture of the field to azure ; Sir John bore the same arms with the addition of a molet gules (257) ; and another Sir John bore, *Gules, a bend cotised between six martlets or* (258).

The same principle is found in Scotland, a notable instance being the arms of Bruce, *Or, a saltire and a chief gules* (102 ; Plate III, 1), which is thus differenced by other families : Jardine, *Argent, a saltire and a chief gules, the latter charged with three stars of the field* (259) ; Kirkpatrick, *Argent, a saltire and a chief azure, the latter charged with three oreillers or* (260) ; and Johnston, *Argent, a saltire sable, on a chief gules three oreillers or*.

259. JARDINE   260. KIRKPATRICK   261. KYRIELL

A canton, or a quarter, ermine, apparently derived from that of the Count of Brittany and Earl of Richmond (300), appears as a difference in the arms of several early families, e.g. De Tateshall, *Checky argent and gules, a quarter ermine.* In the Calais Roll, two De Bassetts bear respectively, *Or, three piles meeting in base gules, a canton ermine,* and, *Or, three pallets gules, a canton ermine*; a further difference appearing in the Roll of Richard II, where Sir John Bassett bears, *Or, three piles meeting in base gules, a canton argent charged with a griffin segreant sable.*

A canton charged with a lion of England occurs in some arms, e.g. Sir Thomas Kyriell, 1460 : *Or, two chevrons gules with a canton gules charged with a lion passant guardant or* (261). In this case the canton was a difference by augmentation for good service to the House of Lancaster.

Differencing which was adopted (so far as is now apparent) simply to avoid identity of arms between persons in no way connected opens a wide field of inquiry. Without doubt it was the need for differencing that led to the introduction of many miscellaneous charges to be borne with the ordinaries and subordinaries. How far some remote degree of kinship, or some subordinate feudal motive now forgotten, may have affected the choice of charges for difference, we cannot now tell ; nor can we always trace the rebus which in many cases dictated the choice. We do know that it rarely happened that different families bore the same arms without difference, and that when identity between arms did occur it was marked with surprise, and on more than one occasion led to a memorable controversy.

The proceedings in the Court of Chivalry, in the suit between Sir Richard Le Scrope and Sir Robert Grosvenor as to the right to the arms, *Azure, a bend or* (Plate II, no. 1), began on the 17th August, 1385, and the final judgment of the King himself on the appeal of the defendant against the finding of the Court was not pronounced until the 27th May, 1390.

On the 15th May, 1389, the judgment of the Court assigned *Azure, a bend or,* to Sir Richard Le Scrope ; and to Sir Robert Grosvenor these arms : *Azure, a bend or within a plain bordure argent.* Thus the Court confirmed to Le Scrope the right to bear the ordinary alone ; and at the same time it was decided that these arms of Scrope should be differenced with a bordure in order that they might become the arms of Grosvenor. Appeal being made to the Sovereign, Richard II determined that a plain bordure argent was a mark of cadency, perfectly sufficient as a difference " between cousin and cousin in blood," but " not a sufficient difference in arms between two strangers in blood in one kingdom." The King therefore cancelled and annulled the sentence of the Court of Chivalry, and in so doing gave a very clear definition of the distinction to be observed between cadency and differencing. Grosvenor thereupon adopted the arms, *Azure, a garb or*. We may assume that the judgment of the Court would have been confirmed by the King had Sir Robert Grosvenor been commanded to place his golden bend between two garbs, or to charge it with one or more garbs, or to make any other decided difference which would be palpably distinct from a mark of cadency.

CHAPTER X

CADENCY

In English heraldry, all persons descended in the legitimate male line from an armigerous ancestor inherit and bear his arms. Nevertheless, it is the essence of heraldry that armorial bearings should be distinctive not only of the family as a whole, but also of its several branches and individual members. This was particularly necessary when arms served the practical purposes of recognition in war and tournament, and denoting identity on seals. To render the common arms of a family distinctive of its various branches and members, a method has been evolved termed " differencing for cadency," i.e. minor differencing of the arms to indicate the position of a cadet in relation to the head of the family, or of a branch in relation to the senior line.

Before the present system of cadency marks is dealt with, the earlier methods of denoting cadency must be considered.

Shields of arms have been differenced for cadency in two ways :

(1) by modifying or adding to the original arms while retaining their principal and distinctive features ; in this case, the arms as modified, while indicating their origin and alliances, become in effect an independent heraldic composition.

(2) by introducing some fresh and minor charge which is not an intrinsic part of the composition, and does not in any degree modify the actual bearings, but may be altered or removed according to changes in the individual's position in the family. This is the basis of the present system of cadency marks.

Differencing by Modifying the Arms

This method was employed at an early date, and preceded the prevalent employment of minor charges to denote cadency. Modifications were effected in various ways, e.g. by change of tincture, variations in the charges, or both ; or the addition of an ordinary, bordure or label, while preserving the main features of the arms.

Modification of Tincture. This might be in the field, e.g. two Furnivals, temp. Henry III, bore their *bend and six martlets gules* the one on *or* and the other on *argent*; or it might be in the charges, e.g. two Bardolfs bore, *Azure, three cinquefoils*, the one *or* and the other *argent*; or the tinctures might be reversed, e.g. temp. Edward III, Le Strange of Knocking bore, *Gules, two lions passant argent*, and Le Strange of Blackmere, *Argent, two lions passant gules* (Plate II, 6). The tinctures of both field and charges might be changed, e.g. two Luterell coats, temp. Edward II : *Or, a bend and six martlets sable ; Azure a bend and six martlets argent.* A change of tincture from argent to ermine was frequent. Thus a variation of the Mortimer coat (**157**) shows an inescutcheon ermine ; another Mortimer substitutes gules for azure in the bars, pallets and gyrons ; others charge the inescutcheon variously.

Modification of Charges. While retaining the identity of the tinctures, differencing was frequently effected by incorporating in the arms some fresh charge or charges of a comparatively subordinate character ; by slightly varying the charges ; by substituting one charge for another ; by introducing insignia from other arms ; the predominance of the original and principal feature of the arms being in all these cases preserved.

As has been shown in the previous chapter, this method of differencing resulted in the enrichment of heraldry by the introduction of fresh charges to be borne in association with the ordinaries or other forms common in early arms. Except when derived from an allied shield, the fresh charges introduced by the early heralds for purposes of differencing do not appear to have been selected on any definite principle, unless it be that a rebus, or charge allusive to the name, was used where practicable. Small crosses were frequently employed, and other charges found include martlets, molets, fleurs-de-lis, escallops, crescents, cinquefoils, sixfoils, roses, billets, and annulets.

These fresh charges were placed either on the field of the shield or on an ordinary, and in the earliest examples they are many times repeated, being scattered over the field or arranged in orle. In this form they were necessarily small. Later they were often reduced in number and drawn larger, and so became secondary charges rather than minor additions. A further stage in differencing was effected by substituting other charges for these secondary charges.

The following groups of arms borne by various members of the

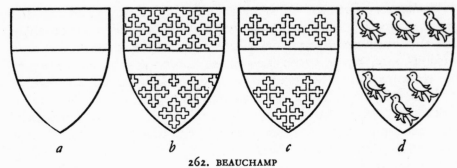

262. BEAUCHAMP

same family are selected from many early examples to illustrate the process :

Beauchamp : *Gules, a fess or ; Gules, crusily and a fess or ; Gules, a fess and six cross crosslets or ; Gules, a fess and six martlets or* (262*a–d*).

Berkeley : *Gules, a chevron argent ; Gules, crusily paty and a chevron argent* (Plate II, 4) *; Gules, crusily paty argent and a chevron ermine* (Plate X) *; Gules semé of cinquefoils (or roses) and a chevron argent.*

Cobham : *Gules, a chevron or,* differenced by various members of the family by the addition on the chevron of *three lioncels, three eaglets, three crosslets, three molets, three estoiles, three fleurs-de-lis* or *three crescents,* all *sable.*

Bassett : *Ermine, on a chief indented gules three molets or ; Ermine on a chief indented gules three escallops or.*

D'Arcy : *Argent, six sixfoils gules ; Argent, within an orle of cinquefoils an inescutcheon gules ; Azure, crusily and three cinquefoils argent ; Azure, crusily and six sixfoils argent ; Argent, within an orle of sixfoils gules an inescutcheon sable.*

De Valence : *Barruly argent and azure ; Barruly argent and azure with an*

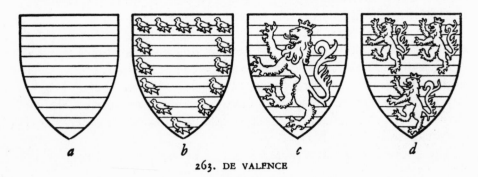

263. DE VALENCE

orle of martlets gules ; Barruly argent and azure, a lion rampant gules crowned or ; Barruly argent and azure, three lions rampant gules crowned or (263a–d).

Differences were applied not only to shields of arms but also to their accessories—crests, mantlings, supporters, and badges. Sir John Daubygné, 1345, bore the arms, *Gules, four fusils cojoined in fess ermine,* with the addition of a pierced molet on each fusil, and on his monument the mantling is powdered with pierced molets, while the crest is a pierced molet within a wreath of olive leaves (264). Animals sometimes have marks of cadency charged on their shoulders, or they are semé of them, and sometimes the marks are formed into collars. The lion crest of Thomas Beaufort, Duke of Dorset, is gorged about the throat with a collar compony ermine and azure, like the differencing border to his shield. Collars appear to have been used for differencing " live " crests when shields were differenced with bordures, and similarly labels were habitually added to crests.

264. DAUBYGNÉ

Modification by Ordinary, Subordinary or Label. The bordure, bend, canton, and chevron were convenient for purposes of differencing. These forms, as well as the label, could readily be added to any shield, and could themselves easily be charged with small objects forming a secondary series of differences. Similarly a chief would sometimes be added to the shield and then charged for difference. Other changes sometimes made for difference were the cotising of ordinaries, and the alteration of a chevron or fess into two or more chevronels or bars, or a bend into two or more bendlets.

The use of a canton or quarter in differencing for cadency may be regarded in many cases as a form of compounding arms (see Chapter XII), the devices charged thereon being frequently taken from some allied coat of arms. In the Calais Roll, Sir William de Warenne bears, *Checky or and azure with a canton of Mowbray* (i.e. *Gules, a lion rampant argent*) (265)[1]. In the Roll of Richard II, Richard de Kyrkeby bears,

---

[1] It is possible that the lion should be ermine and that the canton should be described as " of Nerford " rather than " of Mowbray " [*continued overleaf*]

265. DE WARENNE　　　266. DE ETTON　　　267. HARFORD

Argent, two bars gules, on a canton of the last a cross moline or ; De Etton,
*Barry of twelve argent and gules, a label of three points azure, over all a canton
sable charged with a cross patonce or* (266) ; and Avery Britchebury bears,
Argent, two bars azure, on a canton of the last a martlet or. The Harfords
record the alliance with an heiress of the Scropes by bearing (267)
Sable, two bends argent with a canton of Scrope (i.e. *Azure, a bend or*).

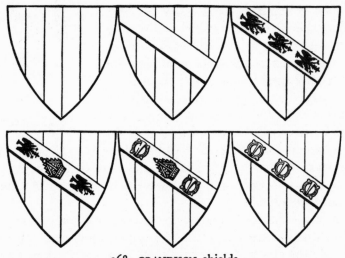

268. GRANDISON shields

for, if Sir William were descended from John de Warenne last Earl of Surrey and
Maud de Nerford, this would fit the case. Sir John Warenne is assigned this coat,
but with an Ermine lion, in Powell's Roll (c. 1350) and he may well have been a
brother or uncle of Sir William. The problem is discussed in the *Herald and Genealogist* (1871), and *History of South Yorkshire* by Rev. Joseph Hunter.

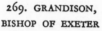

269. GRANDISON,
BISHOP OF EXETER

270. DE HASTINGS

271. EXETER COLLEGE,
OXFORD

The use of the bend in differencing is exemplified by the series of Grandison shields. The original arms were, *Paly of six argent and azure*. To this was first added *a bend gules*, on which William de Grandison charged *three eagles displayed or*. Others substituted for the eagles, *three escallops or*, and *three buckles or*, and a mitre for the middle charge on the bend (268). John de Grandison, Bishop of Exeter, 1327–69, bore, *Paly of six argent and azure, a bend gules charged with a mitre argent between two eagles or* (269). There are many instances of bendlets or bastons as differences.

Robert FitzWalter, a member of the De Clare family, substituted a fess for the middle one of the De Clare chevrons, and bore, *Or, a fess between two chevrons gules* (103). This composition, variously tinctured, was borne by several families, e.g. De Lisle (temp. Edward I) at Rampton, Cambs., *Or, a fess between two chevrons sable*.

The bordure enabled the early heralds to mark cadency distinctly without altering the original composition of the arms, while permitting insignia from other arms to be incorporated. The arms of John of Eltham, *England with a bordure of France* (183), are a fine instance. Examples of bordures from the Roll of Henry III include: John de Hastings, *Or, a maunch gules with a bordure of De Valence* (i.e. *Barruly argent and azure charged with martlets gules*) (270); John de Weston, *Argent, a fess sable and a bordure gules bezanty*; and his son, the same with the bordure indented.

The status of the bordure as a mark of cadency was established in 1390 in connection with the Scrope-Grosvenor controversy (see pages 106–7).

The bordure was freely used by prelates for differencing their arms, e.g. Edmund de Stafford, Bishop of Exeter, 1394–1419, *Or, a chevron gules within a bordure of the same charged with eight mitres argent*. Exeter College, Oxford, bears the arms of its founder, Walter de Stapledon, Bishop of Exeter, *Argent, two bends nebuly sable*, with the addition of *a bordure sable charged with eight pairs of keys addorsed, their rings interlaced or*, from the arms of the See of Exeter (271).

The earliest known label appears on the counter-seal of Saer de Quincey, first Earl of Winchester, who died in 1219. His arms are, *Or, a fess gules, in chief a label of many points* (probably twelve, but it is not easy to determine the exact number). It cannot be shown definitely that this label was borne as a mark of cadency, but Saer was certainly the younger brother of Robert de Quincey.

During his father's lifetime, Edward I charged the shield on his seal with a label, placing it so as to form the chief of the escutcheon, with two of its five points lying alternately over and under the tail of the top lion (280). Edward II as Prince set the label lower on the shield, with longer points.

When first introduced, labels were borne by younger sons as well as by the eldest during his father's lifetime, and in some cases they became hereditary, e.g. in the arms of Courtenay, *Or, three torteaux and a label azure* (Plate II, 10); and Barrington, *Argent, three chevronels gules and a label of three points azure*. Early labels were frequently tinctured so as to contrast effectively with the other tinctures, and they always extend wholly across the shield. The points, broader than the horizontal ribbon, usually numbered three or five, but four are found. There does not seem to have been any significance in the number.

Labels were frequently differenced with charges, e.g. two or three ermine spots, fleurs-de-lis, etc., on each point. George, Duke of Clarence, brother of Edward IV, bore a label with a single canton on each point. Richard II, during his father's lifetime, bore a label with a Cross of St. George on the central point only. Occasionally two distinct groups of differencing charges occur on the same label. Examples of labels borne on shields not of royal rank include (among many plain ones):

Sir James Audley (whose mother was a daughter of William Longespée): *Gules fretty or, a label of Longespée*, i.e. *azure, on each point a lioncel or* (272).

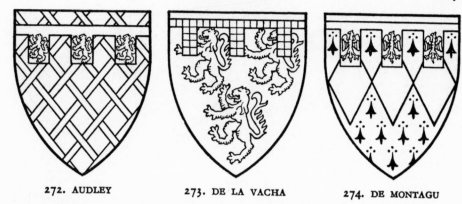

272. AUDLEY   273. DE LA VACHA   274. DE MONTAGU

Sir William Lovel : *Undy or and gules, a label of Valence,* i.e. *the points barruly argent and azure and on each a martlet gules.*

Sir Richard de la Vacha : *Gules, three lioncels argent, a label of Warenne,* i.e. *checky or and azure* (273).

Sir Edward de Montagu : *Ermine, three fusils cojoined in fess gules, a label of Monthermer,* i.e. *or, on each point an eagle displayed vert* (274).

SINGLE MARKS OF DIFFERENCE

Differencing by a single mark of cadency was employed at an early period. As has been shown, the small repeated charges originally introduced as differences soon began to be regarded as intrinsic components of the arms, and they were regularly transmitted with the ordinary or other primary charge. Hence, in more matured heraldry, a single distinct charge of small size for difference became not merely desirable but absolutely necessary to carry out the system of marking cadency. In practice this method of differencing proved to be less satisfactory than was expected ; on the one hand the single small differencing charge was found not always to tell its proper tale with sufficient distinctness and emphasis ; and on the other, even this addition frequently lost its differencing character and assumed a position as a permanent charge.

Sir Fulk FitzWarine differenced the shield of the head of his house, *Quarterly per fess indented argent and gules,* with a molet sable in the first quarter (275). Thomas le Scrope marks his paternal arms, *Azure, a bend or,* with an annulet sable on the bend (276).

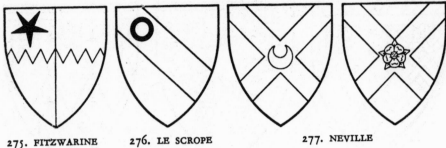

275. FITZWARINE   276. LE SCROPE   277. NEVILLE

The arms of Neville, *Gules, a saltire argent* (Plate II, 9), were variously differenced with labels (plain, compony, and charged with roundles), a single crescent, martlet, molet, fleur-de-lis, cinquefoil, rose, pellet, and interlinked annulets, all except the labels being charged on the centre of the saltire (277, 278). Other charges found as single marks of cadency in various arms include the crosslet, annulet and lozenge.

Modern Marks of Cadency. In the early part of the 16th century, the use of the most common of these charges as marks of cadency was standardized, a particular charge being assigned to denote each son of a family in order of seniority, and (with the exception of Royal Cadency, which is marked exclusively by the label) this remains the practice today. In England and Ireland, the following are the charges which may be borne for cadency by the various sons on their paternal arms (279):

- *a.* The eldest son (during his father's lifetime), a *label.*
- *b.* The second son, a *crescent.*
- *c.* The third son, a *molet.*
- *d.* The fourth son, a *martlet.*
- *e.* The fifth son, an *annulet.*
- *f.* The sixth son, a *fleur-de-lis.*
- *g.* The seventh son, a *rose.*
- *h.* The eighth son, a *cross moline.*
- *i.* The ninth son, a *double quatrefoil,* or *octofoil.*

These marks may themselves be differenced to denote the next generation; e.g. the second son's second son may charge his crescent with another crescent, the third son's fourth son his molet with a martlet, and so on, though in these days this complicated and impracticable extension of differencing is not often employed. Until recently an instance occurred in the peerage, the Earl of Harrington differencing

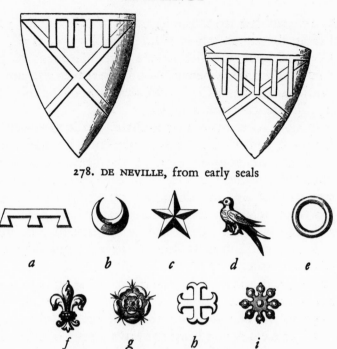

278. DE NEVILLE, from early seals

a   *b*   *c*   *d*   *e*

f   *g*   *h*   *i*

279. Modern Marks of Cadency

the plain coat of Stanhope with a crescent charged with a crescent, for distinction from Earl Stanhope, who differenced the coat with a single crescent; both descended from the Earls of Chesterfield, who bore the undifferenced coat of Stanhope.

A mark of cadency is now generally borne in the chief of the shield, but in the case of a quartered shield it should be placed in the centre so as to overlap all four quarters, unless, of course, it appertains to and has been brought in by one of the quartered coats, when it remains on that coat only. It may be of any tincture, but the rule against placing colour on colour or metal on metal is usually observed.

Except for the eldest son's label, which is removed when his father dies and he becomes head of the family, these marks of cadency are permanent, as hereditary marks of the junior branches, or houses, of the same family. This is practically the only way in which they are employed in these days. Brothers now rarely need to difference their arms during their father's lifetime, but they frequently do so when they themselves become heads of houses.

To take an example from the peerage, the Marquess of Exeter, descended from the eldest son of Lord Burghley (cr. 1571), bears the arms of Cecil without any difference ; the Marquess of Salisbury, descended from Burghley's second son, differences the arms with a crescent ; and Lord Cecil of Chelwood, third son of the third Marquess of Salisbury, differences with a molet.

It is permissible to remove an hereditary mark of cadency should the branch inherit and display a fresh quartering by marriage with an heiress, or receive an augmentation to the arms, because the arms thereby acquire distinction from those of the senior branch.

Daughters do not use the difference marks to denote their own position, but they retain in their paternal arms any permanent mark of cadency borne by their father, and such mark may be included in their marital arms but is usually omitted in any arms they transmit (if heiresses) to their issue.

While in England arms are hereditary to all legitimate descendants of the grantee in the male line, in Scotland the undifferenced coat descends only to the heir male for the time being ; that is, the head of the family.   His eldest son bears the arms with a label for difference. Each younger son must petition the Lyon King of Arms for a differenced version of his father's arms.   This coat, which will have a crescent, bordure, or some such minor addition, then descends to the heir male of the man to whom it is assigned, while his younger sons must petition for a version with some further mark of cadency, such as engrailing or indenting the bordure.   In families with many cadets there will be many versions of the original coat in existence, each with some distinctive variation showing its bearer's particular position in the family.

ROYAL CADENCY

In Boutell's *Manual of Heraldry*, a considerable section was devoted to a list of members of the Plantagenet House and allied families, with the marks of cadency they used at various times.   In this edition it will perhaps be more useful to summarize and present certain conclusions drawn from the facts given by Boutell, rather than to reproduce his list.

The principal additions to the Royal Arms for the purpose of denoting cadency were the label and the bordure.   These were variously tinctured and charged by individuals.   Generally the bordure appears to have

280. EDWARD, son of HENRY III   281. HENRY OF LANCASTER

been regarded as appropriate to the most junior branches, and in a few instances a bendlet was used, e.g. Henry, second son of Edmund, first Earl of Lancaster, bore *England with a bendlet azure* (281).

Edward I (280), Edward II and Edward III, each during the lifetime of his father differenced his arms with a label azure of three or five points. When the arms of France, with their azure field, were quartered in the shield of England, azure became an unsuitable tincture for the label, and the Black Prince, as the eldest son of Edward III, differenced with a label argent. This has been the distinctive mark of all succeeding heirs apparent.

The label was not limited to the eldest son; some of the other sons bore it, of a different tincture, or in many cases charged. Particular labels came to be associated with certain dignities. Thus Edward I's brother, Edmund, first Earl of Lancaster, bore a label of France (*azure, semé-de-lis or*) (282*a*), derived from his marriage with Blanche d'Artois; and this label was borne by his sons and grandson, Earls and Duke of Lancaster. John of Gaunt, Duke of Lancaster, differenced the Royal Arms with an ermine label (282*b*) derived from the ermine shield of Brittany, and his son, Henry Bolingbroke, bore a label of France until his father's death, when he made his label of five points *per pale Brittany and France*, three (or two) of the points being ermine, and two (or three) azure, each charged with three fleurs-de-lis or (282*c* and 368).

On Bolingbroke's accession as Henry IV, the Duchy of Lancaster was merged in the Crown, but its distinctive insignia survives, and has given rise to the arms of the City of Lancaster, *Per fess azure and gules, in chief a fleur-de-lis and in base a lion passant guardant or*; the crest and supporters consisting of lions *azure semé-de-lis or*.

Edward I's second surviving son, Thomas of Brotherton, Earl of

Norfolk, bore *England with a label argent*, and this is quartered by his descendants, the Dukes of Norfolk.

Edward I's third surviving son, Edmund, first Earl of Kent, bore *England with a bordure argent*, which was borne by his two sons, successors in the earldom, and by his descendants through his daughter, the Holland Earls of Kent and Dukes of Surrey. Their kinsfolk, the Holland Dukes of Exeter, the first of whom married a daughter of John of Gaunt, bore *England with a bordure of France*.

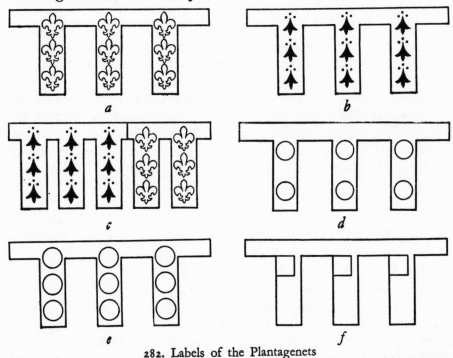

282. Labels of the Plantagenets

Edmund Langley, first Duke of York, fifth son of Edward III, differenced the Royal Arms, *Quarterly France Ancient and England*, with a label argent charged with torteaux, sometimes six in number (282*d*), and sometimes nine. His son and grandson, successors in the dukedom, differenced with a label argent charged with nine torteaux, as also did Edward, fourth duke, who became Edward IV (282*e*).

Similarly a label argent (sometimes ermine) charged with a canton gules became associated with the Duchy of Clarence (282*f*).

The Beauforts, descended from John of Gaunt by Catherine Swynford,

| 283. SIR ROGER | 284. BEAUFORT: | 285. BEAUFORT, |
| CLARENDON | early arms | after legitimation |

after their legitimation bore the Royal Arms with a bordure compony argent and azure, and this was variously charged as a secondary difference by junior branches of the family.

In Tudor times the bordure ceased to be used as a legitimate difference in the Royal Arms. All members of the Royal Family now bear the label argent, uncharged in the case of the Sovereign's eldest son, and charged in various ways by others.

The labels of the present members of the Royal Family are shown in nos. 379–82.

DIFFERENCING FOR ILLEGITIMACY

In modern heraldry certain marks have been commonly used to denote illegitimacy, but the early heralds did not promulgate any particular method of distinguishing the arms of persons of bastard birth or their descendants. Some difference for illegitimacy was held to be necessary, but it might take any form considered best suited to a particular case. Illegitimate persons sometimes altered the position of the charges in their paternal shield; or they marshalled their father's arms on a bend or fess; or they composed for themselves a fresh shield, either using their father's badges or charges from his shield, or adopting devices evidently derived from the paternal bearings; or they bore the father's shield differenced in some peculiarly conspicuous manner. A few examples will illustrate the early practice.

Sir Roger Clarendon, bastard son of the Black Prince, bore, *Or, on a bend sable three ostrich feathers, each piercing an escroll argent* (283); this was derived from his father's "shield for peace" (196). His kinsman,

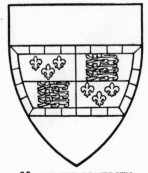

286. SIR JOHN   287. RALPH DE ARUNDEL   288. HENRY SOMERSET,
DE CLARENCE   EARL OF WORCESTER

John de Beaufort, son of John of Gaunt, bore before the Act of
Legitimation in 1397, *Per pale argent and azure, on a bend gules three lions
of England ensigned with a label of France* (284), the tinctures of the field
being the Lancastrian colours.   After legitimation, John de Beaufort
bore the Royal Arms with a bordure compony of these tinctures (285).
Sir John de Clarence, son of Thomas, Duke of Clarence, himself the
son of Henry IV, bore *Per chevron gules and azure, in chief two lions counter-
rampant and in base a fleur-de-lis all or* (286).   Ralph de Arundel, a natural
son of one of the FitzAlans, bore, *Argent, flaunched with FitzAlan and
Warenne quarterly*, that is, the arms are changed on the flaunches, the
centre of the shield being blank (287).

A bendlet sinister was borne by Arthur, Viscount Lisle, son of
Edward IV ; by Henry, Duke of Richmond, son of Henry VIII ; and
by Charles Somerset, Earl of Worcester, son of Henry Beaufort, third
Duke of Somerset.   Henry, legitimate eldest son of this Earl, removed
the bendlet from his father's arms and charged the arms of Beaufort on
a fess on a field argent, thus recognizing the propriety of retaining an
indication of bastard descent though rejecting the bendlet (288).

The arms of the natural sons of Charles II were differenced with the
baton sinister, variously tinctured and charged, except the Duke of
Richmond, who used a bordure for difference.   At the present day
the baton of the Duke of Buccleuch is argent, that of the Duke of St.
Albans is gules charged with three roses argent, and that of the Duke
of Grafton is compony argent and azure.   The Duke of Richmond
bears the arms of Charles II within a bordure compony argent charged

289. DUKE OF RICHMOND   290. EARL OF MUNSTER

with eight roses gules, and gules (289).[1] The Earl of Munster bears the arms of William IV (without the crown of Hanover) with a baton sinister azure charged with three anchors or (290).

In the course of time the baton sinister came to be used as a difference for bastardy only on the Royal Arms. In other cases the customary marks of illegitimacy are in England and Ireland a bordure wavy (sometimes accompanied by a wavy ordinary on the crest), and in Scotland a bordure compony. It should, however, be noted that the bordure wavy is used in Scotland as a legitimate mark of cadency, while in England the bordure compony does not necessarily imply bastardy—in fact, the Beauforts adopted it to mark their legitimation. It is, therefore, inadvisable to jump to conclusions when these bordures are noted in arms.

Persons of illegitimate birth may not assume at will the arms of their putative father with an appropriate difference. They must prove their paternity, and petition for the arms to be granted. If they cannot prove their paternity, or if they prefer not to declare their illegitimacy in their arms, they may petition for an entirely new coat of arms.

Marks of bastardy have sometimes been called abatements, because they abate the status of the arms to the extent of showing that their owner is not in the legitimate line of succession. It should be noted that the word abatement is not used as implying dishonour. There is no such thing as a mark of dishonour in English heraldry.

[1] The illustration shows the arms as assigned to Charles Lennox, 1st Duke of Richmond, by his father on 30th September 1675. By Letters Patent dated 3rd July 1876, Charles Henry Gordon-Lennox (who had been created Duke of Gordon on the 13th January 1876) was assigned quarterings to be borne in the 2nd and 3rd grand quarters, and a crest for Gordon.

DIFFERENCING FOR ADOPTION

If an adopted child is the legitimate issue of an armigerous man, then he may, of course, use the arms of his natural father. On the other hand, if he has no arms, or if the adoptive parents do not want him to bear his father's arms, they may apply for a Royal Licence for the child to be granted the arms of his adoptive father. When such a Licence is granted, and it normally is, the arms are exemplified with two links of a chain as a mark of distinction.

In Canada, the procedure is rather different as all the Sovereign's powers and authority were, by Letters Patent dated 8th September 1947, vested in the Governor General for the time being. Amongst these powers is that relating to the granting and exemplification of arms of persons and families to other persons and families resident in Canada. In 1966 the Governor General expressed a wish that these particular facets of the Royal Prerogative should, in future, be exercised by the King of Arms, acting under a Warrant from the Earl Marshal. In consequence, the Earl Marshal issued a Warrant, dated 15th August 1966, authorizing the Kings of Arms to act in this manner.

DIFFERENCING FOR LEGITIMATION

The Legitimacy Act 1926 provided for the legitimation of bastards by the subsequent marriage of the parents as long as the parents were free to marry at the time of the child's birth. The Legitimacy Act 1959 provides that even if the parents of a bastard were not free to marry when the child was born, thus making it an adulterine bastard, their subsequent marriage still makes the child legitimate in law. However the Acts expressly state that no legitimated child shall be capable of succeeding to or transmitting a right to any dignity or title.

As arms are in the nature of a dignity rather than an item of property, a legitimated child cannot inherit its father's arms. What then must it do? The answer is that it is treated as a bastard and must petition for a Royal Licence to bear the arms of its father with a suitable mark of distinction.

In the first such case to come before the Kings of Arms the arms and crest of the legitimated adulterine bastard were differenced by the addition of a small *saltire couped*. Obviously it is not possible to say whether this creates a precedent which will be followed, but this could well be the case.

291*a*. HOWARD   291*b*. HOWARD   292. PELHAM
                    Augmentation

CHAPTER XI

AUGMENTATIONS

AN augmentation is an honourable addition to armorial bearings. It may take the form of charges added to the arms, or of a complete coat of arms to be borne as a quartering, or it may be an additional crest. Camden tells us that in former times these augmentations were granted, " some of mere grace and some of merit." He instances Richard II's grant of the arms of the Confessor to his kinsmen, the Holland Dukes of Surrey and Exeter, and to Thomas Mowbray, Duke of Norfolk, as examples of augmentation by " mere grace "; while Henry VIII, " for merit," granted to Thomas Howard, Earl of Surrey (second Duke of Norfolk), and his posterity, *the Royal Shield of Scotland, having a demi-lion only, which is pierced through the mouth with an arrow,* to be charged on the bend in the Howard arms (*Gules, a bend between six cross-crosslets fitchy argent*) to commemorate his victory at Flodden, 1513 (291 *a*; *b* shows the escutcheon of augmentation enlarged. See also Plate VIII).

An early example of an augmentation granted " of mere grace " is that by Richard II to Robert de Vere, Earl of Oxford, Marquess of Dublin and Duke of Ireland, *Azure, three crowns or within a bordure argent*, a differenced coat of St. Edmund, at that time apparently regarded as the arms of Ireland ; this was borne quarterly with the arms of De Vere.

Edward IV, as if he felt it to be a point of honour that his Queen should have an heraldic display equal to her Lancastrian rival, Margaret of Anjou, granted to Elizabeth Woodville a series of augmentations derived from the insignia of her maternal ancestry, all to be borne quarterly. This example was improved by Henry VIII in grants of arms to his successive consorts.

The augmentations granted " of merit " are generally the more interesting, because they frequently allude to historic events. The following are examples :

Pelham ; an augmentation granted to commemorate a family tradition that Sir William Pelham captured King John of France at Poitiers in 1356, a tradition which seems to be quite unfounded historically. The coat of augmentation, *Gules two demi-belts* (representing the King's sword-belt) *palewise in fess, their buckles in chief, argent*, is quartered in the second and third with Pelham : *Azure, three pelicans argent, vulning themselves proper* (292).

Clarke ; commemorating the capture of the Duke of Longueville by Sir John Clarke at the Battle of the Spurs, 1513 : to the arms of Clarke, *Argent, on a bend gules between three pellets as many swans proper*, was added on a sinister canton charges from the arms of the Duke, *Azure, a demi-ram salient argent, armed or ; in chief two fleurs-de-lys gold ; over all a baton dexter.*

In 1645 King Charles I, and again in 1660 King Charles II, empowered Sir Edward Walker, the loyalist Garter King of Arms, to grant arms and augmentations to those who had loyally served them. Garter Walker took full advantage of the Kings' Warrants and made many grants and grants of augmentations, of royal insignia, as these examples demonstrate :

Newman ; awarded to Colonel Newman for keeping the gate of Worcester and so enabling Charles II to escape, 1651 : to his arms, *Quarterly sable and argent, in the first and fourth quarters three molets of the second*, was added *an inescutcheon gules charged with a portcullis imperially crowned or* (293).

Lane, of Bently, Staffs. ; in recognition of the courage of Jane Lane in assisting Charles II to escape after Worcester : to the arms of Lane,

Per fess or and azure, a chevron gules between three molets counterchanged, was added *a canton of England* (Plate VIII). Crest: *a strawberry-roan horse salient, couped at the flanks, bridled sable, bitted and garnished or, supporting between his feet a Royal Crown.*

Duppa; Dr. Brian Duppa was a loyal bishop who was translated to Winchester at the Restoration. To his arms, *azure, a lion's paw erased in fess between two bars of chain or,* was added *a canton or, charged with a rose gules* (295*b*). This augmentation of a red rose was frequently used. Among others upon whom it was bestowed were Thomas Kipps, Sir Bartholemew Le Roche and Humphrey Painter.

Wolfe; Sir Francis Wolfe entertained King Charles II after the battle of Worcester, and by special command of the King both his arms and crest were augmented. Over his arms, *gules, a chevron between three wolves' heads erased or,* was placed *an ineuscutcheon gules, charged with a lion of England.* His crest, *a demi-wolf sable,* was honoured by *holding between its forepaws the royal crown proper* (295*c*).

A Scottish peer, Sir John Keith, 1st Earl of Kintore, who preserved the regalia of Scotland during the Commonwealth, was granted: *gules, a sceptre and sword in saltire, in chief the royal crown, within an orle of thistles or.* This was to be borne on an inescutcheon on the arms of Keith: *argent, a chief paly of six or and gules* (294).

Shovel; commemorating Sir Cloudesley Shovel's naval victories, two over the Turks and one over the French, 1692: *Gules, a chevron, in chief two crescents argent and in base a fleur-de-lis or* (Plate VIII).

Churchill; for the services of Sir Winston Churchill to Charles I: to the arms of Churchill, *Sable, a lion rampant argent,* the augmentation

| 293. NEWMAN | 294. KEITH, EARL OF KINTORE | 295. LORD NELSON |

of *a canton of St. George (i.e. argent charged with a cross gules)* ; and to his son, John, Duke of Marlborough, for the victory of Blenheim, 1704, *in chief an inescutcheon of St. George charged with another of France Modern.* The escutcheon is now borne on a shield quarterly Churchill and Spencer (*Quarterly argent, and gules a fret or, over all a bend sable charged with three escallops of the first*) (Plate VIII).

Wellesley, Duke of Wellington, to his arms, *Quarterly 1 and 4, Gules, a cross argent, in each quarter five plates* ; *2 and 3, Or, a lion rampant gules,* as an augmentation *an inescutcheon charged with the crosses of St. George, St. Andrew and St. Patrick combined, being the union badge of the United Kingdom* (Plate VIII).

Byng, Earl of Strafford—see the arms of Lord Byng of Vimy (Plate XXI).

The arms of Nelson, twice augmented in commemoration of the great sailor's victories, provide an instance of a coat which, however it may have gained in honour, has lost in artistic merit by augmentation. His original arms were, *Or, a cross flory sable surmounted by a bend gules. and thereon another engrailed of the field charged with three bombs fired proper,* After the Battle of the Nile, this was augmented by a chief undy containing a landscape consisting of a palm-tree, a disabled ship, and a battery in ruins (295). After his death, a second augmentation was made to the arms, namely *a fess wavy azure charged with the word* TRAFALGAR *or.* The result was to obliterate the original cross flory except for the ends of the vertical limb. The second augmentation was not inherited by the second Earl, who was a nephew of the first Earl to whom it was granted; but it still appears as a quartering in the arms of Viscount Bridport.

In Queen Victoria's reign augmentations were frequently awarded to successful generals and admirals. These usually took the form of a pictorial chief together with a crest of augmentation. Representations of medals were also frequently granted as charges and sometimes supporters were augmented and special mottoes granted. Entire coats of augmentation are rare, but there is a number of examples, perhaps the best known being that granted to the Seymour family by King Henry VIII to commemorate his marriage with Jane Seymour, namely: *Or, a pile of England, between six fleurs-de-lis azure.*

Towards the end of Queen Victoria's reign and during that of King Edward VII few augmentations were granted. In 1911 King George V granted an augmentation to the arms of Sir James Reid, Bart, G.C.V.O.,

K.C.B., who had been a Physician in Ordinary to Queen Victoria and King Edward VII. To his family arms : *Azure, a stag's head erased or, between two torches enflamed proper* was added *on a chief gules, a lion passant guardant or.* After this grant no further augmentations were assigned until in 1956, a year after the City of Cardiff was declared the capital of the Principality of Wales, on this occasion the supporters of the City arms were augmented by the addition of the Queen's royal badge for Wales (Plate XII, no. 4) being suspended from the neck of each by a gold chain.

Since then one further augmentation has been granted, namely, in 1963 a blue canton charged with the crest of Canada (Plate XXVI, no. 2) was added to the paternal arms of the Rt. Hon. Charles Vincent Massey, sometime Governor-General of Canada (295*a*). These are blazoned : *Argent, on a chevron between three lozenges sable, each charged with a fleur-de-lys of the field, as many stags' heads erased or.*

In Scotland the Royal Tressure has been granted as an augmentation both " of mere grace " and " of merit." In the former case, it has been conferred on a number of families descended from the Royal House

295*a*   295*b*   295*c*

in the female line ; the tressure in the arms of Lyon, quartered by H.M. Queen Elizabeth the Queen Mother, is an example. An instance of the tressure as an augmentation " of merit " is provided by the arms of Scott of Thirlestane, *Or, on a bend azure, a molet pierced between two crescents gold,* to which was added the Scottish tressure azure, commemorating the grantee's services at Soutra Edge, 1542.

296. Seal of MARGARET, QUEEN of EDWARD I

CHAPTER XII

MARSHALLING

In the latter part of the 13th century heraldry began to develop a significance distinct from its original motive of personal identification. From the first, some devices, such as the cross, the lion and eagle, and those playing on their bearer's name, possessed a certain symbolic quality, but this was on the whole secondary to their purpose as cognizances.   At length arms came to be used to denote marriage alliances, the possession of two or more lordships by the same man, and the holding of some office.   Such facts were indicated by the grouping together of different arms so as to form one heraldic composition. This practice is known as marshalling.

The combination of two or more coats of arms on one shield to indicate a union of lordships (or sometimes a claim, as when Edward III quartered the arms of France with those of England—Plate V) is historically the most important form of marshalling, because the composite shields this produced became permanent. Furthermore, this practice was carried a stage further in the 16th century, when men began to include in their shields the arms of families whose heiresses their ancestors had married, without regard to whether such unions had brought them lordships and estates. With this aspect of marshalling the question of heraldic inheritance is bound up.

Heraldic arms are a form of property, and the lawful holder of arms has in them a true estate in fee. This possession, however, is subject to two conditions : firstly, the lawful possessor of arms does not possess any right or power to alienate them; and secondly, the inheritance of arms is restricted to heirs who are lineally descended from the first lawful possessor of those arms. In the 14th and 15th centuries deeds of questionable validity were sometimes executed for alienating what may be termed heraldic property, and in the 14th century arms were occasionally granted, without any restriction, to heirs general ; but in our times the general rule obtains that arms cannot be alienated, and can be inherited only by lineal descendants. It is also a general rule of heraldry that the right to hold and use the undifferenced arms of a family appertains to its existing head. In tracing descent for heraldic purposes, male issue always has precedence, and where there exist several male descendants equal in the degree of their hereditary relationship, the eldest always has the preference. Should there be no male heir of direct lineage, a female succeeds ; and if there are several female descendants equal in degree they all inherit equally.

The heir apparent bears the arms of his father with the appropriate mark of cadency (dealt with in Chapter X), which he removes on succeeding to the headship of the family. All the other sons bear their father's arms with their particular mark of cadency.

Children do not inherit the arms of their mother unless she is an heraldic heiress. The conditions and manner of marshalling arms in this case are dealt with below ; but marshalling must first be considered in its historical aspect.

The methods of marshalling have varied at different periods, and in the following pages the subject is dealt with under these headings :

I.   Grouping together of Separate Shields of Arms.
II. Compounding Arms—whereby charges are drawn from two or more
     different shields and blended to form a new and distinct shield of arms.

I. GROUPING TOGETHER OF SEPARATE SHIELDS OF ARMS

A precursor of marshalling was the aggroupment of arms without combination—that is, by arranging two or more shields in such a way that, while each remained separate and distinct, together they formed a connected group. The beautiful and elaborate seals in use in the Middle Ages afford many examples of this. Some of these seals bear an effigy with shields of arms ; others bear heraldic insignia alone.

On seals, as on monuments, effigies of ladies and ecclesiastics, as well as armed men, frequently show armorial devices on costume. In the obverse of her seal, Margaret of France, second Queen of Edward I, wears a tunic emblazoned with the three lions of England; on her right is a shield of France, and on her left a shield charged with a lion rampant (296).

An instance of a seal of an architectural character, with various armorial ensigns in the different compartments, is that of Joan, wife of John de Warenne, Earl of Surrey. She was the daughter of Henry, Count de Barre (in France), and Eleanor, eldest daughter of Edward I and Eleanor of Castile and Leon. On her seal (which is only one-and-a-half inches across) are five lozenges, bearing the arms of Warenne, England, and De Barre. Within the four quatrefoils are the lion of Leon and the castle of Castile (297).

No less rich in its heraldry and Gothic traceries, though measuring only one-and-a-quarter inches across, is the beautiful little counter-seal of Mary de St. Paul, third wife of Aymer de Valence, Earl of Pembroke (298). This lady, who founded Pembroke College, Cambridge, in 1373, was the daughter of Guy de Chatillon, Count of St. Paul, by Mary his wife, daughter of John de Dreux, Duke of Brittany, and Beatrice, sister of Edward I. On her seal the Countess marshals in the centre De Valence (*Barruly argent and azure, an orle of martlets gules*) united with De Chatillon (*Gules, three pallets vair, on a chief gold a label of three points azure*) by the process of dimidiation described later. The roundels bear

297. Seal of JOAN,
COUNTESS OF SURREY

298. Seal of MARY,
COUNTESS OF PEMBROKE

the arms of England, France and De Dreux (*Checky or and azure within a bordure of England, over all a canton of Brittany*—300).

299. Seal of ELIZABETH,
LADY BARDOLF

Elizabeth, wife of John, Lord Bardolf, and daughter of Roger D'Amory, being a descendant of Edward I and Eleanor of Castile through Joan, wife of Gilbert De Clare, Earl of Gloucester, displayed on her seal a shield of the arms of Bardolf (*Azure three cinquefoils or*—Plate II, 3), surrounded by roundles bearing the arms of D'Amory (*Argent, three bars undy gules, over all a bend azure*), De Clare (*Or, three chevronels gules*), De Burgh (*Or, a cross gules*), Castile and Leon (299).

This system of grouping together several shields of arms on one seal led naturally to the grouping of several coats of arms on one shield (dealt with in section III).

II. COMPOUNDING ARMS

But before it became the practice to marshal two or more distinct coats of arms on one shield, so that they preserved their identity while forming a single heraldic composition, the combination of two or even three coats of arms was frequently effected by taking the principal features or charges from each and blending them together in one shield so as to form a new coat of arms. Many early heraldic shields were produced by this process of "compounding" arms. The arms of

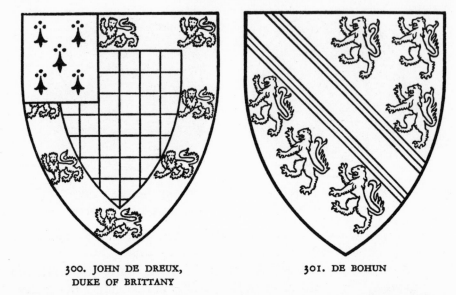

300. JOHN DE DREUX,   301. DE BOHUN
DUKE OF BRITTANY

John de Dreux, Duke of Brittany and Earl of Richmond, son of John
mentioned on page 132, provide an example (300). His mother was a
daughter of Henry III. The component parts of the arms which he
bore at the siege of Caerlaverock in 1300 are: *Checky or and azure*
(for De Dreux), *a bordure gules charged with eight lions passant guardant
or* (for England), and *a canton ermine* (for Brittany). · Similarly the arms
of the De Bohun Earls of Hereford, *Azure, a bend agent cotised or between
six lions rampant gold* (301), are thought to be compounded of the arms
attributed to Milo, Earl of Hereford, *Gules, two bends, one or and the
other argent*, and those of Longespée, Earl of Salisbury, *Azure, six lions
rampant or*, with whom the De Bohuns were connected.

The shield of Prince John of Eltham, *England within a bordure of
France* (183), is a simple example of this compounding of arms. A
modern instance of compounding is the blending of the cross of St.
George and the Saltires of St. Andrew and St. Patrick in the Union Flag.

III. The Arrangement of Two or More Distinct Coats of Arms on a Single Shield

(a) Historical

It was an easy step from the grouping of several shields on one seal
to the grouping of two or more coats of arms on one shield. The

302. DE VALENCE   303. CORNWALL dimidiating
dimidiating CLAREMONT-NESLÉ   DE CLARE

simplest method, applicable where only two coats were concerned, was
by impalement, the shield being divided palewise and one coat being
placed in each half.

The primitive method of impalement was dimidiation, whereby the
shields of husband and wife were each cut in half vertically, the dexter
half of the husband's being then joined to the sinister half of the wife's.
This practice appears to have been introduced into English heraldry
during the reign of Edward I.   An instance has already been noted in
the dimidiated arms of De Valence and De Chatillon on the seal of
Mary de St. Paul, Countess of Pembroke.   No. 302 shows De Valence
dimidiating the French coat of Claremont-Neslé, *Gules semé of trefoils,
two barbels hauriant addorsed or*, only half the De Valence orle of martlets
and one of the barbels being shown.

Another example (303) shows the dimidiated arms of Edmund, Earl
of Cornwall (d. 1300): *Argent, a lion rampant gules crowned or within
a bordure sable bezanty*, and his wife Margaret, daughter of Richard, Earl
of Clare, who bore, *Or, three chevronels gules*.   This clearly shows the
unfortunate effects of dimidiation, as the chevronels have become
bendlets and the coat is no longer identifiable as that of De Clare.

Two examples of dimidiated coats which are still in use occur in
civic heraldry, namely, the arms of the Cinque Ports, consisting of
England dimidiating, *Azure, three ships' hulls fesswise in pale argent* (304);
and Great Yarmouth : *England* dimidiating, *Azure, three herrings naiant
in pale argent finned or*.   The result is that the fore-halves of the lions
appear to be cojoined in the one case to ships' sterns and in the other
to fish-tails.

304. CINQUE PORTS

305. D'AUBIGNY
impaling SCOTLAND

Dimidiation was abandoned because it was found in many cases to affect and even destroy the distinctive character of the arms, and therefore to impair the significance of marshalling. Its place was taken by simple impalement, whereby the whole of each of the two coats was placed in its appropriate half of the shield. No. 306, from the monumental brass of Thomas, Lord Camoys, and his wife Elizabeth Mortimer, at Trotton, Sussex, 1410, marshals Camoys (*Argent, on a chief gules three plates*) impaling *Mortimer* (157). Dimidiation has left a trace in the treatment of bordures and tressures in impalement; they are not shown complete, but the side of a bordure or tressure that adjoins the line of impalement is omitted; e.g. the arms of D'Aubigny (*Azure, three fleurs-de-lis or within a bordure gules charged with eight buckles gold*) impaling *Scotland* (305). Modern rules with regard to impalement are dealt with later.

Another method of marshalling two or more coats of arms on one shield is the quartering of arms. Here the shield is divided quarterly, a coat of arms being placed in each of the four divisions. If there are only two coats of arms to be quartered, the more important is placed in the first and fourth quarters, and the other in the second and third (Plate X). In the case of three coats of arms, the principal one (normally the paternal coat) is placed in the first quarter and repeated in the fourth, the others being placed in the second and third in order of their importance or acquisition. Should it be necessary to quarter more than four coats on one shield, it may be divided into quarterly of six, eight, nine or more. A quarter may itself be quartered, in which

case it is termed a grand quarter, and the shield is
said to be quarterly quartered.

306. THOMAS,
LORD CAMOYS

The earliest example known in England of a
quartered shield is that on the monument of Eleanor,
Queen of Edward I, at Westminster. It bears,
Quarterly Castile and Leon. Its date is 1291.

On the fourth Great Seal of Edward III, adopted
in 1340, the Royal Arms appear as *Quarterly of
France Ancient (Azure, semé-de-lis or), and England*;
and about 60 years later the number of fleurs-de-lis
was reduced to three, this being termed *France Modern*.

One of the first English subjects who is recorded to have quartered
arms is Sir Symon de Montagu, whose shield is blazoned in the Falkirk
Roll (1308): *Sire Symon de Montagu, Quartile de argent e de azure, en les
quarters de azure les griffons de or, en les quarters de argent les daunces de goules.*
Here the *daunce* is a variant of *three lozenges cojoined in fess*, the usual form
of the arms of Montagu. In modern blazon these arms would be,
Quarterly, 1 and 4, Argent, a fess dancetty gules; 2 and 3, Azure, a griffin or.

Another early instance is the coat of arms of Laurence Hastings, Earl
of Pembroke, who is shown on the Hastings brass at Elsyng, Norfolk,
1347, with a jupon *Quarterly Hastings and De Valence*. In no. 307
these arms are shown impaling the Royal Arms, for the second Earl,
who married Margaret, daughter of Edward III.

During the second half of the 14th century, both impaling and
quartering gradually became established as heraldic usages, and shields
thus marshalled became frequent; later, quarterings became numerous in
many shields.

Other early examples of impalement and quartering include the
following:

Eleanor de Bohun, wife of Thomas of Woodstock, Duke of
Gloucester (brass at Westminster, 1399): *Quarterly France and England,
all within a bordure argent*, impaling *Quarterly Milo and De Bohun, Earl
of Hereford*. Here the border is not cut off by the impalement. The
practice with regard to bordures and tressures was at this date variable.
On the same brass is the shield of Eleanor de Bohun's father and
mother, *De Bohun*, impaling *Quarterly FitzAlan (Gules, a lion rampant
or) and Warenne (Checky or and azure)*.

John of Gaunt, on one of his seals: *Quarterly Castile and Leon,*

307. JOHN HASTINGS,
EARL OF PEMBROKE

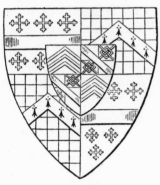

308. RICHARD BEAUCHAMP,
EARL OF WARWICK

impaling *Quarterly France and England with a label ermine*. Here, in
honour of his royal consort, Constance of Castile and Leon, he places
her arms on the dexter side. In his other seals bearing impaled shields,
his own arms occupy the dexter side.

Henry VII, in his Chapel at Westminster: *Quarterly France Modern
and England*, impaling *Quarterly quartered*, 1 *France and England quarterly;
2 and 3 Ulster; 4 Mortimer*, the sinister side being the arms of Elizabeth of York, declaring her descent from the Houses of York and
Clarence.

Richard Beauchamp, Earl of Warwick (d. 1439), on his Garter-plate
at Windsor: *Quarterly Beauchamp and Newburgh* (*checky or and azure, a
chevron ermine*), and on an escutcheon of pretence, *Quarterly De Clare and
Le Despencer*, for his wife Isabelle, daughter and heiress of Thomas
Le Despencer, Earl of Gloucester (308).

(b) Present System

The present system of marshalling arms has now to be described. It
discriminates between a combination of arms which is only temporary
and is to end with the lifetime of the bearer, and one which is to be
permanent and hereditary.

The temporary and non-hereditary combinations are: (i) those

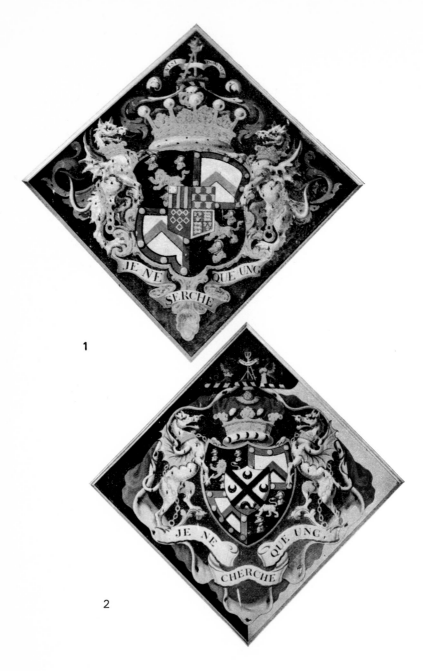

1

2

Plate IX

HATCHMENTS

Plate IX

HATCHMENTS

(See Chapter XII, pp. 148–50)

1. The hatchment of James Compton, 5th Earl of Northampton, who died 3rd October 1754. He married Elizabeth, sister and heiress of Robert Shirley, Viscount Tamworth. She inherited the baronies of Ferrers of Chartley, Bourchier, Louvaine and Basset of Drayton and died 13th March 1740/1. As she was an heiress, her arms are shown on an escutcheon of pretence (Shirley quartering Ferrers and France and England quarterly within a bordure argent) and, as she predeceased her husband, the entire background of the hatchment is painted black.

2. The hatchment of Charles Compton, 9th Earl and 1st Marquess (created 1812) of Northampton. The Marquess died in 1828, but as his wife survived him the sinister half of the hatchment is painted white. Strictly speaking the Marquess was not entitled to the supporters for these pertained to the barony of Compton which, on the death of James, 5th Earl of Northampton (see above), passed to his only daughter and heiress, Charlotte, Baroness Ferrers of Chartley. The matter was put right in 1858 when supporters of a dragon and an unicorn were granted to Charles, 3rd Marquess. The wife of the first Marquess was Maria, daughter of Joshua Smith of Erle Stoke Park, Wiltshire. Her arms, which were not granted until 1804, she having married in 1787, are incorrectly portrayed and should be blazoned: *Argent, on a saltire between three crescents azure, and in base a dolphin of the last, finned or, an escallop gold.* The arms shown were possibly used before the grant was made, but as hatchments were usually painted by local craftsmen the heraldry is often incorrect and should always be carefully checked. Both the hatchments shown in the illustration are in Compton Wynyates Church, Warwickshire.

produced by the union of the arms of husband and wife in all cases
where the wife does not possess in her own person hereditary rank,
or is not an heiress or representative (or coheiress or co-representative)
of any family ; and (ii) those produced by the union of arms appertaining to an office (e.g. that of a Bishop or King of Arms) with the
personal arms of the holder of such office for the time being. In both
cases the combination is effected by impalement (Plate XXII).

Firstly, with regard to husband and wife : clearly when a woman
has brothers to inherit and hand down the paternal arms, there would
be no justification in her transmitting them to her children. Furthermore, if in every instance the wife's arms, as well as the husband's,
were hereditary, there would speedily arise such complexity in armorial
bearings as to render marshalling impracticable. Normally, therefore,
in the case of marriages where the wife has no hereditary rank of her
own and is not an heiress or representative of her family, her arms are
not transmitted to her children or their descendants. The husband's
arms are placed on the dexter side of the impaled shield, and the wife's
on the sinister side, and they are thus borne together by the husband
and wife [1] while they both live. The children bear and inherit only
their father's arms. Some heralds have taken the view that a man
should impale only his wife's pronominal coat, and not any quarterings
she may possess, but in practice a quartered coat is often found impaled.

A widower ceases to impale the arms of his late wife. However,
on a memorial or hatchment (see page 148) the impaled shield may be
exhibited; and, if he marries again, he may impale the arms of both
wives in the sinister half of the shield; either the sinister half may be
parted palewise, the first wife's arms being placed to the dexter of the
second wife's, or it may be parted fesswise, the first wife's arms being
placed in chief and the second wife's in base. This practice, only
customary on memorials, is now uncommon. The position of a widow
is dealt with later (page 148).

Secondly, with regard to official arms : Archbishops and Bishops
may impale the arms of their province or see (Plate XXII), Heads of
Colleges those of the college, and Kings of Arms, Deans of Cathedrals,
and Regius Professors at Cambridge the arms of their office, with
their personal arms. In the case of a county, borough, urban or rural

---

[1] For convenience, the use of arms by women is dealt with in detail in a later
section.

district council, it has been permissible for the mayor or chairman (as the case may be), during his term of office, to impale the arms of the council with his personal arms (see p. 300). In all these cases, the official arms are placed on the dexter side of the impaled shield. The combination ends with the termination of the tenure of office. It would obviously be misleading for a man to continue to use official arms after vacating the office they indicate, and for his descendants to bear such arms.

A permanent and hereditary combination of arms occurs when a man marries an heiress or coheiress, and has children who succeed in due course to the arms of their mother as well as of their father. The term heiress in heraldry does not necessarily imply the possession of real estate or wealth : the inheritance of an heiress may consist of only her paternal arms. Not only must her father be dead, but all her brothers (if any) must have died without leaving any sons or daughters. If she has sisters, she and they are all coheiresses. As there is no male to carry on the line, an heiress or coheiress is the representative or co-representative of her family, and in order that the arms of that family shall not become extinct she carries them to her husband, and after her death to her children and descendants, as a permanent possession. A woman may become an heiress after her death, called 'an heiress in her issue', if the male line of her family fails after her decease, leaving her descendants the inheritors of her paternal arms.[1]

The rules and methods of marshalling arms must be given here in detail, because they are necessary to the understanding of many shields which may come under the student's notice. At the same time it should be pointed out that in these days the practice of incorporating the arms of heiresses is, by custom and taste, restricted. There has been a reaction against the elaborate genealogical escutcheons of the period of heraldic ostentation, when people searched their pedigrees for marriages entitling them to display additional quarterings, regardless of the fact that some of the heiresses may have represented only junior branches of large families of which the senior branches continued. The heraldic taste of the present day is opposed to quartering for its own sake, and considers that the simple dignity of a single coat may be impaired rather than enhanced by quartering. People who are technically entitled, but not required, to quarter the arms of other families with their paternal coat should consider whether the alliances to which the

[1] See page 296.

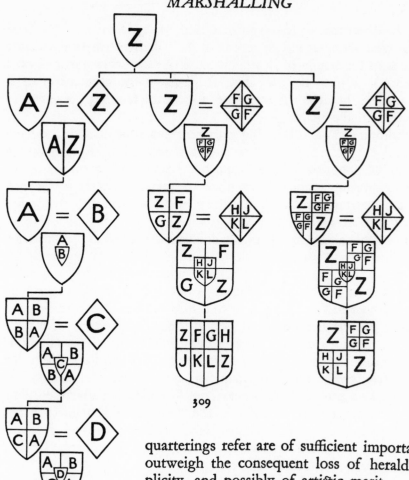

309

quarterings refer are of sufficient importance to outweigh the consequent loss of heraldic simplicity, and possibly of artistic merit.

The accompanying diagram (309) shows the principle of marshalling the arms of husband and wife, and the transmission of the arms of an heiress to her descendants.

A marries Z, who is not an heiress because she has a brother. The arms of A and Z are therefore impaled, and their son inherits only the arms of A.

This second A marries B, an heiress. He thereupon places the arms of B on an escutcheon of pretence in the centre of the shield of A, because he pretends to the representation of the family of B, there being no male member left to represent it. (If there are two or more coheiresses of the family of B, the husband of each bears the arms of B in pretence.) When the wife dies, A removes the escutcheon of B from his shield, because the representation of the family of B passes to the children of the marriage.

The children of A and B, being truly representative of their mother's family, and not only pretenders to such representation, do not use the escutcheon of pretence. At their mother's death, they incorporate her arms by quartering them. They place their father's arms in the first and fourth quarters, and their mother's in the second and third, and bear *Quarterly A and B*.

Assuming that a son (or other male descendant) of the above marriage, bearing *Quarterly A and B*, marries a woman who is, or becomes, the heiress of her family, C, the husband would bear *Quarterly A and B with C in pretence*; and their children in due course would proceed to quarter the coat of C, placing it in the third quarter of the shield, and so bearing *Quarterly*, 1 *and* 4, *A;* 2, *B;* 3, *C*. Similarly, if a male descendant bearing the last shield marries the heiress of the family of D, he will place the arms of D in pretence, and his children will in due course quarter them, and bear *Quarterly A, B, C, and D*. And so the process might continue, a fresh quartering being added after the others for every marriage with an heiress, the division of the shield being increased to quarterly of six, eight, etc., as necessary, and the pronominal coat of A being repeated in the last quarter if required to make up a convenient number of quarterings.

So far we have considered the marshalling of the arms of heiresses only where they consist of single coats without any quarterings accruing to them. But suppose now that a man, Z, marries the heiress of the family of F, who is also representative of the family of G, and bears *Quarterly F and G*. The husband will place the quartered coat of F and G, in pretence on the shield of Z, and the children of the marriage will inherit their mother's arms, including the quartering accruing thereto. The normal English practice is to break up their mother's arms into the component coats, and range these in the shield after their father's; they will thus bear *Quarterly* 1 *and* 4, *Z;* 2, *F;* 3, *G*.

However, there may be reasons why the quarterly coat of F and G cannot be broken up and rearranged in this way. It may be of such

long standing as to have acquired the status of a single and indivisible
coat of arms ; or it may have been quartered in the first instance by
Royal Licence as a condition of inheritance to an estate under a "name
and arms" clause, in which case it is indivisible, or impartible. In
such circumstances it must be treated as a single coat, and the children
of the marriage will therefore bear *Quarterly quartered, 1 and 4, Z ; 2
and 3 grand quarters, quarterly F and G.* This method of marshalling is
generally employed in Scotland, where arms combined by quartering
are usually regarded as constituting an indivisible shield, and indeed
may be made so by a border placed round all four quarters, or some
other addition, for cadency.

In the diagram, each method is carried a stage further by assuming
a further marriage with an heiress bearing *Quarterly H, J, K, and L.*
It will be seen that, according to the normal English practice, the result
is a shield of eight quarters (the pronominal coat being repeated in
the eighth) ; while where the principle of the indivisible coat is applied,
the result is a coat of four grand quarters, two of them being sub-
quartered. (It is, of course, possible for all four grand quarters to be
sub-quartered.)

The usual English practice of breaking up a quartered shield and
redistributing the coats avoids repetition of quarterings and results in
a simpler composition. This has practical and artistic advantages, but
it less accurately reflects the genealogical circumstances which gave
rise to the quartered shield. All that can be told from the coat of eight
quarters in the diagram is that the arms are those of a man Z who,
through his marriage or the marriages of his ancestors, represents the
families of F, G, H, J, K, and L. The shield in itself gives us no
further clue as to how the coats came together. Without the pedigree
before us, we might suppose that men of the family of Z had successively
married the heiresses of F, G, H, J, K, and L (in that order) ; or that a
Z had married an F, and their descendant a G, who already possessed
and "brought in" the H, J, K, and L quarterings ; and there are
several other possibilities.

But the corresponding shield produced by the other method tells us
definitely, without reference to the pedigree, that the arms came
together by the following stages : F married the heiress of G ; men
of the family of H successively married the heiresses of J, K,
and L ; men of the family of Z married first the heiress of F and

then the heiress of H, and these heiresses " brought in " the other coats.

It is not necessary for a man to use all the quarterings to which he is entitled. He may make a selection from them, but if he does so, he may include a particular quartering which has been brought in by an heiress only if he also includes the one which brought it in. For instance, in the shield of eight quarterings in the diagram, Z can only quarter G if he also quarters F.

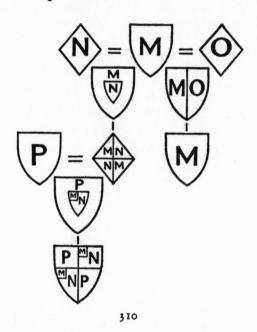

310

Bordures and tressures (affected by impalement) are not affected by quartering ; where they form part of a coat to be marshalled quarterly with other coats, no part is to be omitted. Thus, in the Royal Arms the tressure of Scotland is shown complete in the second quarter.

If a man M marries an heiress N and has by her a daughter, and then marries a non-heiress O and has by her a son, the daughter inherits the quartered arms of her father and heiress mother, and the son inherits only his father's arms (310). In this case the daughter is the heiress of her mother and not of her father. Accordingly she cannot transmit the quartered arms of her father and mother to her husband P, and the proper course is for him to bear in pretence her mother's arms charged with a dexter canton of her father's pronominal coat, and their children will quarter these arms in the usual way.

The widower of an heiress does not continue to bear his late wife's arms. However, on memorials a first wife's arms are sometimes found in pretence on a coat impaling the arms of a second wife; or, if the second wife was also an heiress, the arms of both wives may be found on an escutcheon of pretence party per fess, the arms of the first wife being placed in chief.

A man who himself has no coat of arms can make no use of his wife's arms, since he has no heraldic shield on which to bear them, either impaled or in pretence. Similarly, the children of a non-armigerous father cannot inherit the arms of their mother (she being an heraldic heiress) because they have no paternal arms with which to quarter their mother's coat. The remedy is, of course, for a man who marries an heiress to petition for a grant of arms for himself, so that he may preserve and transmit to his descendants the arms of his wife's family.

IV. The Grouping and Arrangement of Two or More Distinct Shields of Arms so that they form a Single Heraldic Composition

Marshalling sometimes requires special treatment having regard to the inclusion of insignia which appertain to one partner in the marriage but not to the other.

A man holding an office to which official arms appertain, and impaling such arms with his own, should not bear his wife's arms on the same shield. For example, a King of Arms, Head of a College, Regius Professor, or Mayor, may impale (on the dexter side) the arms of his office, college or corporation, with his personal coat, placing above the shield his personal crest, and in the case of a King of Arms his crown (see page 187). To include his wife's arms in his achievement, he must use two shields placed side by side, that to the dexter bearing the official arms impaled with his own, and that to the sinister bearing his personal arms combined with those of his wife, impaled or in pretence.

An Archbishop or Bishop, who impales his personal arms (on the sinister side) with those of his province or see, ensigning the shield with a mitre, may in theory bear a second shield displaying his own arms and those of his wife, but this is not a common practice.

Knights of the Garter, and knights, commanders and companions of other orders who are entitled to place the insignia of the order round their shields, if married display two shields, one bearing their paternal arms and encircled by the appropriate insignia, and the other bearing their arms with those of their wife in pretence or impaled. To give artistic balance to the composition, a wreath or garland, provided it has no significant character, may be placed round the second shield. (This is dealt with more fully in Chapter XVIII.)

The position of a Peeress in her own right is dealt with in section VI.

Royal Persons, when married, bear their paternal arms alone on one shield, which is placed to the dexter; and a second shield bears the arms of the spouse, or the impaled arms of husband and wife, the arms of the person of the higher rank being impaled on the dexter side.

V. THE TREATMENT OF CRESTS AND ACCESSORIES

Although crests, like arms, are hereditary, they are not necessarily transmitted by heiresses. There are cases of a second crest, brought in by marriage with an heiress, being recorded at the Visitations, and this is regarded as authority for the descendants at this day to bear the two crests. An additional crest may also be borne by special grant from the Crown, e.g. as an augmentation, and by the Royal Licence permitting a person to bear the name and arms of another family in addition to his own. It is, however, irregular to assume an additional crest without due authority.

When two crests are displayed, the helms on which they are placed may either both face to the dexter (Plate X), or they may face one another, in which case the dexter crest will have to be turned about.

The principal crest is the crest of augmentation (if there is one) or, failing this, the crest appertaining to the arms in the first quarter of the shield. The principal crest is placed to the dexter, or in the centre if three crests are displayed.

The display of any badges to which a man may be entitled by inheritance or grant is not a matter for definite rules. Badges may be grouped in the achievement (but not, of course, combined with any part of it) according to artistic taste.

Supporters and other accessories are dealt with elsewhere.

Plate X

QUARTERED ARMS WITH TWO CRESTS

(See Chapter XII, pp. 136–46; see also p. 154)

PORTMAN quartering BERKELEY.

Arms : Quarterly, 1 and 4, **Or,** a fleur-de-lis azure (for PORTMAN) ;
2 and 3, Gules, a chevron ermine between ten crosses paty
argent (for BERKELEY).

Crests : 1, a talbot sejant or (for PORTMAN) ; 2, a unicorn
passant gules, armed and crined gold (for BERKELEY).

Plate X

QUARTERED ARMS WITH TWO CRESTS

VI. THE BEARING OF ARMS BY WOMEN (see Plate XI)

Unmarried daughters bear their paternal arms, including the quarterings and any mark of cadency the father may use, but they add no mark of cadency (as their brothers may do) to denote their own relative position in the family. They bear the arms on lozenges, without the crest or accessories. The lozenge was in use as early as the 15th century. It is a most inconvenient form for the purpose of displaying armorial bearings, frequently resulting in inartistic distortion of the design. A permissible variation is a roundle or oval. The lozenge of an unmarried woman sometimes has a knot of ribbon on top, but this is merely decorative.

An unmarried woman holding the office of Head of a College or Mayor may, while she holds such office, impale the arms of the college or corporation with her own on a lozenge, the official arms occupying the dexter side.

A married woman bears on a shield her paternal arms marshalled with those of her husband, by impalement or escutcheon of pretence. But a new circumstance has now to be considered which was not contemplated when Boutell wrote, namely, that in these days of sex-equality, when women frequently have public and other activities and interests distinct from those which they share with their husbands, a married woman may wish to use arms for her own personal purposes.

The husband for his own exclusive affairs may use his own arms without his wife's coat impaled or in pretence, but it is not open to a married woman to use only her maiden arms. She cannot use her married arms on a lozenge, because this is the style appropriate to widowhood. The matter has been carefully considered by Fox-Davies, having regard to such precedents as are available, and he has expressed the view that the most satisfactory course for a married woman wishing to use arms for her own particular purposes is to place the combined arms of her husband and herself on a shield with a knot of ribbon above it. The impalement, or escutcheon of pretence, will show that they are married arms, and the knot will show that they are those of a woman. This practice, however, has no official sanction.

A married woman serving in the office of Mayor will use an impaled shield with the Corporation arms on the dexter side, and on the sinister her husband's arms with her own impaled or in pretence as the case may be. (In this case it is clear that the arms are those of a woman mayor, as a man holding the office does not impale his wife's arms on the shield bearing the corporation's coat.)

A widow continues to bear the combined arms of her late husband and herself, hers being impaled or in pretence as the case may be, but she places them on a lozenge without helm or crest, though if she is the widow of a peer she may use the supporters and appropriate coronet. If a widow marries a second time, she normally ceases to bear her first husband's arms.

A woman whose marriage has been dissolved bears on a lozenge her paternal arms charged for distinction with a mascle, which may be of any metal or colour and placed wherever convenient. If she remarries, the mascle is removed.

A peeress in her own right bears her hereditary arms on a lozenge, with coronet and supporters but without helm or crest. If she marries a peer, both her arms and her husband's are fully marshalled and the shield and lozenge with their respective supporters, coronets, and the husband's crest, are grouped together to form a single comprehensive achievement, the armorial bearings of the husband being placed to the dexter of the other.

If a peeress in her own right marries a commoner, her husband charges her paternal arms, ensigned with her coronet, in pretence on his own, and she also bears her own achievement of arms, distinct and complete as she bore it before her marriage; and the lozenge and the shield are grouped together, the lozenge yielding precedence.

VII. Hatchments (see Plate IX)

It was formerly the custom, when an armigerous person died, to paint his or her armorial bearings on a lozenge-shaped panel of canvas or wood, enclosed in a black frame, and to place this on the house-front as a sign of mourning. Such paintings were termed hatchments (from " achievement ") or funeral escutcheons (312). The custom is not now common, but as many hatchments were, after the period of mourning, removed to the parish church, and there remain, they are an object of interest to students of heraldry, and the practice with regard to them must be explained.

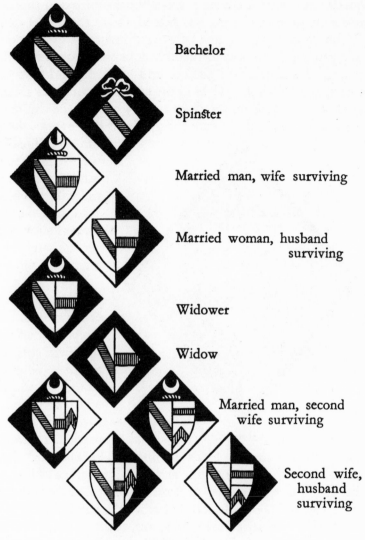

Bachelor

Spinster

Married man, wife surviving

Married woman, husband
surviving

Widower

Widow

Married man, second
wife surviving

Second wife,
husband
surviving

311. Funeral Hatchments

Hatchments contained the full armorial bearings of the deceased person, including, in the case of a married person, the arms of both husband and wife; but the motto was usually replaced by *Resurgam*, or some similar phrase. The usual rules of marshalling were observed;

quarterings were included; crests were omitted in the case of women, and sometimes a cherub was placed above the shield or lozenge.

The special significance of a hatchment lay in the treatment of the background; this was painted black behind that part of the arms which related to the deceased person, and white behind that part relating to a person still living. Thus in the case of an impaled shield, if the background was black on the dexter and white on the sinister side, the husband was dead and the wife survived; if the reverse, the wife was dead and the husband survived. Where the whole background behind the arms of husband and wife was black, both were dead, and the use of shield or lozenge showed to which partner the hatchment particularly referred (311).

312. Hatchment

In the case of deceased single persons, the background was, of course, all black, except in the case of arms impaled with an official coat, when the background behind the latter would be white, because the office survives. There were variations of the practice in particular circumstances, but the principle that a black section of background denotes the deceased person is constant, and this, together with the details of the achievement—shield or lozenge, impaled or otherwise, crest or none, etc.—tells the observer whether the hatchment refers to the death of a bachelor, married man, widower, maid, married woman, or widow.

Occasionally a "death's head" was placed over the shield instead of a crest, and this is said to have indicated that the deceased person was the last of his or her line.

Plate XI

THE USE OF THE LOZENGE IN HERALDRY

(See Chapter XII, p. 147)

1. Arms of a peeress in her own right.

   The arms of Louise Renée de Penancoet de Keroualle (usually called Louise de Queroualle), a mistress of King Charles II who was created Duchess of Portsmouth for life in 1673. The lozenge of an unmarried woman is surmounted by the coronet of a duchess and flanked by supporters, a privilege of peerage, which were granted to the Duchess 8th June 1674. They are : *Two ermines, about the neck of each an ermine scarf.* This illustration is taken from the actual record at The College of Arms.

2. Arms of a spinster.

   The arms of Elizabeth, second daughter of John Young of Milton, Oxfordshire, and a grand-daughter of John Young, Bishop of Rochester (1578–1605). These arms were entered on the certificate taken after her funeral at St. Andrew's, Holborn, London, on 20th June 1633. The lozenge of a spinster is surmounted by a true lover's knot. This ornament has no official sanction but is a conceit often employed when depicting the arms of an unmarried woman.

3. Arms of a widow.

   The arms entered on the funeral certificate of Mrs. Jane Archbold, widow of the Rev. William Archbold, D.D., sometime pastor of St. Peter in Cornhill, London, where she was buried on 14th January 1635. She was the daughter of William Billingsley of Stepney and niece of Sir Henry Billingsley, Lord Mayor of London. Her maiden arms are impaled by those of her husband and shown upon a lozenge.

4. Arms of a widow who is an heiress.

   The arms of Frances Herbert, dowager Viscountess Nelson. She was the only child and heiress of William Woollward, and was granted arms on 20th December 1805 after the death of her husband, the famous admiral. These arms are shown on an escutcheon of pretence over the arms of Viscount Nelson and the whole is placed in a lozenge. As the widow of a peer she would be entitled to use his coronet and supporters.

5. Arms of a corporation.

   The arms granted to Girton College, Cambridge, on 14th February 1928. This is an heraldic solecism for a Corporation, whether or not its members are all women, is regarded in heraldry as being masculine and should bear arms on a shield in the ordinary manner.

PLATE XI

THE USE OF THE LOZENGE IN HERALDRY

313. Helm and shield of
RICHARD I

314. Crested helm of RICHARD II
in Westminster Hall

CHAPTER XIII

THE CREST AND ITS ACCESSORIES

A CREST is a device which was mounted on the helm or bascinet in the days of chivalry, and is still so displayed in modern heraldry. In its fully-developed form, the crest was an ornament fashioned of wood or leather, and was probably worn more in pageantry and tournaments than in war, since it must have been rather cumbersome. The forerunner of the crest was the fan-like plate set on edge on the top of some helms in the 12th and 13th centuries, perhaps intended to break the force of a sword-cut. This plate was sometimes decorated with a device. Richard I's second Great Seal, c. 1195, shows such a plate with a lion passant painted on it, the rudiment of the Royal Crest of England (313). The development of the crest was carried a stage further when the plate was cut to the outline of the device it bore, producing a flat figure which could be seen properly only in profile;

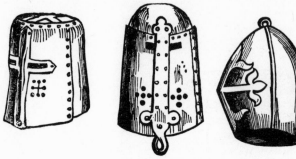

315. Types of Helm

and this was followed in the late 13th and early 14th centuries by a small modelled crest fitting the top of the helm. The elaboration of the modelled device, and its accompaniments of torse and mantling, produced the large heraldic crest associated with armorial display.

Before considering the crest in detail, it will be convenient to deal with its accessories : the helm on which it is borne ; the torse (or crest-wreath), chapeau and crest-coronet ; and the mantling which hangs from the helm and forms a decorative feature of the achievement.

THE HELM

The helm (heaume or helmet), which in heraldry is usually placed above the shield of arms, not only serves as a means of displaying the crest, but also has a significance of its own, since its type denotes the rank of the person bearing the arms.

Helms, like shields, were of different patterns at various periods. The type commonest in the 13th century was the cylindrical pot-helm with a flat or pointed top, slits to see through, and holes for ventilation (315). This was worn over a chain-mail coif or a close-fitting steel cap, and the helm would only be used in action, being at other times slung from the saddle. In the 14th century the bascinet was introduced —a pointed, steel cap to which was attached the camail, or chain-mail protection of neck and shoulders (316). The pot-helm, or great helm, was worn over the bascinet when necessary, but this proved to be clumsy, and accordingly the bascinet itself was strengthened and provided with a vizor, while the camail was replaced by a plate gorget (318). In the 15th century the great helm was used only in tournament. There

316. Bascinet and camail from
the Black Prince's effigy

317. Crested helm of THOMAS,
second EARL OF LANCASTER

were three types: the tilting helm, which was permanently closed
except for a slit to see through; a helm with a vizor which could be
opened, for combats on foot; and one with an aperture before the
face, protected by bars or lattice, for use in the *mêlée*, where the weapons
were sword or mace. These were the types of helm which bore the
great crests of tournament and heraldic display, and they are the ones
still associated with armorial bearings. In later times, fantastic helms
of a type which could never have been used were introduced in heraldic
achievements, but it is now the usual practice to show a helm of a
type which could have been actually worn in tournament.

In the early 17th century, regulations were adopted regarding the type
and position of helms in achievements, having regard to the rank of the
person bearing the arms.

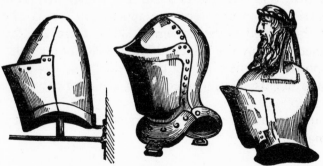

318. Helms from Cobham Church, Kent

The Sovereign has a barred helm of gold and this is placed affronté. This applies also to Princes of the Blood Royal (Plate I).

Peers have barred helms of silver decorated with gold, placed sideways and showing five bars (Plate XXI).

Baronets and knights have vizored helms of steel adorned with silver, placed affronté, the vizor raised.

Esquires and gentlemen have either closed helms, or vizored helms with the vizor down; these are of steel, and are placed sideways. A corporate body possessing a crest places it on an esquire's helm.

In practice the steel helms of baronets, knights, esquires and gentlemen are sometimes garnished with gold, and all open helms may be shown with lining material of any suitable colour, representing the silk covering of the inside padding.

While the use of different types of helm to denote rank has an interest, the rule that helms of certain ranks must be shown affronté, and others in profile, produces unfortunate results. We find crests in profile on helms set affronté, and *vice versa*. The crest of a demi-griffin segreant, being itself in profile, is suitably displayed on the sideways helm of the Marquess of Cholmondeley, but looks wrong on the full-face helm of Cholmeley, Baronet, since it is obviously anomalous that the creature in a crest should face a different way from the man who bears it. Equally unsuitable is Lord Willoughby de Broke's crest of a Saracen's head affronté placed on his peer's helm set sideways. To a great extent this problem has been overcome by twisting the helm and the crest a little so that they are more or less aligned, yet the blazon of the crest remains unambiguous.

Two or more helms may be placed above a shield where the owner has more than one crest (as in Plate X). They may both or all face to the dexter, or they may face one another, in which case the dexter crest must be turned with its helm. When there are three or more crests, sometimes only the principal one is placed on a helm, the others being disposed " in the air " on either side.

A helm is not usually included in an achievement unless there is a crest for it to bear.

In monuments, the crested helm frequently forms a rest for the head of the effigy.

The Torse, Chapeau and Crest-Coronet

The crest was laced or bolted on the helm, and to hide the unsightly join various decorative means were employed. The simplest was a plain fillet or ribbon. Another was the *contoise* or scarf, possibly a lady's favour, which was sometimes worn with the ends flowing loose (317). The twisting of such a scarf round the helm, perhaps in imitation of the turban, would give rise to the torse, or crest-wreath, which appeared about the middle of the 14th century. In other cases the *capelot*, or *chapeau*, worn on the helm before the development of mantling, was used as the basis for the crest. Finally there was the decorative circlet which became the crest-coronet. Every crest now granted is to be borne with a torse, chapeau, crest-coronet, or circlet. The last is a modern innovation, and may be plain or charged.

The torse is now shown as a twisted ribbon of two or more tinctures which appear alternately in the folds, of which six are visible in representation. Unless other tinctures are specified, the torse, like the mantling, is of the colours, i.e. of the principal metal and the principal colour in the arms, or, in the case of a quartered shield, of the first quarter. These tinctures will be those of the field if it is party, or otherwise of the field and the principal charge, and they will generally be those first mentioned in the blazon. If one of the principal tinctures is a fur, the dominant metal or colour of the fur is taken; thus, ermine gives argent, erminois or, and ermines sable. The first fold of the torse on the dexter side is of the metal. In a few early instances a wreath appears as a decoration of the bascinet, unaccompanied by a crest, e.g. Lord Willoughby d'Eresby, 1409, has his pointed bascinet encircled by a wreath of roses (319).

The chapeau has rarely been granted in modern times. It is usually tinctured gules turned-up ermine, and this is presumed unless other tinctures are specified (see page 298). Edward III's crest showed the lion statant guardant on a chapeau, and this remained the form of the Royal Crest until the reign of Henry VIII (314). The lion crests of the Dukes of Norfolk and Northumberland are also displayed on chapeaux.

The crest-coronet is misleadingly blazoned as a ducal coronet. It has no relationship to ducal rank, and little resemblance to the coronet worn by a duke. Early examples take various floral and foliated forms (322, 323, 324). The modern ducal coronet (i.e. ducal crest-coronet)

319. Crest-wreath:
LORD WILLOUGHBY D'ERESBY, 1409

320. Helm and crest of
SIR GEOFFREY LOUTERELL, 1345

has four strawberry-leaves, three being visible in the flat. It is now rarely granted in connection with new crests, but in some cases a crest may be granted issuing from a mural, naval or eastern crown. (These types are described later.) There are a few instances of crests issuing from coronets associated with particular rank in the peerage, e.g. Forbes, Bart., of Pitsligo : *Issuing out of a baron's coronet, a dexter hand holding a scymetar proper.* This is misleading, and such coronets would not now be granted.

The crest-coronet was originally an alternative to the torse, and they were seldom borne together, but instances of both in the same crest do occur in ancient and modern heraldry, and if the blazon specifies that the coronet is on a torse, both should be shown.

THE MANTLING OR LAMBREQUIN

The mantling was a small mantle attached to the helm and hanging down over the shoulders of the wearer, perhaps to protect his head and shoulders from the sun's heat. It has become a decorative accessory to the crest and shield. Following the fashion for scalloping the edges of garments, the mantling was frequently depicted with scalloped or jagged edges, and in this treatment fanciful writers have seen the cuts and rents which it would have received in battle. In ancient examples mantlings vary considerably in treatment. They are of two tinctures, generally a colour on the outside and metal or fur in the lining. Mantlings are sometimes decorated with charges from the arms or badges; for example, that of John Daubygné, 1345, is semé of molets (264). Other instances of mantlings so treated are:

George, Duke of Clarence: semé of white roses of York.
Henry Bourchier, Earl of Essex, d. 1483: the outside billetty, and the lining semé of water-bougets (361).
John, Lord Beaumont: semé-de-lis like the field of his shield.

In some cases the material of the crest, especially if a textile, was continued below the crest-coronet or torse so as to form the mantling. Thus Sir Richard Woodville, Earl Rivers, has for crest a demi-man in a garment semé of trefoils, and this garment is prolonged to form a mantling similarly semé. Likewise the skin of the black boar's-head crest of Sir Ralph Bassett continues into a sable mantling. Sir Simon de Felbrigge's mantling is feathered ermine like his panache (324). There are several examples of feathered mantling resulting from the continuation of a crest consisting of the head of a swan or griffin. In many cases the tinctures of the mantling were those of the arms or crest, but this does not seem to have been a rule in early mantlings.

During the 16th and 17th centuries nearly all mantlings were gules lined argent. Towards the end of the 17th century the custom changed and mantlings, like wreaths, were almost invariably "of the colours", that is, the principal colour and metal in the arms. After World War II there was a return to medieval practice and wreaths and mantlings today are frequently of different tinctures from the arms and from each other. Mantlings parted of two colours, or two metals, or both, are not uncommon and the badge may be strewn over the mantling as was sometimes done in past ages. The mantling of the Heraldry Society affords an early example of this return to first principles; it is *parted gules and azure semy of the badge, doubled or* (394). Peers are permitted a mantling *gules doubled ermine* and the Sovereign's mantling and those of royal princes is *or doubled ermine*.

THE CREST

It has been shown that the crest, in its early form, consisted in the painting of a device on the fan-shaped plate rising from the helm. As late as 1345, Sir Geoffrey Louterell bore such a plate on his helm (320), charging it with a bend and six martlets as his shield was charged. (In this case the crest was flanked by two long spikes, perhaps used to

321. SIR THOMAS DE
ST. QUINTIN, 1420

322. Helm with panache:
SIR EDWARD DE THORPE,
1418

323. Panache of
JOHN, LORD SCROPE

display a contoise.) A number of equestrian seals, e.g. those of
Humphrey de Bohun, Earl of Hereford, 1301, and Richard FitzAlan,
Earl of Arundel, 1301, show such plates on the helm, and sometimes
also on the horse's head, without any apparent decoration, though it
is probable that they were painted in distinctive colours. The Garter-
plate of Hugh, Lord Burnell, c. 1421, shows a ribbed fan, each rib
ending in a tassel.

At an early date the panache makes its appearance as a form of crest.
This was an arrangement of many feathers, usually rising in tiers on
the top of the helm, but sometimes forming a cluster fastened by a
brooch to the front of the helm as in the brass to Sir Thomas de St.
Quintin at Harpham, 1420 (321). A panache of peacock's feathers
appears on the helm of Sir Edward de Thorpe, 1418 (322). Cocks'
and swans' feathers were also used. The panache usually rose to a
point, but sometimes it was spreading, as in the Garter-plate of Sir
Simon de Felbrigge (324).

Feathers arranged in only one or two rows are sometimes referred
to as a plume or bush of feathers. The panache and plume were
occasionally tinctured as the arms ; the Mortimers matched the azure of

324. Arms and crest of SIR SIMON DE FELBRIGGE, from his Garter stall-plate. These face the sinister as it was customary for the knights' achievements in St. George's Chapel to face the high altar, thus those on the gospel side of the choir were reversed.

their arms with a panache of many azure feathers rising from a crest-coronet; and Waldegrave bears for arms, *Per pale argent and gules,* and for crest, *out of a crest-coronet or,* a *plume of five feathers per pale argent and gules.*

Preference was shown for " live " crests: beasts, birds or monsters, or their heads. In some cases these consisted in a repetition of a charge in the arms, as Richard I's lion crest accorded with the lions in his shield; but often the charges in arms did not lend themselves to use in crests, and consequently it became a common practice to use a crest in no way resembling the arms.

Examples of various types of crest are:

Human Figures

Lord Stourton : a demi-monk grasping a scourge—a canting crest referring to the family of Moyne. (Brass at Sawtry, Hunts.)

Henry Bourchier, Earl of Essex, 1483 : a Saracen's head wreathed about the temples and wearing a tasselled cap encircled by a coronet. (Brass at Little Easton—361.) Lord Bourchier, standard-bearer to Henry V, surmounted the Saracen's cap with a Catherine wheel from the arms of the Roets, with whom he was connected.

325. Crest of LORD DYNHAM

326. Seal of RICHARD,
EARL OF ARUNDEL, 1397

Beasts

Howard, Duke of Norfolk : on a chapeau, a lion statant guardant or, ducally gorged argent, tail extended ; granted by Richard II to Mowbray, Duke of Norfolk.

Percy, Duke of Northumberland : on a chapeau, a lion statant, tail extended, or.

Neville, Earl of Westmorland : from a wreath, a dun bull's head and neck erased proper.

Ralph, Lord Bassett, of Drayton : out of a crest-coronet, a boar's
 head sable armed or (Garter-plate).
Lord Dynham : on a cap of estate, an ermine (325).

Birds

Humphrey, Earl of Stafford, 1429 : out of a gold crest-coronet, a
 swan's head and wings proper (Garter-plate—64).
Thomas de Beauchamp, Earl of Warwick, 1344 : out of a crest-coronet,
 a swan's head and neck (seal—6).
Stanley, Earl of Derby : on a chapeau, an eagle, wings addorsed, or,
 hovering over an infant in its nest, proper, swaddled azure and
 banded gold (Garter-plate). The Stanleys derived this crest from
 the Lathams, who bore it in allusion to a story that one of the heads
 of their house adopted as his heir a child which had been exposed
 in Latham Park, and had been nurtured by an eagle.
Sir Richard Pole : on a wreath, a cormorant trussing a fish (Garter-
 plate).

Monsters

Roger de Quincey, Earl of Winchester, d. 1265 : a wivern (seal).
Richard, Earl of Arundel : out of a gold crest-coronet a griffin's head
 argent, beaked gules, between a pair of wings erect (326).
Thomas, Earl of Lancaster, 1301 : a wivern (seal).
William de Montagu, Earl of Salisbury, d. 1344 : out of a crest-coronet,
 a griffin's head and wings (seal).

Objects

John, Lord Lysle : a millstone argent with a sable centre and thereon
 a fer-de-moline or (Garter-plate ; no torse, coronet or chapeau).

Marks of cadency were displayed on crests as well as shields ; the
lion statant (but not guardant) on the helm of the Black Prince has a
silver label about its neck. Such marks are still placed on the crests
of members of the Royal Family, but otherwise their use in crests,
while permissible, is unusual.

The seal of Richard Neville, the King-maker, 1428–71, gives an early
instance of the use of two crests. He was Earl of Salisbury, and in
right of his wife also Earl of Warwick, and he displays two helms

facing one another, one bearing the Beauchamp swan for the earldom of Warwick, and the other the Montagu griffin for Salisbury.

It appears that crests were originally a mark of special dignity, perhaps restricted to persons of a rank or status entitling them to take part in tournaments. Later, however, their use became unrestricted, except as regards women. Today a crest is a normal part of armorial bearings granted to a man; it is only granted in conjunction with arms, or to a person who has inherited arms but no crest. Corporate bodies do not necessarily have crests granted to them when they obtain arms, and some heralds have taken the view that a crest is a personal device and should not be granted to a corporate body.

In England a crest is intended to be as distinctive of a particular family as arms, and though duplication has occurred, the heralds aim at avoiding it. In Scotland, however, it is possible for two or more different families to bear the same crest. The result is that while Scottish crests have remained comparatively simple, English crests have tended to become complicated through the introduction of minor differences to make each crest distinctive.

When the day of the modelled crest passed, and the crest became merely a device to be painted "in the flat," its original character was overlooked, and the heralds of the 16th and later centuries produced crests which could never have been borne on a helm. An instance is the crest of Sir Francis Drake, commemorating his circumnavigation of the world: *out of a wreath, a ship drawn round the globe with a cable-rope by a hand issuing out of clouds, all proper, and in the ship a dragon gules regarding the hand*; and above it the motto, *Auxilio Divino*.

Still more impracticable is the crest granted to the former London and North-Eastern Railway: the figure of Mercury rising from a cloud of steam. Nowadays the heralds are mindful that crests, like helms, should be of a type that could actually have been modelled and worn, and where they must have insubstantial things, such as a cloud of steam, or one object disjointed from the rest, it has sometimes been the practice of the Kings of Arms to grant the crest in the form of a roundel painted with the device.

327. Seal of THOMAS, DUKE OF GLOUCESTER, 1395

CHAPTER XIV

BADGES AND KNOTS

BADGES are heraldic insignia which, like arms and crests, are distinctive of a person or family, but unlike them are not associated with the shield or helm. While they may be displayed in conjunction with arms in a complete achievement, they are nevertheless independent devices, complete in themselves and capable of being used alone or with only a motto. They are sometimes found on a roundel of the livery colours, or on a standard, and occasionally they are placed decoratively on mantlings, but they may be displayed without any particular background of form and colour. They frequently appear on seals in association with shields of arms ; for example, a seal of one of the Berkeleys, 1430, has a mermaid on each side of the armorial shield.

Badges existed before armorial shields came into use, and were displayed on pennons and seals. In some cases these early badges developed into arms ; the seal of John Mundegumbri, c. 1175, contains a fleur-de-lis (not placed on a shield), and his descendants, the Montgomery Earls of Eglintoun, bore three fleurs-de-lis as arms. In other cases, such as the *Planta genista* adopted by Geoffrey of Anjou (207), these devices did not become arms, but continued as badges. At a later stage a device which had been used as a badge was sometimes placed on the helm and became a crest; or a crest device came to be used as a badge, the torse or crest-coronet being omitted.

Badges were sometimes adopted to commemorate a remarkable exploit, or to denote some feudal or family alliance, or to indicate some territorial right or pretension. Many were allusive to names. Some were taken from the charges in the bearer's arms, or had some reference thereto. Even where the motive for the selection of a certain device has not been discovered, it may be assumed that one existed. Traces of marshalling and feudal difference are found in badges. It was not uncommon for a man or family to use more than one badge, and sometimes two or more badges were combined to form a single device.

While arms and crests were personal to their bearers, and might be worn only by themselves and (with due difference) by members of their families, badges might be used in a variety of ways for which personal insignia were unsuitable, notably as marks or cognizances worn by retainers or adherents. In the 14th and 15th centuries badges were habitually used for the decoration of costume, military equipment, horse-trappings, household furniture and plate. They also appear on seals as accessories of shields of arms, and sometimes as diapers.

A distinction must be drawn between badges used (often in connection with livery colours) to distinguish followers and retainers—the "household badge" to which Shakespeare refers—and those which a nobleman might adopt and retain for his own private use. Badges of the former class were well-known, and were intended to proclaim to the world their wearer's allegiance; some, indeed, like Richard II's white hart (328), were so popular that they were hung outside taverns and are still in use as inn-signs. But a badge of a more personal character was restricted in use to its owner. It might be assumed with some subtle significance not to be blazed to the world; its purpose might be to disguise rather than declare identity—for example, at a joust, masque or pageant in which some great man might prefer to take part *incognito*.

The use of badges reached its height during the dynastic wars which took their names from rival badges—the Wars of the Roses. The rose first appears as a royal badge of Edward I, who bore it gold, while

328. White Hart Badge of
RICHARD II

329. Sunburst Badge of
RICHARD II

his brother, Edmund Crouchback, by way of difference bore it gules
and so transmitted it to his descendants, the House of Lancaster. The
white rose of York, perhaps derived from Mortimer, was opposed to
the rose of Lancaster in token of the Yorkist claim to the throne by
descent from Edward III in the senior line through Roger Mortimer,
Earl of March. Edward IV placed the white rose en soleil, i.e. on the
sun, which was another Yorkist badge, and it was the confusion
between this badge and the silver star of De Vere, Earl of Oxford,
that lost the Lancastrians the Battle of Barnet in 1471—an instance of
the importance of distinctive badges at that time. Henry VII united
the red and white roses in the Tudor rose when he married Elizabeth
of York.

The ostrich feather badge, perhaps introduced by Philippa, Queen of
Edward III,[1] was used by that King, and with various differences
by several of the Plantagenets. Edward, the Black Prince, bore
as his " shield for peace," *Sable, three ostrich feathers quilled argent and
passing through scrolls of the same bearing the words* ICH DIEN (196—his
" shield for war " bore the quartered arms of France and England
with a label). Here the feathers are displayed on a shield, but that
they were regarded as badges is shown by the Black Prince's will, where
they are referred to as " *nos bages des plumes d'ostruce.*" No doubt it
was the sable field of the shield and surcoat on which he displayed his
feathers that earned him his nickname. On two of his seals the Black

---

[1] There is no contemporary evidence to support the legend that the Black Prince
won the feathers from the blind King of Bohemia at Crécy.

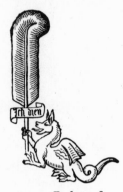

330. Badge of
HENRY OF BOLINGBROKE

331. Badge of
PRINCE EDWARD (after-
wards Edward V)

332. Badge of
PRINCE ARTHUR,
son of Henry VII

Prince placed his quartered arms between two feathers. He also mentions in his will, " swans, ladies' heads, and mermaids of the sea " as his badges.

Richard II made frequent use of the feathers, and granted them as marks of special favour to Thomas Mowbray, Duke of Norfolk. John of Gaunt bore the feathers sometimes argent and sometimes ermine, and again with chains lying along their quills. Henry of Bolingbroke entwined the feather with a garter bearing the word SOVEREYGNE (330), and as Henry IV he placed a shield charged with three feathers among the insignia on his Great Seal. Thomas, Duke of Gloucester, laid a garter along the quill of his feather (327), and the Beauforts made the quill compony argent and azure like the bordure to their arms. The feathers were otherwise differenced by other of the Plantagenets. They were borne by Lancastrians and Yorkists, without being particularly associated with any one member of the Royal House. However, in Tudor times they gradually assumed a distinctive character as the special badge of the heir to the throne. On the seal of Edward, Prince of Wales (afterwards Edward V), the feather is held by a lion (331). Prince Arthur, son of Henry VII, used a feather held by a dragon (332). The latter also placed a coronet above his feather, and Prince Edward, afterwards Edward VI (who was never Prince of Wales), appears to have been the first to place the group of three feathers within a coronet, the form in which they are used today. Ostrich feathers appear in the

2   1   3

5   4   6

7   8   9

10

PLATE XII

HERALDIC BADGES

Plate XII

HERALDIC BADGES

(See Chapter XIV)

ROYAL BADGES

1. For the United Kingdom of Great Britain and Northern Ireland. (*p.* 218)
2. For England. (*p.* 218)
3. For Scotland. (*p.* 218)
4. For Wales. (*p.* 218)
5 and 6. For Ireland. (*pp.* 85, 218)

OTHER BADGES

7. The Heir Apparent. (*p.* 219)
8. The portcullis of the Beauforts and Tudors, now the badge of Portcullis Pursuivant. (*pp.* 97, 212, 263)
9. The Stafford Knot. (*p.* 169)
10. The standard of Lord Marchwood. The family (Penny) arms are in the hoist and the badge, crest (shown twice) and motto in the fly.

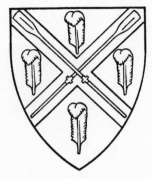

334. DE BOHUN Badge in
Westminster Abbey

333. BOROUGH OF BARNES

arms of the Borough of Barnes in reference to Edward, Prince of Wales
(subsequently Duke of Windsor), who was born there (333).

Reference is made to other Royal Badges in the chapter on Royal
Heraldry.

The swan badge of the De Bohuns (334) was derived, with the earldom of Essex, from the Mandevilles, who may have adopted it in token
of descent from Adam FitzSwanne. Through the marriage of the co-
heiresses of the last De Bohun Earl of Hereford and Essex with Henry IV
and Thomas of Woodstock, the swan passed as a badge on the one hand
to Henry V and on the other to the Stafford Dukes of Buckingham.
From the latter it has found its way into civic heraldry as a charge in
the arms of the Borough of Buckingham and Buckinghamshire County
Council. This is a good instance of heraldic continuity.

The famous badge of the Earls of Warwick, a bear chained to a
ragged staff, was produced by uniting devices which were originally
separate. They appear on the brass of Thomas, fourth Beauchamp
Earl of Warwick (15), the bear at his feet and the ragged staff on his
elbow-plates and scabbard; and they are united in the seal of the
fifth Earl of Warwick (335). Though said to have been of greater
antiquity, these badges are first recorded as having been borne by the
Earls of Warwick of the Beauchamp family. Shakespeare tripped when
he made Richard Neville, Earl of Warwick, (the King-maker) say:

" my father's badge, old Nevil's crest,
The rampant bear chain'd to the ragged staff,"
Henry VI, *pt.* **2**, *v*, 1.

335. Seal of RICHARD DE BEAUCHAMP,
fifth EARL OF WARWICK, d. 1439

336. Seal of WALTER,
LORD HUNGERFORD, 1432

for the King-maker derived this badge not from his father but, with
the earldom of Warwick, from his wife, the heiress of the last Beauchamp
Earl. The King-maker's father, Richard, Earl of Salisbury, bore as
his crest a demi-griffin inherited from the Montagues, and if he used a
badge it would appear to have been the Neville bull.

The bear and ragged staff was used in the 16th century by the Dudley
Earls of Warwick, and survives as a crest of the present Earl, and as a
charge in the arms of the Warwickshire County Council (187).

The following are examples of other badges [1]:

Arundel—an acorn; a swallow (*hirondelle*).

Askew—an ass's head.

Babyngton—a " man-tyger " (probably intended as a baboon in
allusion to the name).

Beaufort—a portcullis with the motto, *Altera Securitas*.

Clinton—a gold molet.

De La Warr—the crampet of a scabbard; commemorating a part in
the capture of the French King at Poitiers.

Douglas—a red heart (as in the arms).

Howard—a white lion.

[1] The list of badges given by Boutell is here supplemented by examples from
Fox-Davies's *Heraldic Badges*.

Plate XIII

MILITARY HERALDRY

(See Chapter XIV, p. 171)

1. Badge of Northern Command, U.K., 1939–45 : a shield sable with the cross of St. George charged with five lions of England ; based on the arms of the City of York.

2. Badge of G.H.Q., Home Forces, 1939–45 : a roundel per fess gules and azure charged with a gold winged lion passant within the Scottish tressure, also gold.

3. Badge of H.Q., 21st Army Group, 1943–45, then of the British Army of the Rhine : gules, a cross azure and over all two gold swords in saltire, points downward.

4. Royal Corps of Signals : the figure of Mercury.

5. No. 3 Company Colour, Welsh Guards : the Arms and Dragon of Wales in the form of an heraldic standard.

6. Badge of the King's Own Yorkshire Light Infantry : the Light Infantry bugle-horn with a white rose.

7. Sovereign's Colour of the 3rd Battalion Coldstream Guards. The pile wavy from the canton distinguishes the colour from that of the 2nd Battalion. In the 1st Battalion colour the canton of the Union is omitted.

1

2

3

4

5

6

7

Plate XIII

MILITARY HERALDRY

Hungerford—a sickle; Sir Walter de Hungerford, who bore this badge, married the coheiress of Thomas Peverel whose badge was a garb (perhaps originally an allusive pepper-sheaf), and united the two badges to form his crest: a garb between two sickles (336).

Mauleverer—a greyhound (*levrier*).

Mowbray—a mulberry tree.

Peché—a peach charged with the letter *e* (253).

Pelham—a buckle; from a coat of augmentation granted in connection with the capture of the French King at Poitiers (292).

Percy—a silver crescent; a double manacle.

Scrope—a Cornish chough.

Stourton—a drag or sledge; still borne by Baron Mowbray, Segrave and Stourton.

337. WHEATHAM-
STEDE

Talbot, Earl of Shrewsbury—a talbot.

Welles—a bucket with chains.

Wheathamstede, Abbot of St. Albans—three ears of wheat (337).

Intertwined cords, termed knots, constitute a small and distinct class of badges, often associated with other devices. The best known of these, here illustrated (338), are:

(*a*) The Stafford knot, borne as a badge by the Earls of Stafford and Dukes of Buckingham; now a charge in the arms of Staffordshire County Council, and of several towns in the county (see also Plate XII, 9).

(*b*) The Bourchier knot.

(*c*) The Heneage knot, borne with the motto, " Fast tho' untied."

(*d*) The Wake or Ormonde knot; on the assumption that the Wake family are descended from the famous Hereward, called " Wake," the Wake knot has been attributed to him, and commemorates him in the crest of the Isle of Ely County Council.

(*e*) The Lacy knot, allusive to the name; this appears on the counter-seal of Roger de Lasci, Constable of Chester, 1179–1211.

(*f*) The Bowen knot—four bows, allusive to the name.

(*g*) The Harrington knot or fret, derived from the arms, and perhaps intended to suggest a herring net.

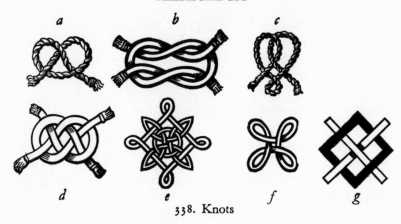

338. Knots

A badge of the Lords Dacre of Gilsland consisted of a knot gules linking a silver escallop (from the Dacre arms) with a ragged staff argent (339); the staff may allude to the barony of Greystock, united by marriage with that of Dacre.

In the badge of the Lords Hastings and Hungerford, a knot unites the Hungerford sickle with the garb of the Peverels (340).

Advocating a revival in the use of badges, Boutell said: " Unlike crests, which must necessarily be associated with helms, and the wearers of helms, and consequently have both a military and a medieval character, badges are equally appropriate for use by ladies, as well as by men of every profession, and they belong alike to every age and period." He also pointed out the unsuitability of using a crest, which should be borne on a helm, as a device on such things as livery buttons. Since he wrote, heraldic badges have again come into use.[1] An armigerous

339. Badge of
LORD DACRE OF GILSLAND

340. Badge of
LORD HASTINGS AND HUNGERFORD

[1] The practice of granting badges was instituted by an Earl Marshal's Warrant dated 18th June, 1906.

person may now obtain a grant of a badge or badges, which may be used alone or on a standard (see Flags, Chapter XXII). The assumption of an heraldic badge without authority is irregular.

A distinction must be drawn between personal badges forming part of true heraldic insignia, and impersonal devices such as are extensively used today by the Services of the Crown, sporting associations, schools, and societies of various kinds. These can be noticed only briefly.

Regimental badges, specimens of which are shown in Plate XIII, go back in some form to the beginnings of the standing Army, and may be regarded as successors to medieval badges in their military application. In the two great wars of the 20th century there has been an interesting revival of the use of insignia for military purposes. It became necessary to devise means of readily recognizing the personnel and transport of any unit or formation, while avoiding giving information to the enemy; and consequently, army, corps, divisional and unit " signs " were introduced in the 1914–18 war, and continued with increasing scope and application in the 1939–45 war. Many of these signs were heraldic in origin and character. Examples are given in Plate XIII. For further information the reader is referred to *Divisional and Other Signs*, by V. Wheeler-Holohan (published by Messrs. John Murray), dealing with the first World War; and to *Heraldry in War : Formation Badges, 1939–1945*, by Lt.-Col. H. N. Cole (Messrs. Gale & Polden).

In 1918, consequent on the unofficial adoption of badges by some ships of the Royal Navy, the Board of Admiralty appointed a commission to consider the matter and to assign approved badges to ships. Major Charles ffoulkes, F.S.A., Curator of the Imperial War Museum, prepared designs for nearly 300 of these badges, which he presented to the Admiralty. These generally referred to the ship's name, e.g. a hand grasping a sword for " Vindictive," a torch and laurel wreath for " Renown," an ancient lamp (symbol of truth) for " Verity," a human eye surrounded by rays for " Wakeful," an ark with a crown for " Ark Royal," and the letters E R with a crowned rose per pale gules and argent for " Queen Elizabeth." The panel containing the badge has a gold border moulded to represent a rope, and is ensigned with a gold naval crown, composed of the sails and sterns of ships. Up to August, 1942, the shape of the panel varied with classes of ships: circular panels for capital ships, pentagons for light cruisers, shields for destroyers, and lozenges for auxiliaries and small craft; but on that date a common shape and size was adopted irrespective of the class of ship. All ships' badges approved since August, 1942, are displayed on round panels, the lozenge being reserved for Shore Stations and the pentagon for Royal Fleet Auxiliaries. Examples are shown in Plate XIV.

Information about ships' badges, and photographic prints of them may be obtained from the Admiral Superintendent, H.M. Dockyard, Chatham, who is authorized to grant permission for their reproduction on behalf of the Controller of H.M. Stationery Office, in which the Crown copyright is vested. A royalty fee is charged in respect of each design reproduced, for the purpose of acknowledgment of Crown copyright. One of the Officers of Arms is a member of the Ships Badges Committee, and Adviser to the Navy Department on Heraldic Questions.

The use of badges by units of the Royal Air Force dates from shortly after its formation in the first World War. Arising from the desire for some emblem to express the identity and corporate spirit of units, these badges were at first adopted at will and used unofficially. In due course, as a result of officers writing to the Air Ministry to ask whether there was any objection to the practice, it was decided that badges of a suitable character should be recognized, and that their adoption and use should be subject to some control. On April 1st, 1936, an Inspector of Royal Air Force Badges was appointed, their connection with traditional heraldry being acknowledged by the selection of one of the Officers of Arms to fill the post. Since that date, any unit wishing to have a badge has arrived at its design in consultation with this Inspector. A painting of the badge suggested is submitted to Her Majesty, and if she approves of it she personally signs it, and the painting is then presented to the unit on parade. The badge is displayed on the aircraft, transport, and other Government property of the unit, and unofficially on notepaper, Christmas cards, etc.

The expansion of the Royal Air Force in the second World War resulted in a great increase in the number of these badges, which were sanctioned not only for squadrons, but also for commands, groups, stations, training schools, etc. Badges were also granted to units of the Canadian, South African, Australian, New Zealand, and Royal Indian Air Forces.

All badges consisted of a circular frame in which the title of the unit appeared, ensigned with the Royal Crown and having a motto on the

Plate XIV

NAVAL AND AIR FORCE HERALDRY

(See Chapter XIV, pp. 171–3 *and p.* 188*)*

NAVAL BADGES

1. Badge of H.M.S. "Laburnum." The laburnum tree is said to have been the *arc bois* from which bows were made.

2. Badge of H.M.S. "Vindictive." The hand and sword is taken from the badge of a former ship of the same name. The clouds commemorate the smoke screen through which the "Vindictive" steamed to lay alongside the Mole at Zeebrugge on St. George's Day, 1917.

3. Badge of H.M.S. "Argus." In Greek mythology, Argus, a son of Zeus, had a hundred eyes. On his death these were transferred to the tail of the peacock.

4. Badge of H.M.S. "Renown."

5. Badge of H.M.S. "Witch."

6. Badge of H.M.S. "Queen Elizabeth."

The variation in the shape of ships' badges to differentiate between the various classes of ship is no longer observed. All newly devised badges are round, the lozenge and pentagon being used for shore establishments.

AIR FORCE BADGES

7. Badge of No. 59 Squadron, Royal Air Force. This commemorates an incident in the first world war. An enemy limbered gun was being galloped away when its crew was attacked by machine-gun fire from an aircraft of No. 59 Squadron. The gun was abandoned on the road, where it was taken over by the advancing infantry. The gun was subsequently presented to the Royal Air Force as a trophy.

8. Badge of No. 6 Squadron, Royal Australian Air Force. The boomerang, with the motto *Nous Reviendrons,* has a double significance : it typifies a force which flies through the air, achieves its purpose, and returns ; it also expresses Australia's willingness, as shown in two world wars, to return to assist the Mother Country in her hour of peril.

1   2   3

4   5   6

7   8

Plate XIV

NAVAL AND AIR FORCE HERALDRY

scroll below it. The frame varied in design according to the Force —laurel for Great Britain, maple leaf for Canada, protea flower for South Africa, wattle for Australia, fern for New Zealand, and lotus for India. Within the round frame was placed the distinctive emblem of the unit. Some of these emblems referred to past achievements of the unit, others to operational functions or location, and many were symbolic of the qualities and aims of the Force (Plate XIV).

Since the practice of granting badges was revived in 1906, badges have been granted to corporations as well as individuals. For example, the British Transport Commission was granted three badges in 1956.

By a Royal Licence dated 1st January 1963 the arms and badges then granted were assigned to the British Railways Board, which was established by the Transport Act 1962 to provide railway services and such ancillary services as appear expedient. For a long time, the railways freely used one of the badges, namely: *Out of a coronet composed of two oak leaves as many roses barbed, seeded, stalked and leaved, as many thistles stalked and leaved and as many leeks set upon a rim or, a demi lion gules, holding between the paws a railway wheel argent.* Recently, however, British Railways Board has abandoned its many heraldic devices in favour of a curiously dull non-armorial symbol. The Society of Dyers and Colourists has a badge consisting of a Purple Iris Flower within a gold hexagon; Vickers Ltd. was granted *Out of an ancient crown or, two ostrich feathers forming the Roman letter V azure*; a cross formy charged with four ermine spots and interlaced with a Stafford knot is the badge of Wolverhampton Girls' High School and in 1962 Uganda was granted a badge consisting of an African elephant affronty holding erect in his trunk a thunderbolt.

The members of a corporation may be equated with the retainers of a feudal lord and should therefore use the badge rather than the arms. For centuries crests have been wrenched off helmets and used as badges, but now that badges are once more obtainable there is every reason why they should be used. A badge is particularly useful to municipal authorities, for these receive frequent requests from local organizations, such as bowling clubs, boy scouts, fire brigades and so forth, for permission to use the arms of the authority. Unfortunately, even if the local authority wished to help the applicant, it is not within its power to permit another body to use its arms. However, if it has a badge it may license its use. In this way heraldry is used correctly.

CHAPTER XV

MOTTOES

MOTTOES, or *mots*, seem originally to have been associated with badges. In a few cases they may have been derived from a war-cry, for example the royal *Dieu et mon Droit*, and the FitzGeralds' slogan, *Crom a boo*; but for the most part mottoes were brief phrases expressing some pious, loyal or moral sentiment, and often playing on the name of the bearer or alluding to the device they accompanied. In the 15th century they were sometimes associated with crests, e.g. Sir Simon de Felbrigge's *Sans muer*, borne with his ermine panache.

It was not uncommon for the sword-blade to bear some legend, e.g. that of the Earl of Shrewsbury: *Sum Talboti pro vincere inimicos meos*, "I am Talbot's, to conquer my enemies." De Setvans, whose arms were winnowing fans, alluded to them in the motto, *Sic dissipabo inimicos Regis mei*, "Thus [like chaff before the fan] will I scatter the enemies of my King."

Instances of mottoes playing on names include:

Ne vile velis, "Form no mean wish"—Neville.
Forte scutum salus ducum, "A strong shield is the leaders' safeguard"—Fortescue.
Templa quam dilecta, "How dear are the Temples"—Temple.
Cavendo tutus, "Safe through caution"—Cavendish.
Set on—Seton.
Reddite Deo, "Render unto God" [the things that are God's]—Redditch Urban District Council.
Adhuc hic hesterna, "The things of yesterday are still here"—Chichester Rural District Council.

Of many which refer to devices, the following examples are selected:

Cassis tutissima virtus, "Valour is the safest helm"—Cholmondeley; alluding to two helms in the arms.
Alte fert aquila, "The eagle soars aloft"—Lord Monteagle; two eagles are the supporters.

At spes infracta, "Yet Hope is unbroken"—Hope; the crest is a broken terrestrial globe with a rainbow above it.

Deus major columna, "God is the greater support"—Major-Henniker; three columns are borne in the arms.

Some mottoes allude to national or family history :

Caen, Cressy, Calais—Radclyffe.

Pro Magna Charta—Le Despencer.

Fuimus, "We have been"—Bruce, once Scotland's royal house.

Zealous—Hood; Captain Hood commanded the "Zealous" at the Battle of the Nile.

A motto may be in any language. In the past Latin has been chiefly favoured, but there is now a growing preference for English mottoes.

In England no authority is needed to use a motto, and it does not form part of a grant of armorial bearings.[1] Any suitable motto chosen by the grantee may be included in the painting of the arms in the margin of the patent, but not in the blazon; it is usually placed on a scroll below the shield, but a permissible variation is to place it above or behind the crest, which is appropriate where the motto alludes to the device forming the crest. Occasionally the motto encircles the shield, but where this is done the scroll should not be given the appearance of a garter or other form of insignia. A motto may be changed at will, but there is naturally a tendency to retain and transmit one which has become traditional in a family. More than one motto may be used.

In Scotland the motto forms a definite part of the armorial bearings. It can only be borne by authority, and changed by re-matriculating the arms ; and it must be placed in the position specified in the blazon, i.e. in the compartment below the shield, or above the crest.

The tinctures of the scroll and lettering are a matter of taste, and the scroll may be reversed of a different tincture from the front. The principal tinctures of the arms are often carried into the treatment of the scroll and lettering.

[1] Generally speaking this is true, but as the following illustrates, there can be exceptions. On 17th July 1615, a crest and motto were granted to Randolf Bull, chief horologer and a servant in ordinary to King James, in the following terms : " Forth of a Clowde a Sphere Gold with this Italian musicall Motto Sol : Re : Mi : fa ; alluding that as the Celestiall Sphere conteyneth in itselfe an Harmony supernaturall to be ascribed unto God only So this Artist imitating God in his worke by a Concordance artificiall acknowledgeth the kings Matis bounty to be the cause of his harmony and maketh him to sing Sol : re : mi : fa ; videlicet *Solus Rex me facit* being the Allegory of his song."

341. Arms of JASPER TUDOR from his Seal

CHAPTER XVI

SUPPORTERS

SUPPORTERS are figures which stand on either side of the shield, as if upholding and guarding it. They may be angelic or human beings, or any kind of living creature, natural or imaginary. They may be identical (Plate XXIV) or dissimilar, e.g. the lion and unicorn which flank the Royal Arms (Plate I). There are also occasional instances of a single supporter placed behind the shield. In French heraldry, the term *supports* applies to animals, human figures holding up a shield being termed *tenants*.

These honourable accessories of the heraldic shield are said to have been introduced in the reign of Edward III, but they cannot be traced with certainty before the reign of Henry VI. Their actual origin is conjectural, and must probably be assigned to a combination of several factors, including the desire to display personal badges in association with shields of arms ; the grouping together on a seal of a shield and an effigy ; and (perhaps most significant) the practice of seal designers

176

Plate XV

ARMS OF H.R.H. THE PRINCE OF WALES

ARMS OF H.R.H. THE PRINCE OF WALES

(See Chapter XIX, pp. 218–19)

This is the approved design of the arms of the heir-apparent for use by H.R.H. Charles Philip Arthur George, Prince of Wales, Duke of Cornwall and Rothesay, Earl of Chester and Carrick, Baron of Renfrew, Lord of the Isles and Great Steward of Scotland. Worked into the compartment are H.R.H.'s badge as heir-apparent (Plate XII, 7), the red dragon badge for Wales differenced by a label argent and the arms of the duchy of Cornwall.

(This illustration is from an original painting by Mr. Geoffrey Mussett.)

342. Seal of THOMAS HOLLAND,
EARL OF KENT, 1380

343. Seal of MARGARET BRUCE,
LADY DE ROS, 1280

in filling the space between the shield and the border with some animal
or lizard-like monster, " not, however," as Planché remarks, " without
some heraldic intention."

Animals and birds, either the same as those in the shields they accom-
pany, or derived from some allied coat of arms, together with personal
and family badges, are common on seals long before the regular appearance of true supporters. They are placed in various positions. An
early example is the imperial eagle, holding in his beak the guige and
forming a background to the shield, on the seal of Richard, Earl of
Cornwall, c. 1290 (195). On the seal of Humphrey de Bohun, 1322, the
guige of the shield passes over the back of a swan, which was the badge
of the Earls of Hereford. Thomas Holland, Earl of Kent, half-brother
to Richard II, has on his seal his shield with the guige buckled round
the neck of a white hind, clearly allied to the white hart which was
King Richard's favourite badge (342).

Human and angelic figures are also found. In the seal of Margaret
Bruce of Skelton, Lady de Ros, 1280, her effigy with outspread arms
supports escutcheons of the arms of De Ros and Bruce (343). On
Devorguilla Crawford's seal, c. 1290, a female figure holds a shield by
its guige. In some seals a shield of arms is flanked by two armorial
banners, and where these banners are supported by beasts we have the
immediate predecessors of supporters of the arms. Such examples,

344. Seal of EDMUND MORTIMER, EARL OF MARCH, 1400

345. Seal of WILLIAM DE WYNDESORE, 1381

together with the angels grouped round the shield of Richard II in Westminster Hall, and the creatures introduced into seals by early engravers, all take part in preparing the way for supporters.

The seal of Henry, first Duke of Lancaster, c. 1350, has the shield placed between two lions sejant with their backs to it. Two of the FitzAlan Earls of Arundel, 1375 and 1397, have on their seals the one two lions and the other two griffins, and these creatures actually uphold the crested helm above the shield (326). Similarly the lions on the seal of Edmund Mortimer, Earl of March, support the helm and are themselves supported by the shield (344). In the seal of William de Wyndesore birds, perched on the mantling, fill the space between the helm and the surrounding inscription (345).

And so a series of progressive examples might be carried on until it would merge into the systematic use of true supporters of the shield in the middle of the 15th century. A good example is provided by the seal of John, Earl of Arundel (346).

In Scottish heraldry, supporters, originally entitled bearers, appear at about the same period as in England, and were developed under much the same conditions, the marked distinction being a more frequent use of single supporters in the earliest examples. On several Scottish seals of the close of the 13th century the shield is displayed on the breast of an eagle, and many other varieties of single supporters are in use. Savage men frequently act as supporters of Scottish shields; also animals taken from the shields, and various human and allegorical

346*a*. Seal of JOHN, EARL OF ARUNDEL

figures. A few Scottish supporters are allusive, e.g. the conies of Cunningham, Earl of Glencairn, and Lord Oliphant's elephants. There are even examples of inanimate supporters, such as the two wheat-sheaves on a compartment of stubble proper, in the arms of the first and only Lord Boyd-Orr.

The right to bear supporters is now restricted to those to whom they have been granted, recorded or (in Scotland) matriculated, and this is normally confined to the following classes :

Peers of the Realm : the supporters to descend with the peerage ; life peers do not transmit supporters to their descendants (see page 297). Spiritual peers do not use supporters.

Knights of the Garter, the Thistle, and St. Patrick, and Knights Grand Cross or Knights Grand Commanders of other orders, and Bailiffs and Dames Grand Cross of the Most Venerable Order of the Hospital of St. John of Jerusalem : the grant is personal, and the supporters are not hereditary.

County, city, district and town councils, and certain corporations.

Some baronets have in the past been granted supporters.

Supporters, unless otherwise blazoned, are represented in an erect posture. Their function is to guard and uphold the shield and it is wrong materially to vary their attitude.

The supporters themselves must have some support. Having the task of holding up the shield, they must be given something to stand on. A piece of floral scroll-work (nicknamed " gas-bracket ") was at one time common, and pediments of an architectural character have been tried. The scroll which bears the motto is still often used, with an unfortunate appearance of instability. " An energetic lion, or a massive elephant, and, in a certain class of achievements of a comparatively recent date, a mounted trooper, or a stalwart man-of-war's man, probably with a 24-pounder at his feet, are made to stand on the edge of the ribbon that is inscribed with the motto . . . Let us produce something better than this support for our Supporters." [1]

The best solution of the problem, now usually employed, is to depict a mound on which the supporters can stand and rest the shield. This may be treated in some manner consistent with the supporters ; it is usually shown as a grassy knoll, but sometimes as a pebbly beach when the supporters are sailors or fishermen ; or as marshy ground when they are herons, and so on. An excellent example is shown in the achievement of Viscount St. Davids, whose supporting knights stand on the top of a battlemented wall. The blazon of the arms of Scotland specifies that the unicorns shall stand on a compartment (as the ground is termed) from which issue thistles. Recently the English Kings of Arms have taken against supporting supporters. Since about 1965, in Letters Patent where supporters are shown, they are depicted as if suspended in the air. If a compartment is included then it is blazoned. However, it seems doubtful whether a person entitled to supporters, even if they are shown sans compartment in the Patent granting them, would be wrong in placing them on a conventional grassy mount, " gas-bracket " or motto scroll if he so wished. On the other hand if a compartment formed part of the actual grant it would probably be incorrect to omit it when displaying the supporters.

In the Royal Arms the cojoined rose, thistle and shamrock are frequently shown in the compartment, and the proclamation of 1921 assigning arms to the Dominion of Canada lays down that under the shield there shall be a wreath of roses, thistles, shamrocks and lilies. As these examples show, the compartment may be used for the display of badges.

Many of the supporters in use at the present day are figures traditional

[1] *English Heraldry.*

Plate XVI

CROWNS AND CORONETS

Plate XVI

CROWNS AND CORONETS

(See Chapter XVII, pp. 183–9)

1. Baron.
2. Viscount.
3. Earl.
4. Marquess.
*5. Heir-Apparent to the throne.
6. Duke.
*7, 8, and 9. Conventional representations of the Royal Crown.
10. Sovereign's sons and daughters (except the Heir Apparent), and brothers and sisters.
11. Type of foreign crown.
12. Sovereign's grandchildren : issue of sons in the direct line.
13. Sovereign's grandchildren : issue of younger sons ; also sons of Sovereign's brothers.
14. King-of-Arms.
15. Sovereign's grandchildren : issue of the Sovereign's daughters having the style of Highness.

* In recent representations of these crowns, the jewels shown on the rim are usually a sapphire in the centre between two emeralds, and two rubies on the outside ; while the mound is shown as gold and not as green banded with gold.

in heraldry—wild men, knights in armour, beasts of all kinds, birds and monsters, variously charged for difference. A few of the less usual are here selected to show how supporters are drawn from many fields, lands, and periods of history, and so constitute an increasingly varied and interesting branch of armory. (The full blazons of peers' supporters will be found in *Burke's* or *Debrett's Peerage*.)

A Roman knight and a Moorish prince—Earl Annesley.

Two gladiators—Lord Rothermere.

Two Norsemen—Norman, Bart.

Two knights in English armour of the middle of the 14th century— Earl St. Aldwyn.

An armed knight with a lance, and a knight " in the disguise of a countryman " with a corn-fork—Cunyngham, Bart.

Two 14th-century mariners, one with an astrolabe and the other with a sounding-line—Horne, Bart., of Stramannan.

A scribe and a printer of the time of Caxton—Lord Iliffe.

A pirate with a cutlass and a fisherman holding a net—Corporation of Penzance.

Two Bengal Lancers—Lord Wigram.

Two Canadian War Indians—Earl Amherst.

A Tartar soldier and a Matabele Zulu—Lord Loch.

A diver and a Mexican peon—Viscount Cowdray.

Two electrical mechanics—Lord Ashfield.

A mason and a carpenter—Lord Ashcombe.

Two whifflers of the Corporation of Norwich—Lord Mancroft.

Thor and Vulcan—City of Sheffield.

Neptune and a sea-horse—Lord Hawke.

Two heraldic sea-bulls—Burney, Bart.

Two Centaurs—Lord St. Audries.

A Chinese dragon and a peacock—Hart, Bart.

A rhinoceros and Hercules—Viscount Colville.

A salmon and a seal—Lord Rowallan.

The supporters of Lord Brabazon of Tara, a pioneer of both motoring and aviation, deserve special mention because literally and metaphorically they carry armorial bearings into the field of the air. They consist of two flying seagulls holding the shield in their beaks and rising with it above water. The blazon is, *on either side, a Gull volant over water, supporting the shield with its beak, all proper*. An example of supporters accompanying the arms of a Peer will be found in Plate XXI.

Although supporters are usually granted only to those classes of people and corporations detailed on page 179 an exception was made in the case of Captain Mark Phillips, Princess Anne's husband. He was granted a winged lion and a winged horse each gorged with his wife's coronet. The supporters were to be borne by him and the heirs male of his body by Princess Anne (346*b*).

The arms of Heriot-Watt University (formerly College) in Scotland afford an example of a single supporter; the arms are shown supported by a steam engine.

346*b*. Arms of CAPT. MARK PHILLIPS

Supporters for Canadians

Since December 1971 it has been within the discretion of Garter King of Arms to grant supporters to such distinguished Canadians as the Governor General of Canada may recommend or to whom Garter may consider a grant of supporters to be fit and proper. There is also a list of specific categories of people to whom such grants can be made, viz : the Governor General of the Dominion and the Lieutenant Governors of the Provinces, those entitled to the prefix " Right Honourable," Commanders of the Order of Canada, Chief Justices and Justices of the Supreme Courts of the Dominion and of the Provinces, Privy Councillors, Senators, the Speakers of the Senate and House of Commons and Major-Generals and above in the Army and those holding equivalent ranks in the other armed forces.

347. Edward II's crown

348. Henry IV's crown

CHAPTER XVII

CROWNS AND CORONETS

THE Royal and Imperial Crowns of Great Britain have undergone many changes in their form and enrichment. From coins it appears that before the Norman Conquest crowns took various forms; the most usual seems to have been a simple circlet with four uprights (three shown in representations), each surmounted by a ball. The Saxon crown is so depicted when it occurs in modern heraldry. A coin of Canute shows a crown with three trefoils on the circlet, and some of the Confessor's coins exhibit an arched crown, which may also be intended by the ornamental cap represented on his Great Seal. The crowns of Harold and the first three Norman kings also appear to have had low arches connecting the middle point with the two outer ones. Stephen's crown had four fleur-de-lis heads (three visible), connected by ornamental and possibly jewelled arches, but after his reign the arches disappear until the time of Henry V.

The type of crown in Plantagenet and later times is shown by monumental effigies, as well as seals, coins and illuminations. The early Plantagenet crowns were richly-jewelled circlets heightened with ornaments resembling the heraldic strawberry-leaf. The crowns of Richard I and Berengaria have four large leaves only; those of Henry II and Eleanor of Aquitaine have smaller leaves alternating with the four large ones; those of John, Henry III and Edward I have eight trefoils alternately large and small, and the last two have slight points between

349. Henry VII's crown in
King's College Chapel, Cambridge

350. Crown from the monument of
Margaret, Countess of Richmond,
in Westminster Abbey

the trefoils. A further development is seen in the crown of Edward II on his effigy at Gloucester (347), with four large and four small strawberry-leaves and little trefoils between them. In small representations on coins, crowns of this period show three fleur-de-lis heads alternating with points or balls.

Froissart states that Henry IV, at his coronation, was crowned with St. Edward's crown, " which is close above " (other texts say " arched in a cross " or " arched in three "). This arched crown seems to have been used only for the coronation, for on his effigy at Canterbury Henry IV wears an open crown (348). Here the jewelled circlet is heightened by eight strawberry-leaves and eight fleurs-de-lis, the whole alternating with sixteen small groups of pearls, three pearls in each group.

The crown began to assume its present form in the reign of Henry V. Henry's crown consisted of a jewelled circlet heightened by four square-ended crosses alternating with eight fleurs-de-lis in pairs, and two arches springing from behind the crosses and supporting at the top a mound and cross. Henry VI placed alternate crosses paty and fleurs-de-lis on the rim, and this has continued as the characteristic of the Royal Crown. In some reigns additional arches were used, and the number of crosses paty and fleurs-de-lis was varied. The sculptured representation of Henry VII's crown in King's College Chapel, Cambridge, is a fine example of the period ; here the royal motto is charged on the circlet (349).

Charles I's crown had four crosses paty alternating with four fleurs-de-lis, and also four arches rising almost to a point, the arches being studded with pearls. Charles II reduced the arches to two, and depressed them at the point of intersection. This was the form taken by " St. Edward's Crown," made in his reign to replace the ancient coronation crown which had been destroyed during the Commonwealth, and intended to be as similar to it as possible. On this pattern the Royal Crown of heraldry was based until the reign of Victoria.

The State Crown made for Queen Victoria differed from its predecessors in enrichment rather than design ; the arches were fashioned like wreaths of roses, thistles and shamrock, and though flattened they were not actually depressed. About 1880, after Queen Victoria became Empress of India, it was felt that the heraldic crown should be given an imperial form, and this was effected by making the arches semi-circular. (Plate XVI, 8). This type

351. The present heraldic Crown

of crown continued to the end of King George VI's reign.

In the present reign there has been a return to the form of heraldic crown with arches depressed under the mound (Fig. 351). It consists of a circlet jewelled with rubies, emeralds and sapphires ; thereon four crosses paty (one and two halves being visible) and four fleur-de-lis heads (two visible) ; nine pearls on each half of the complete arch, and five pearls on the visible half of the other arch ; the mound gold ; and the cap of crimson (not purple, as in the case of the real State Crown), its ermine lining appearing below the rim.

ROYAL CORONETS (Plate XVI).

The coronet of the Heir Apparent differs from the Royal Crown in having only one arch.

The coronets of the sons and daughters (except the Heir Apparent), and brothers and sisters of the Sovereign, consist of a circlet heightened with crosses paty and fleurs-de-lis alternately, but with no arches. The circlet is chased as though jewelled, but not actually set with gems.

Grandchildren of the Sovereign who are issue of the Heir Apparent substitute strawberry-leaves for two of the crosses paty ; sons, not bearing the rank of Duke and daughters of the Sovereign's younger

352. Coronet of THOMAS FITZALAN, EARL OF ARUNDEL, 1445

353. Coronet of EARL AND COUNTESS OF ARUNDEL, 1487

sons, and sons of the Sovereign's brothers, have four crosses paty and four strawberry-leaves; and children of the Sovereign's daughters four fleurs-de-lis and four strawberry-leaves. In each case the cap (if worn) is crimson lined with ermine, and has a gold tassel.[1]

Peers' Coronets (Plate XVI)

Coronets as insignia of the higher nobility came into use in the 14th century, but were limited to dukes and marquesses until 1444, when they were granted to earls. At this period they do not appear to have had any distinctive pattern. The coronets of two Earls of Arundel, 1445 and 1487, are shown in nos. 352 and 353. Coronets were first granted to viscounts by James I, and to barons for the coronation of Charles II, 1661. The baron's coronet was then specified as to consist of a circle of gold with six pearls. The pattern of all coronets has now been laid down as follows:

Dukes: a silver-gilt circlet, chased as jewelled but not actually gemmed, heightened with eight gold stylized strawberry-leaves, of which five are seen in representations. (The coronet of a duke must not be confused with the so-called ducal coronet used as a charge and crest-coronet.)

Marquesses: a circlet as above, heightened with four gold strawberry-leaves alternating with four silver balls which are slightly raised on points above the rim; three leaves and two balls are shown in representations.

Earls: a circlet as above, with eight lofty rays (five visible) each topped with a silver ball, and between each pair of rays a gold strawberry-leaf.

[1] Royal Warrant, 19 November, 1917.

PLATE XVII

THE ORDER OF THE GARTER

Plate **XVII**

THE INSIGNIA OF THE MOST NOBLE ORDER
OF THE GARTER

(See Chapter XVIII, pp. 193–4*)*

The GARTER is of blue velvet, and is worn below the left knee, buckled and looped as here illustrated. Ladies of the Order wear it above the left elbow.

The COLLAR is of gold and enamel, and has the GEORGE pendent from it.

The STAR is of chipped silver, gold and enamel.

The LESSER GEORGE is of plain gold, and is worn from the ribband of Garter blue, four inches wide, which passes over the left shoulder, the gold badge resting on the right hip.

The Star and Lesser George are never worn with the Collar.

Viscounts : a circlet as above set with sixteen silver balls touching one another (nine being seen in representations).

Barons : a plain silver-gilt circlet set with six large silver balls, of which four are visible.

All these coronets are normally worn about a crimson cap with a gold tassel, which is guarded with ermine appearing below the rim of the coronet. The cap may be omitted in representations.

The silver balls on coronets are termed pearls, and in heraldry they are so represented, but the use of imitation pearls is banned, as also is the setting of any jewel or precious stone in a peer's coronet.

In an achievement of arms, a peer's coronet may be shown (with or without the cap) resting on the shield, with the helm and crest rising above it. It is often shown encircling the base of the helm, in disregard of their relative sizes. Ideally, the coronet should be of a size that would fit the head inside the helm.

Kings of Arms : the crown of a King of Arms is of silver-gilt and has sixteen leaves, which are generally held to be oak, but which many consider are more properly acanthus, alternating in height, set erect on a circlet which bears the legend, *Miserere mei Deus secundum magnam misericordiam tuam.* Nine leaves and the first three words are shown in representations (389–391). The crown may be shown either with or without a cap, which is the same as that of a peer.

CROWNS AND CORONETS IN ARMS AND CRESTS

In addition to the foregoing insignia of royalty and rank, there are crowns and coronets which are found as charges in arms or as part of crests. The crest-coronet of " ducal " type has already been dealt with (Chapter XIII). The special forms of coronet dealt with below may also be used as the basis for crests.

There are a few instances of the Royal Crown in arms and crests. That of Douglas is well known (Plate III, 3). In 1677, the Earl of Kintore was granted a Royal Crown in a coat of augmentation commemorating his preservation of the regalia of Scotland. Lane of Bently was granted the Crown as part of a crest acknowledging Jane Lane's assistance in Charles II's escape after Worcester. In the crest of the Borough of Eye (Suffolk), the Royal Crown is surmounted by an estoile charged with an eye.

354. Mural Crown　　　355. Astral Crown　　　356. Naval Crown

Where a crown is blazoned without any type being specified, an open crown in the form of a ducal or crest-coronet, or a crown of fleurs-de-lis may be drawn. The arms attributed to St. Edmund, King of the East Angles, are, *Azure, three crowns or* (360).

Of the special forms of crown or coronet, the MURAL CROWN is most frequently found, being widely used in civic heraldry and also in the arms of distinguished soldiers. The crest of augmentation of Byng, Earl of Stafford (Plate XXI) affords an example. Various forms of mural crown are used, but it is invariably embattled and masoned, sometimes of a different tincture from the crown itself (354). In 1914 the arms granted to the London County Council were ensigned by a mural crown in lieu of a crest. This created a precedent which has been followed in grants to other County Councils (see page 236). In Scotland burghs are not now granted crests, their arms being ensigned by mural crowns of various tinctures. A police burgh has a crown azure, masoned argent ; a burgh of barony has a crown gules, masoned argent and a royal burgh a crown of eight battlements proper (i.e. grey stone), masoned sable. The arms of Scottish County Councils are ensigned by a crown composed of eight points alternating with a like number of garbs set about a circlet (359 *a*).

The NAVAL CROWN is a circlet on which are mounted the sterns and sails of ships alternately (356). This has been granted as a crest-coronet or charge to distinguished sailors, including Lord Nelson, and figures in the insignia of some towns with naval associations, e.g. Chatham and Plymouth. It is used to ensign ships' badges of the Royal Navy (Plate XIV), and forms part of the badge of the Merchant Navy. This is curious in view of the fact that there is an old version of the naval crown, now called the Merchantile Crown, which has been used occasionally to signify a connection with the Merchant rather than the Royal Navy. It was used to gorge the supporters granted to John Tatem, 1st Lord Glanely, a considerable shipping magnate, in 1918. It is similar to the naval crown but consists solely of sails set about a rim.

The ASTRAL CROWN consists of a circlet on which are mounted four stars (three visible), each star being placed between a pair of elevated

357. Crown Vallary 358. Palisado Crown 359. Eastern Crown 359a. Scottish County Councils' Crown

wings (355). This crown is reserved for distinguished people and institutions connected with aviation.

The CROWN VALLARY and the PALISADO CROWN, both derived from defensive works, are very similar to one another and the terms are often used interchangeably (357 and 358).

The EASTERN CROWN has eight points, of which five are seen (359). It has been granted as a mark of distinguished service in the East, e.g. to Sir James Outram, Bart., "the Bayard of India." In Scottish heraldry, a precisely similar form is termed the ANTIQUE CROWN, found in the arms of Grant (Plate III, 8). This has no special significance.

The CELESTIAL CROWN is similar to the Eastern Crown but has a star at the point of every ray.

The ANCIENT CROWN is a coronet consisting of four fleurs-de-lis raised above a circlet, one and two halves being visible. This is a recent blazon, originally applied to an ancient diadem first granted to The Heraldry Society in 1956 (394).

In the years following World War II a crest-coronet consisting of a rim, on which various charges were set, became very fashionable, especially in civic heraldry. Some years ago the Kings of Arms discontinued the granting of such coronets as they considered that they were too facile a way of differencing similar crests.

360. Arms of ST. EDMUND, at St. Albans

361. HENRY BOURCHIER, EARL OF ESSEX, 1483,
with crested helm, Yorkist collar, and mantle of the Garter

CHAPTER XVIII

ORDERS OF KNIGHTHOOD AND INSIGNIA OF HONOUR

KNIGHTHOOD has been defined as " a distinction of rank amongst freemen, depending not upon birth or property, but simply upon the admission of the person so distinguished, by the girding of a sword or other similar solemnity, into an order of men having by law or usage certain social or political privileges," and also an appropriate title. Knighthood thus implies the possession of certain qualifications, and conferment by a personage endowed with competent power and authority.

In feudal times the qualifications for knighthood were distinguished military or other services rendered to the King and the realm, and also the holding of property in land of a certain value by the feudal tenure of personal military service. It has, however, been disputed whether there was any necessary connection between the degree of knighthood and the knight-service of feudal tenure. During the Norman period, knighthood was conferred not only by the King or his representative, but also by the great barons and prelates; but after the accession of

Henry III it appears to have become the general rule in England that no persons should be created knights except by the King or his personal representative.

Knightly rank carried with it not only dignity but duties. In particular, all knights were required to make suitable provision to render military service, and to take part in chivalrous exercises. Men who were qualified for knighthood by feudal tenure, but were unwilling to take up the dignity with its military obligations, were required to pay a fine as an alternative. This practice became common with the increase in the number of military tenants of small tenures, many of whom were unsuited to the degree of knighthood and had no inclination to the profession of arms.

Knights of the Middle Ages may be grouped in two classes. Firstly, there were persons who had been admitted to the general degree of knighthood; and secondly, there were those who, in addition to their knightly rank, were members of some particular fraternity, companionship or order of chivalry. The general body of knights had no special insignia; they were known only by their military accoutrements, though in due course gilded spurs came to be distinctive of knighthood. The knights of particular orders, however, wore the insignia of their order.

Two orders of priestly soldiers with distinctive insignia originated in the Crusades. These were the Knights of St. John of Jerusalem, or Hospitallers, and the Knights of the Temple, or Templars.

The Hospitallers, formed as an Order about 1092 and introduced into England a few years later, wore a black habit charged with a silver cross of eight points. They were not originally a military order, but first existed to assist pilgrims and to care for the sick. Later the Order was reconstructed on a military basis, and in the latter part of the 13th century, when engaged in military duties, the Hospitallers wore a red surcoat with a straight white cross. The knights acquired the Sovereignty of the Island of Malta in the 16th century but were dispossessed by Napoleon. However, they still exist, The Grand Majistry being in Rome. The order is strictly Roman Catholic and the Pope approves the election of the Grand Master. It is generally known today as "The Order of Malta".

The Templars, instituted in 1118, were introduced into England about 1140. Their habit was white with a red cross of eight points worn on the left shoulder. Their war-cry was *Beau Seant*, and this was also

the name of their banner, *Per fess sable and argent*. They displayed on
their lances a second banner of white charged with the cross of the
Order. As badges they bore the Agnus Dei, and a device consisting
of two knights riding on one horse in allusion to the original poverty
of the Order. (The latter has, by a curious corruption, become a
Pegasus in the arms of the legal fraternity of the Inner Temple in
London.) In 1312 the Order was abolished by Pope Clement V.

The Order of St. Anthony, established on the Continent and represented in England in the 14th century, had as its symbol the Tau Cross,
or Cross of St. Anthony (119). This is found worn as a knightly badge
on a few monumental effigies.

362. Collar of Esses

Collars composed of various heraldic devices
were in use late in the 14th and during the 15th
century. These were not insignia of any order,
but rather decorations of honour, usually denoting
political partizanship. The Lancastrian Collar
consisted of a row of SSS, the meaning of which
is uncertain, though it is clearly connected with
Henry IV's SS badge, and may have been adopted
as the initial of his personal motto, *Sovereygne* (362).
This collar sometimes had the swan of De Bohun
as a pendant. Henry VII modified the collar by
alternating the SS with portcullises, and added a Tudor rose or a
portcullis as a pendant. Henry VIII restricted the collar to knights.
It survives, with some modifications, as insignia of the Heralds, the
Lord Chief Justice, and the Lord Mayor of London.

The Yorkist Collar consisted of alternate suns and white roses, either
set on a ribbon or linked by a chain (361). The pendant was usually
the white lion badge. A variation has the roses en soleil and a white
boar as a pendant.

Private collars charged with the personal devices of their owners
were also worn ; Thomas, fourth Baron Berkeley, is shown on his brass
at Wootton-under-Edge wearing a collar of mermaids. This was a
Berkeley badge, perhaps indicating attachment to the Black Prince, who
included " mermaids of the sea " among his devices.

From these insignia showing adherence to a person or cause, we
pass to insignia denoting membership of the various orders of chivalry.
Such insignia have become elaborate in the course of time, e.g. the

premier Order, originally distinguished only by the Garter, now has its collar and " George," ribbon and " lesser George," star, habit, mantle and hat. Here we are concerned only with those parts of the insignia of the various orders which may be displayed in an achievement of arms. These are the Garter or (in the case of other orders) the circlet bearing the motto, the collar, the badge and the ribbon.

Early in the 15th century, and perhaps within a few years of the foundation of the Order of the Garter c. 1348, the knights of the Order sometimes encircled their shields with the Garter; but the practice did not become general until the reign of Henry VII. As other orders were formed, their members adopted the same practice with their insignia.

Knights of the Garter may now encircle their shields with the Garter, and (if they please) they may place outside the Garter the collar of the Order with its pendant " George."

Knights and Dames, and Companions or Commanders, of other orders may surround their shield (or lozenge) with the circlet (bearing the motto) of their order, and suspend below it the badge of the order by its appropriate ribbon. (In the case of Knights of the Military Division of the Bath, the circlet is enclosed by a laurel wreath.) Knights and Dames Grand Cross, and Knights Grand Commanders, of the various orders may also place outside the circlet the collar of the order with its pendant badge. Officers and Members of orders, below the rank of Companion or Commander, do not surround their shield with the circlet, but may suspend below it the badge of their grade by the appropriate ribbon.

THE MOST NOBLE ORDER OF THE GARTER

The premier Order of Chivalry was founded by Edward III in c. 1348. The stall-plates, or Garter-plates, of its members, emblazoned with their armorial bearings and affixed to their stalls in the Chapel of St. George at Windsor, go back to the early part of the 15th century, and form one of the most valuable and interesting of our national heraldic records. The insignia of the Order are shown in Plate XVII.

The Garter, formerly light blue but deep blue since the beginning of George I's reign, is edged, buckled and adorned with gold, and bears in letters of gold the motto : HONI SOIT QUI MAL Y PENSE.

The collar is gold, and consists of 26 Garters each encircling a red rose, enamelled in colour, alternating with interlaced knots. (Fewer pieces may be depicted in heraldic representation.)

The badge which hangs from the collar, known as the George, represents St. George on horseback slaying the dragon. This is also enamelled in colours.

The ribbon is the blue of the Garter.

THE MOST ANCIENT AND MOST NOBLE ORDER OF THE THISTLE

While greater antiquity is claimed for it, this Order in its present form was instituted by James II in 1687, lapsed in the following year, and was revived by Queen Anne in 1703. Its chapel (which is modern) is in St. Giles's Church, Edinburgh, and contains the heraldic stall-plates of the Knights. The chain, badge and jewel are shown in no. 363.

The circlet of the Order is green edged with gold, and bears in gold letters the motto : NEMO ME IMPUNE LACESSIT.

The collar is gold, and consists of 16 sprigs of thistle and rue (*Andrew*) alternating, all enamelled in proper colours.

The badge contains the figure of St. Andrew enamelled in colour, his gown green and surcoat purple, bearing before him his white saltire, the whole surrounded by gold rays forming eight points. The ribbon is green.

THE MOST ILLUSTRIOUS ORDER OF ST. PATRICK

This Order was instituted by George III in 1783. There are now no Knights of the Order but, as the Sovereign has not dissolved it, presumably it still exists. The chapel of the Order was in St. Patrick's Cathedral, Dublin, and the banners and stall-plates of the arms of the knights may still be seen there.

The circlet is sky-blue edged with gold, and bears in letters of gold the legend, QUIS SEPARABIT : MDCCLXXXIII.

The collar is gold, and consists of a crowned harp as the central piece (the crown enamelled in colours), and alternate harps and roses linked with one another and with the crown by four-fold tasselled knots. The roses are alternately of white petals within red and red petals within white (364).

The badge has on a white centre the red saltire of St. Patrick surmounted by a green shamrock-leaf charged with three gold crowns,

Plate XVIII

BADGES OF THE ORDERS OF CHIVALRY

(See Chapter XVIII)

1. THE MOST HONOURABLE ORDER OF THE BATH, Military Division. (*p.* 196)
2. THE MOST HONOURABLE ORDER OF THE BATH, Civil Division. (*p.* 196)
3. THE MOST EXALTED ORDER OF THE STAR OF INDIA. (*p.* 197)
4. THE MOST DISTINGUISHED ORDER OF ST. MICHAEL AND ST. GEORGE. (*p.* 197)
5. THE MOST EMINENT ORDER OF THE INDIAN EMPIRE. (*p.* 198)
6. THE ROYAL VICTORIAN ORDER. (*p.* 198)

PLATE XVIII

BADGES OF THE ORDER OF CHIVALRY

363. Insignia of
the Order of
the Thistle

364. Insignia of
the Order of
St. Patrick

the whole within the circlet and motto (as above), around which is a gold border studded with green shamrock leaves.

The ribbon is sky-blue.

THE MOST HONOURABLE ORDER OF THE BATH

Among the ceremonials attending the admission of aspirants to knighthood, one of the most important was the symbolic act of bathing. An order of knights characterized by this rite is said to have been founded by Henry IV at his coronation in 1399, and the present Order of the Bath, formed by George I in 1725, is supposed to have been a revival of the earlier institution ; but it is doubtful whether the " Knights of the Bath " of the 15th century constituted a definite order.

In the 18th century the Order consisted of Knights only, but in 1815 it was divided into Military and Civil Divisions, each having three classes —Knights Grand Cross, Knights Commanders, and Companions. King Henry VII's Chapel in Westminster Abbey has been the chapel of the Order since 1725 and here the Knights Grand Cross may erect banners and stall-plates of their arms.

The circlet is of red edged with gold, and bears in gold letters the motto, TRIA JUNCTA IN UNO. For the Military Division, the circlet is enclosed by two branches of laurel enamelled in colour, issuing from a blue scroll bearing the words ICH DIEN in gold letters.

The collar consists of nine gold Imperial Crowns, each with four arches, alternating with eight groups of the cojoined rose, thistle and shamrock enamelled in colours and issuing from a gold sceptre, this device being linked with the crowns by white knots.

The badge of the Military Division (Plate XVIII, 1) consists of a gold eight-pointed cross enamelled white, with small gold lions of England between the limbs, the centre being the laurel-wreath and circlet as above, enclosing the cojoined rose, thistle, shamrock and sceptre between three Imperial Crowns as in the collar.

The badge of the Civil Division (Plate XVIII, 2) is of plain gold, and consists of the circlet (without laurel-wreath) enclosing the same design.

The ribbon is crimson.

THE ORDER OF MERIT

This Order, founded in 1902 by Edward VII on the occasion of his coronation, is a special distinction for eminent men and women, without conferring a knighthood or any precedence. It has two divisions—Military and Civil—each with its distinctive badge.

The badge of the Civil Division is a cross paty with curved ends, forming part of a circle; the cross has a blue edge and red panels and a blue centre enclosed by a green laurel-wreath; the cross is ensigned with the Imperial Crown in colour. On the centre are the Sovereign's cypher in gold on one side, and the words For Merit in gold on the other side.

The badge of the Military Division is similar, with the addition of crossed swords, points upwards, appearing between the limbs of the cross; their blades silver and pommels and hilts gold (Plate XX, 1).

The ribbon is Garter-blue and crimson.

The Most Exalted Order of the Star of India

This Order was instituted by Queen Victoria in 1861. It has three classes—Knights Grand Commanders, Knights Commanders, and Companions. There have been no appointments since 1947.

The circlet is fashioned and enamelled in the form of a pale blue ribbon knotted at the bottom, and bearing in letters of diamond the motto, Heaven's Light our Guide.

The collar is composed of united red and white roses alternating with lotus-flowers, with palm branches crossed and tied between each rose and lotus, all enamelled in proper colours and connected by a double gold chain; in the centre is the Imperial Crown from which depends the badge.

The badge consists of a five-pointed star set with diamonds, and below it an oval medallion containing an onyx cameo profile bust of Queen Victoria, encircled by the motto in diamond letters on an enriched border of light blue enamel (Plate XVIII, 3). In the case of Knights Commanders and Companions the star in the badge is of chipped silver.

The ribbon is light blue edged with white.

The Most Distinguished Order of St. Michael and St. George

This Order was founded in 1818 to bestow honourable distinction on natives of Malta and the Ionian Islands. It has been reconstituted, and is now chiefly conferred on members of the Diplomatic and Colonial services, and latterly upon soldiers for services in connection with the foreign affairs of the Commonwealth. It has three classes—Knights

Grand Cross (banners of whose arms may be seen in the chapel of the Order in St. Paul's Cathedral, London), Knights Commanders, and Companions.

The circlet is blue edged with gold and bears the motto, AUSPICIUM MELIORIS ÆVI, in gold letters.

The collar consists of alternate crowned lions of England in gold and Maltese crosses enamelled white, linked by gold chains and the letters SM and SG alternately; the centre-piece is composed of the Crown over two winged lions counter-passant guardant, each with a nimbus about its head and holding a book and seven arrows.

The badge is a cross of 14 points of white enamel edged with gold, ensigned with the Imperial Crown, and has in the centre on each side the circlet and motto, and therein St. Michael trampling on Satan on one side, and St. George slaying the dragon on the other, both in coloured enamel (Plate XVIII, 4).

The ribbon is Saxon-blue and scarlet.

THE MOST EMINENT ORDER OF THE INDIAN EMPIRE

This Order, founded in 1877, has three classes—Knights Grand Commanders, Knights Commanders, and Companions. There have been no appointments since 1947.

The circlet is Imperial purple (or purple-blue) edged with gold, and bears in gold letters the motto, IMPERATRICIS AUSPICIIS.

The collar has a central Imperial Crown flanked by two elephants facing it, the rest being composed of Indian roses, peacocks, and lotuses alternately, linked by double chains. The collar is of plain gold and not enamelled.

The badge is an heraldic rose enamelled in scarlet petals and green sepals, and ensigned with the Imperial Crown in gold; in the centre is the circlet (as above) containing the head of Queen Victoria in gold (Plate XVIII, 5).

The ribbon is purple-blue.

THE ROYAL VICTORIAN ORDER

This Order, instituted by Queen Victoria in 1896, has five classes —Knights Grand Cross and Dames Grand Cross, Knights Commanders and Dames Commanders, Commanders, and Members of the Fourth and Fifth Classes. The chapel of the Savoy, London, is the chapel of the Order.

The circlet is blue, edged and bearing the word VICTORIA in gold.

The collar is of gold, composed of alternate octagonal and oblong pieces, the octagonal pieces being blue, each with a gold rose jewelled with a carbuncle, and the oblong pieces forming ornamental frames, each containing a portion of the inscription, VICTORIA—BRITT. REG. —DEF. FID.—IND. IMP. In the centre of the collar is an ornamental gold frame containing an octagonal piece enamelled blue, edged with red, and charged with a white saltire, and thereon a gold medallion of Queen Victoria.

The badge consists of a white enamelled cross of eight points, bearing in the centre the circlet (as above) ensigned with the Imperial Crown in colour, and within the circlet the cypher VRI in gold on crimson (Plate XVIII, 6).

In the case of the Fifth Class, the cross in the badge is frosted silver.

The ribbon is dark blue edged with three narrow stripes, red, white and red.

THE ROYAL VICTORIAN CHAIN was instituted by Edward VII in 1902. It is bestowed only on special occasions, and confers no precedence.

THE MOST EXCELLENT ORDER OF THE BRITISH EMPIRE

Founded in 1917 and divided into Military and Civil Divisions in the following year, this Order is open to men and women, and has five classes—Knights Grand Cross and Dames Grand Cross, Knights Commanders and Dames Commanders, Commanders, Officers and Members. The insignia are illustrated in Plate XIX.

The circlet is scarlet, edged and lettered in gold with the motto, FOR GOD AND THE EMPIRE.

The collar is of silver-gilt, and consists of alternate medallions of the Royal Arms and the cypher GRI connected by a design of interlacing knots passing through the Imperial Crown, which is placed between two heraldic sea-lions, counter-rampant reguardant, each grasping a trident.

The badge, which is silver-gilt, consists of a cross patonce of pearl grey enamel, ensigned with the Crown and charged with the circlet (as above) surrounding a medallion which now bears the crowned effigies of King George V and Queen Mary.

In the case of Officers, the badge is silver-gilt without any colouring in enamel. Members have silver badges.

The ribbon is rose pink edged with pearl grey, and in the case of

the Military Division it has a narrow vertical pearl grey stripe down
the centre. (The ribbon was originally purple, with a red stripe
for the Military Division.)

The Order of the Companions of Honour

This Order, instituted in 1917 at the same time as the Order of the
British Empire, is open to a limited number of men and women who
have performed conspicuous national service. It carries no title or
precedence.

The badge is oval, ensigned with the Imperial Crown enamelled in
colours; it has a blue circlet bearing in letters of gold the motto,
In Action Faithful and in Honour Clear. In the centre is a gold
oblong plaque bearing a representation of a knight on horseback and
an oak-tree from which hangs the Royal Shield. The ribbon is carmine
with gold edges (Plate XX, 2).

The Distinguished Service Order

This Order, dating from 1886, is bestowed on Commissioned Officers
in the Royal Navy, the Army, the Royal Marines or the Royal Air Force.

The badge consists of a gold cross formed of curves, of white enamel
with a gold edge; it bears on each side a green laurel wreath; this
encircles a gold Crown on a red centre on one side, and the Royal
Cypher on the other. The cross is suspended from a straight clasp
through which is passed the ribbon, which is red edged with blue.
Bars may be added to the ribbon as further awards. Any such bars
should be shown when the badge is suspended below the shield.

The Imperial Service Order

This was founded in 1902 and now consists of the Sovereign and
740 Companions of either sex. It is awarded to those who belong to
the Civil Service, Foreign Service and the Civil Services throughout
the Commonwealth. The badge for men consists of a gilt star of
seven rays, with a central medallion ensigned with the Imperial Crown
and bearing the Royal Cypher and the words, For Faithful Service,
in blue lettering. In the badge for women, a laurel wreath takes the
place of the star. The ribbon is crimson with a blue centre.

In addition to the insignia of Orders of Chivalry, there are other
badges of rank and office, and also decorations, which may properly be
displayed in an heraldic achievement.

Plate XIX

INSIGNIA OF THE MOST EXCELLENT ORDER OF THE BRITISH EMPIRE

(*See Chapter XVIII, pp.* 199–200)

Reading from the top downward.

1. Badge of Knights and Dames Grand Cross on riband of the Military Division. The riband for knights is four inches broad, that of dames two and a quarter.

   Star of Knights and Dames Grand Cross.

   Collar of Knights and Dames Grand Cross.

   Star of Knights and Dames Commander.

   Badge of Knights and Dames Commander and of Commanders, suspended from the riband of the Military Division as worn round the neck by men.

   (*Left*) Badge of Officers, and (*right*) Badge of Members, both on riband of the Military Division.

   British Empire Medal with Military riband.

2. Star of Knights and Dames Grand Cross.

   Collar of Knights and Dames Grand Cross with badge pendent.
   Badge of Knights and Dames Commander and of Commanders, suspended from the riband of the Civil Division as worn round the neck by men.

   (*Left*) Badge of Officers, and (*right*) Badge of Members, both on riband of the Civil Division and suspended from a bow as worn by women.

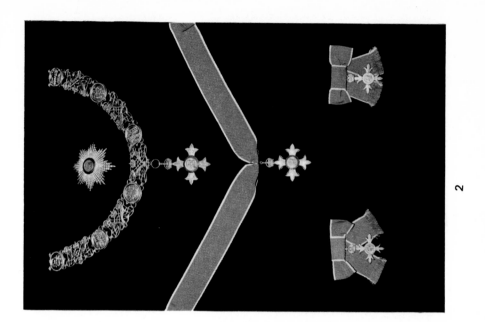

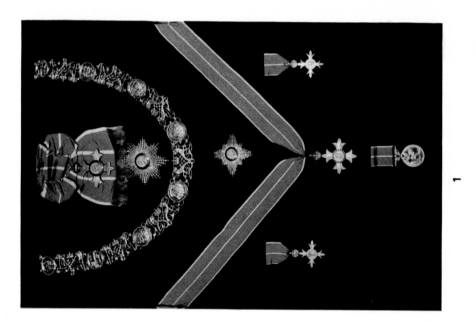

PLATE XIX

THE ORDER OF THE BRITISH EMPIRE

KNIGHTS BACHELOR

As their title implies, Knights Bachelor are not attached to any order, but represent the ancient knighthood which existed before particular orders came into being. Until 1926 they had no insignia, their achievements of arms being distinguished only by the affronté helm. In that year George V sanctioned a badge for Knights Bachelor, consisting of an oval medallion of vermilion enclosed by a scroll, and thereon a cross-hilted sword, belted and sheathed, pommel upwards, between two spurs, rowels upwards, the whole set about with the sword-belt, all gilt (Plate XX, 3). This is worn on the left breast without a ribbon. By a Royal Warrant dated 19th July 1973 Knights Bachelor were permitted to wear the badge approved by King George V round the neck suspended from a vermilion riband edged with gold, and to wear it in miniature. They were also permitted to suspend the badge beneath their arms. What they are not permitted to do is to wear badge both round the neck and also on the breast.

BARONETS

The order of Baronets is an hereditary rank or degree below the peerage. Baronets were first created in 1611 by James I in connection with the colonization of Ulster, and Baronets of England and Ireland (or " of Ulster ") consequently bear as an augmentation to their arms an escutcheon or canton *Argent, a sinister hand erect, coupled at the wrist and appaumé, gules* (Plate XXV).

The Baronets of Scotland were instituted in 1625 in connection with the colonization of Nova Scotia, and are sometimes referred to as Baronets of Nova Scotia. These were authorized to add to their arms, either on a canton or an inescutcheon, the arms of the Province of Nova Scotia, *Argent, on a saltire azure an escutcheon of the Royal Arms of Scotland*, together with crest, supporters and motto, which in practice were generally omitted. By a grant of Charles I, Baronets of Nova Scotia were entitled to wear, pendent from an orange-tawny ribbon, a badge bearing the arms of Nova Scotia as above ensigned by the Royal Crown, all within a blue circlet edged and lettered in gold, with the motto, FAX MENTIS HONESTÆ GLORIA. This badge (Plate XX, 5) is suspended below the holder's shield.

Since the union of England and Scotland in 1707, all new creations were designated Baronets of Great Britain then, after the union with Ireland in 1801, they were styled Baronets of the United Kingdom. Such Baronets all bear "the bloody hand" as an augmentation to their arms.

Until 1929, only Baronets of the Scottish creation possessed a badge which could be worn on the person. In that year George V granted to all Baronets, other than those of Nova Scotia, a badge containing a shield argent charged with the sinister hand gules as above blazoned, and ensigned with the Imperial Crown, all within a blue border variously decorated—with roses for Baronets of England; shamrock for Baronets of Ireland; roses and thistles for Baronets of Great Britain; and roses, thistles and shamrocks for Baronets of the United Kingdom. The badge is worn round the neck on an orange-tawny ribbon with a dark blue edge (Plate XX, 4), and may also be suspended beneath the arms.

INSIGNIA OF OFFICE

The relatively few cases of persons who hold offices to which official arms belong have been dealt with in the chapter on Marshalling. The following are instances of other insignia of office which may be included in an achievement :

> *The Earl Marshal and Hereditary Marshal of England* (the Duke of Norfolk) : two batons of gold tipped with black, placed in saltire behind the shield (422).
>
> *The Hereditary Lord High Steward of Ireland* (the Earl of Shrewsbury) : a white wand in pale behind the shield.
>
> *The Hereditary Keeper of Stirling Castle* (the Earl of Mar and Kellie) : a key and a baton in saltire behind the shield.
>
> *The Lord Chief Justice of England, and Sergeants at Arms :* a collar of SS encircling the shield.
>
> *The Kings of Arms* (in addition to their official arms and crowns): a silver-gilt collar of SS, showing a portcullis on each shoulder, round the shield.
>
> *The Heralds* have a silver collar of SS, which they may place around their arms. The *Heralds* and *Pursuivants* are entitled to wear an oval medallion suspended from a scarlet ribbon round their necks on occasions where decorations are normally worn. There is no ruling as to whether these may be suspended beneath their arms.

Decorations and Medals

The Victoria Cross, the George Cross, the Albert Medal, and other decorations and medals awarded by the Sovereign, suspended by their appropriate ribbons may be placed below the shield in their correct order of precedence, the senior being to the dexter. A person having the Sovereign's leave to wear in this country the insignia of any foreign order may, by courtesy, display such insignia in the appropriate manner in his heraldic achievement.

The Order of St. John of Jerusalem

Among insignia which may be displayed in association with arms are those of the Most Venerable Order of the Hospital of St. John of Jerusalem in the British Realm. This Order, a revival of the Grand Priory in England dissolved in 1559, has received a Royal Charter. The Order exists to promote ambulance, hospital and other charitable work. The grades are, Bailiffs and Dames Grand Cross, Knights and Dames (of Justice and Grace), Commanders and Officers of both sexes, and Serving Brothers and Sisters. Membership does not confer any rank, title or precedence. The insignia of the Order is worn in the customary manner on all suitable occasions. The badge of the Order is a white cross of eight points embellished in the four principal angles alternately with a lion passant guardant and a unicorn passant. This is suspended from a black ribbon, which is worn over the right shoulder by Bailiffs and Dames Grand Cross, round the neck by Knights, Dames and Commanders, and on the left breast by others. In an achievement of arms, Bailiffs, Knights, Dames and Chaplains may display their shields on the badge of the Order, while others may show the badge suspended below the shield by its appropriate ribbon. Bailiffs and Dames Grand Cross may bear as a chief of augmentation on their arms the arms of the Order, viz. *Gules, a cross argent, in the first quarter a representation of Her Majesty's crest.*

The Marshalling of Insignia

These insignia and decorations may be worn only by the men and women on whom they are conferred; consequently, in heraldic display they may be associated only with the arms of the recipient, and not with the arms of the recipient's spouse. Except where the order or office is hereditary (e.g. baronetcies) the insignia are not transmitted to descendants.

In the chapter on Marshalling, it has been shown that a married man holding an office to which arms appertain may impale these arms with his own paternal coat only ; he bears on a separate shield, to the sinister, his paternal arms marshalled with those of his wife. Similarly in the case of a married man who is entitled to place a collar or circlet round his shield : he must use only his paternal arms for this purpose, bearing his arms marshalled with those of his wife on a separate shield to the sinister. A wreath or garland of a purely conventional character may be placed round the second shield to balance the design. A Knight Grand Cross places his supporters so as to flank the pair of shields.

In the case of a married woman entitled to the collar or circlet of an order, as she cannot bear arms other than the married arms of her husband and herself (marshalled by impalement or inescutcheon), the insignia encircle the married escutcheon, and this is placed to the sinister of a separate shield bearing the husband's arms. This arrangement shows that the insignia belong to the wife and not to the husband.

With regard to badges and decorations which are suspended below the shield, where these represent distinctions restricted to men they may be placed below a shield on which the arms of husband and wife are marshalled, because there can be no doubt which partner they belong to. But in the case of badges of orders open to both men and women, two shields must be used, one bearing the husband's and the other the married arms, the husband's insignia being placed below the former, and the wife's (if any) below the latter.

It is permissible, though today unusual, to place round the shield, or suspend below it, the insignia of more than one order. Most people displaying insignia in this way are content to exhibit only those of the principal order to which they belong. However, if various insignia are to be included in an achievement, only one circlet—that of the senior order—should be used, and if there is more than one collar, that of the senior order should be next to the circlet, and that of the lesser order outside. Below the shield, the badge of the senior order should be centred, the other badges being ranged dexter and sinister according to seniority.

It should be noted that only decorations and not campaign medals may be shown in an achievement of arms.

365. Arms attributed to the Norman kings

CHAPTER XIX

THE ROYAL HERALDRY OF GREAT BRITAIN AND IRELAND

THE Royal Arms and Crest of England date from the reign of Richard I. Some of the earlier monarchs may have possessed personal marks or badges, but we have no certain evidence of the systematic use or hereditary transmission of such devices. Nevertheless the heralds in the 13th century assigned arms to English kings who lived before the days of heraldry. We cannot dismiss these attributed arms so summarily as those other heraldic anachronisms, the arms assigned to Biblical characters. Fictitious though they are, the arms credited to the pre-Conquest kings occasionally have a basis of fact in some tribal emblem. Furthermore, some of them have been actually used as commemorative arms in heraldic times, or have formed the basis of true armorial bearings. For example, the arms attributed to Edward the Confessor (1) were marshalled with the Royal Arms by Richard II; those assigned to the East Anglian kings (particularly St. Edmund) are the basis of the arms of Oxford University (217), the See of Ely, and Bury St. Edmunds; and the horse, regarded as the arms of the Kentish kings, is of frequent occurrence in the civic heraldry of Kent.

205

We have therefore to note these insignia attributed to English kings of the pre-heraldic period, remembering that they had no contemporary use as true armorial bearings, and have only acquired such a character through the use made of them in later times.

KINGDOMS OF THE HEPTARCHY

NORTHUMBRIA—
    BERNICIA : *Paly of eight or and gules.*
    DEIRA : *a lion rampant.*
    The combined kingdom : *a cross between four lions.*
MERCIA : *a saltire.*
EAST ANGLES : *Azure, three crowns or* (360).
MIDDLE and EAST SAXONS : *Gules, three seaxes barwise proper, pommels and hilts gold.*
KENT : *Gules, a horse salient argent.*
SOUTH SAXONS : *six swallows.*
WESSEX : *a dragon gold.*

SAXON AND DANISH KINGS OF THE ENGLISH

The kings of the English from Egbert, 802–39, to Edwy, 955–59, are credited with the arms, *Azure, a cross moline argent* (sometimes a cross flory).

The kings from Edgar, 959–75, to Ethelred, 978–1016, are said to have borne, *Azure, a cross flory between four doves or.*

The Anglo-Danish kings, 1017–42, are said to have borne *a raven.*

Edward the Confessor : *Azure, a cross flory between five doves or* (1).

This was apparently based on a coin bearing a cross between four birds, the fifth being added when the arms were devised, so as to fill the tapering shield then used.

Harold : *Gules crusily argent, two bars between six leopards' faces, 3, 2, 1, gold.*

NORMAN KINGS OF THE ENGLISH

We have no direct evidence as to the insignia of the Norman kings, but there are several indications that a lion was a royal badge long before the emergence of the three lions as the English Royal Arms.

As we have seen, Henry I gave his son-in-law, Geoffrey of Anjou, a shield bearing golden lions (2). The descendants of Henry's illegitimate sons, Robert, Earl of Gloucester, and Reginald, Earl of Cornwall, bore lions.

Of Henry II's sons, John bore on his seal two lions passant guardant in his father's lifetime; Richard I bore a lion and possibly two (as shown below); and William Longespée, an illegitimate son, bore six lions rampant (3). Henry, the eldest surviving son, is credited by Matthew Paris with, *Per pale gules and sable, three lions passant guardant or*.

It is conjectured that a lion was a badge of Henry I, and that Henry II may have borne two lions as arms. At a later date, *Gules, two lions passant guardant or* became established as the arms of the Duchy of Normandy, and these have been assigned as arms to William I, William II, Henry I and Henry II (365).

The third lion does not appear in the arms of the English kings until the end of Richard I's reign, and the theory that Henry II derived it from the arms of Aquitaine in right of his wife has nothing to support it.

On their seals, William II and Henry I have flowers, the former of five foils, and the latter of eight, and these have been cited as badges; but it is doubtful whether they were anything more than decorative additions to the seals.

Stephen appears to have used a Sagittary, or Centaur, as a badge, and he has been credited with arms, *Gules, three Sagittaries or*.

THE HOUSE OF PLANTAGENET

ROYAL ARMS (Plate V)

On the first Great Seal of Richard I, a lion rampant to the sinister is seen on the visible (dexter) half of the rounded shield. It has been conjectured that there was a corresponding lion rampant to the dexter on the hidden half of the shield, making his early arms *Gules, two lions combattant or*, but there is no actual evidence for this.

In 1198 (and perhaps rather earlier) his arms were *Gules, three lions passant guardant in pale or*. This coat is referred to briefly as *England* (366; Plate V). It was borne by all the later Plantagenet kings.

England was borne alone until 1340, when Edward III, adopting the new practice of quartering, took the arms of France, *Azure, semé-de-lis or*, termed *France Ancient*, and bore *Quarterly France Ancient and England* (367; Plate V). These arms expressed his claim to the French throne.

366. ENGLAND   367. The Royal Arms, 1340–c. 1400

These continued as the Royal Arms until about 1400. Then Henry IV,
following the example of the French King, reduced the number of
fleurs-de-lis to three, i.e. *France Modern*. The Royal Arms then became
Quarterly France Modern and England (370). They are occasionally
found in the form, *Quarterly England and France Modern*.

Richard II bore, *The Confessor* impaling *Quarterly France Ancient and*

368. Arms of HENRY BOLINGBROKE,
1399, and later (only with France
Modern) of JOHN, DUKE OF BEDFORD,
at King's Langley

369. Shield of HENRY, PRINCE OF
WALES, afterwards Henry V

370. The Royal Arms, c. 1400-1603   371. Arms of RICHARD II

England (371), and Edward IV sometimes quartered the coat attributed to the Confessor with his Royal Arms.

The Garter, charged with the motto of the Order, *Honi soit qui mal y pense*, has encircled the royal shield since the reign of Edward III, though the practice was not at first so general as it became later.

Henry VI first used *Dieu et mon Droit* consistently as a motto.

ROYAL CREST

A lion passant was painted on the plate on Richard I's helm (313). From the reign of Edward III to that of Henry VII the Royal Crest was, *on a chapeau gules turned up ermine, a lion statant guardant crowned or*. The crest on the Black Prince's helm at Canterbury shows the lion not guardant but looking straight ahead. It seems probable that this was the usual form of the crest in the days when it was actually used on a helm, the guardant position being adopted on seals and sculptures under the influence of the lions guardant in the shield, and becoming permanent as the crested helm ceased to be actually worn.

On the seals of Edward V, Richard III and Henry VII the chapeau is encircled by a coronet.

The mantling was gules and ermine.

Edward III bore an eagle as a second crest.

ROYAL BADGES

Henry II—*Planta genista*, or broom-plant (207); a genet between two sprigs of broom; an escarbuncle; a sword and an olive branch.

Richard I—*Planta genista*; a star above a crescent [1]; a mailed arm and hand grasping a broken lance, with the motto, *Christo Duce*; a sun over two anchors.

John and Henry III—*Planta genista*; a star above a crescent.[1]

Edward I—*Planta genista*; a golden rose with a green stalk.

Edward II—a castle (of Castile).

Edward III—a sunburst, or rays issuing from a cloud; the stock of a tree eradicated and couped (for Woodstock); a falcon; a griffin; an ostrich feather (see Chapter XIV); a fleur-de-lis; a sword; a sword erect on a chapeau, its blade enfiled with three crowns; a boar.

Richard II—a sunburst (329); a sun in splendour; an ostrich feather; a white hart lodged, ducally gorged and chained or (328— from his mother, Joan of Kent); the stock of a tree erased and couped or; a white falcon; a sprig of broom, the cods open and empty; the sun clouded.

Henry IV—the monogram SS; a crescent (so Hollingshed; but Fox-Davies suggests that it should be a cresset—cf. Henry V's fire-beacon); a fox's tail; the stock of a tree; an ermine, or gennet, between two sprigs of broom; a crowned eagle; an eagle displayed; a crowned panther; an ostrich feather encircled by a scroll bearing the word SOVEREYGNE (330); a columbine flower; the red rose of Lancaster; a sun in splendour; a rose en soleil (a combination of the last two badges); a white swan (from De Bohun, 334); a white antelope. Colours (of Lancaster), argent and azure.

Henry V—an ostrich feather argent; a chained antelope with the motto *Dieu et mon Droyt*; a chained swan; a fire-beacon; a stock of a tree eradicated; the red rose of Lancaster; a fox's tail. Colours (of Lancaster): argent and azure.

Henry VI—a chained antelope; a spotted panther; two ostrich feathers in saltire, one silver and the other gold.

Edward IV—a black bull (of Clarence); a black dragon (of Ulster); a white wolf and a white lion (of Mortimer); a white hart; a falcon and fetterlock (of York); the sun in splendour; a white rose, and the same en soleil; a red rose en soleil, and a red and white rose en soleil

---

[1] In describing this badge as a star and crescent, I follow Boutell, but for reasons which I have given in *The Romance of Heraldry*, we incline to the view that the emblems were intended for the sun and moon.—C. W. S.-G.; J. P. B.-L.

(referring to his marriage with Elizabeth Woodville, of the Lancastrian party).

Edward V—a white rose; a falcon within a fetterlock.

Richard III—a white rose; a sun in splendour; a white boar; a falcon with a virgin's face holding a white rose.

ROYAL SUPPORTERS

The definite use of supporters dates from the reign of Henry VI, but supporters have been attributed on doubtful authority to some of the earlier sovereigns. As will be seen, there was a close relationship between supporters and badges. In the following list, the dexter supporter is in each case the first mentioned.

Edward III (attributed)—a lion and a falcon.

Richard II (attributed)—two white harts.

Henry IV (attributed)—a lion and an antelope; an antelope and a swan.

Henry V (attributed)—a lion and an antelope.

Henry VI—two antelopes argent; sometimes dexter a lion, and sinister a panther, antelope, or heraldic tiger.

Edward IV—a lion or and a bull sable; a lion argent and a hart argent; two lions argent.

Edward V—a lion argent and a hart argent, gorged and chained or.

Richard III—a lion or and a boar argent; two boars argent.

THE HOUSE OF TUDOR

ROYAL ARMS

Quarterly France Modern and England; the shield being encircled with the Garter.

During Mary's reign, the arms were impaled to the sinister with those of Philip of Spain.

ROYAL CREST

Henry VII—*on a chapeau encircled by a coronet, a lion statant guardant crowned or.*

Henry VIII and the later Tudor Sovereigns removed the chapeau, and bore, *on the Royal Crown proper, a lion statant guardant or, also crowned proper.*

Mantling: gules and ermine until the reign of Elizabeth I, who adopted gold and ermine.

Royal Motto

All the Sovereigns used *Dieu et mon Droit.*
In addition, Mary I used as a personal motto *Veritas Temporis Filia*,
and Elizabeth I used *Semper Eadem.*

Royal Supporters

Henry VII—a dragon gules and a greyhound argent; two grey-
hounds argent; a lion or and a dragon gules.
Henry VIII—a lion or and a dragon gules; a dragon gules and a
bull sable, a greyhound argent, or a cock argent.
Edward VI—a lion or and a dragon gules.
Mary I—a lion or and a dragon gules; a lion or and a greyhound
argent. When the Royal Arms were impaled with those of Philip of
Spain, the supporters were an eagle and a lion.
Elizabeth I—a lion or and a dragon or; a lion or and a greyhound
argent.

Royal Badges

Henry VII—a gold portcullis (Plate XII, 8), also crowned and with
the motto, *Altera Securitas;* a white greyhound courant; a red dragon
(of Cadwallader); a dun cow (of Warwick); a crowned hawthorn
bush (alluding to his having been crowned after Bosworth with
Richard III's crown, which was found under a hawthorn) with the
cypher HR; a crowned Tudor rose; a crowned fleur-de-lis; flames of
fire; a sunburst; a falcon standing on a fetterlock. Some of these
badges were used in conjunction with the Tudor colours, argent and
vert.
Henry VIII—a portcullis; a fleur-de-lis; a Tudor rose; a white
cock; a white greyhound courant.
Edward VI—a Tudor rose; a sun in splendour.
Mary I—a pomegranate (from Catherine of Aragon); a pomegranate
and rose cojoined; the Tudor rose impaling a sheaf of arrows ensigned
with a crown and surrounded by rays.
Elizabeth I—a crowned falcon with a sceptre (from Anne Boleyn); a
crowned Tudor rose with the motto, *Rosa sine spina;* a sieve; a gold
crowned harp, stringed argent (for Ireland); a phœnix; a gold crowned
fleur-de-lis.

BADGES OF HONOUR AND OF RANK

Plate XX

BADGES OF HONOUR AND OF RANK

(*See Chapter XVIII*)

1. The Order of Merit, Military Division. (*p.* 197)
2. Companion of Honour. (*p.* 200)
3. Knight Bachelor. (*p.* 201)
4. Baronet of the United Kingdom. (*pp.* 201–2)
5. Baronet of Nova Scotia. (*p.* 201)

372. The Royal Arms,
1603–88

373. Arms of the
Commonwealth

374. The Royal Arms of
WILLIAM III and MARY II

THE HOUSE OF STUART

ROYAL ARMS

On the accession of James VI of Scotland to the English throne, the royal heraldry of Scotland was marshalled with that of England in the Sovereign's achievement, and at the same time the arms of Ireland were introduced.

The Royal Arms of Scotland are, *Or, a lion rampant within a double tressure flory counter-flory gules* (Plate VI). It is believed that the arms consisted originally of the lion only, the tressure being added by Alexander II.

The arms of Ireland are, *Azure, a harp or stringed argent* (235). These were adopted in the reign of James I and VI, and based on the badge used for Ireland in Tudor times.

The Royal Arms of the Stuart kings were: *Quarterly,* 1 *and* 4 *grand quarters, France Modern and England quarterly;* 2, *Scotland;* 3, *Ireland* (372); the shield encircled with the Garter.

In Scotland the Royal Arms were marshalled, *Quarterly,* 1 *and* 4, *Scotland;* 2 *grand quarter, France Modern and England quarterly;* 3, *Ireland;* the shield encircled with the collar of the Thistle and the badge of St. Andrew pendent below it. This practice of giving the Scottish quarter precedence in Scotland later lapsed for a time, but has now been resumed.

William III, as an elected king, placed upon the Royal Arms his paternal arms of Nassau, *Azure billety and a lion rampant or* (Plate V).

Mary II bore the arms of the Stuart Sovereigns undifferenced, and during their joint reign there are one or two examples showing the arms of William and Mary impaled (374), but on the Great Seal, the coinage and elsewhere the arms of the joint sovereigns are simply the Royal Arms with Nassau in pretence.

Anne bore the Stuart Royal Arms until 1707, when in consequence of the Union with Scotland the arms were re-marshalled as follows: *Quarterly, 1 and 4 grand quarters, England impaling Scotland; 2, France Modern; 3, Ireland* (375). The shield on the Great Seal adopted on the occasion of the Union bore only *England impaling Scotland.* (The dexter side of the Scottish tressure was cut off by the impalement.)

ROYAL CREST

In England—*on the Royal Crown proper, a lion statant guardant or, regally crowned proper.*

In Scotland—*on the Royal Crown proper, a lion sejant affronté gules, regally crowned or, holding erect in the dexter paw a naked sword proper and in the sinister a sceptre or.* (From about 1385 to 1550, the Royal Crest of Scotland was *a lion statant guardant gules.*)

Mantling: gold and ermine.

ROYAL MOTTOES

In England—*Dieu et mon Droit,* though Queen Anne used *Semper Eadem.*

In Scotland—above the crest, *In defens*; below the shield, *Nemo me impune lacessit.*

ROYAL SUPPORTERS

In England—dexter, a lion rampant guardant or, regally crowned proper (for England); sinister, a unicorn argent, armed, unguled and crined or, gorged with a coronet composed of crosses paty and fleurs-de-lis gold, a chain affixed thereto of the last passing between the forelegs and reflexed over the back (for Scotland.) The original Royal Supporters of Scotland were two lions guardant.

In Scotland the supporters were transposed so as to place the unicorn on the dexter side; the unicorn was regally crowned (as well as gorged), and supported between the forelegs a banner of St. Andrew; while the lion, on the sinister side, supported a banner of St. George.

Royal Badges

James I—the Tudor rose ; the thistle (for Scotland ; first used by James III of Scotland) ; the conjoined red and white rose dimidiated with a thistle and ensigned with the Royal Crown, with the motto, *Beati Pacifici* ; a harp ; a fleur-de-lis.

Charles I, Charles II and James II—the same as James I without his motto.

Anne—a rose branch and thistle growing from one stalk and crowned.

THE COMMONWEALTH

During the Commonwealth, the Royal Arms were superseded by a shield bearing, *Quarterly,* 1 *and* 4, *Argent, the cross of St. George gules* (for England) ; 2, *Azure, the saltire of St. Andrew argent* (for Scotland) ; 3, *Azure, a harp or stringed argent* (for Ireland) ; *and on an inescutcheon, Sable, a lion rampant argent* (Oliver Cromwell's personal coat) (373). On the Great Seal, 1655, this appeared with the Royal Helm and Crest ; the motto, *Pax quaeritur bello* ; and as supporters, dexter, a crowned lion, and sinister, a dragon.

THE HOUSE OF GUELPH OR HANOVER

Royal Arms

The succession of the House of Hanover (a branch of the line of Guelph) led to a place being assigned in the royal shield to the arms of Hanover. These are : *Tierced in pairle reversed :* 1, *Gules, two lions passant guardant in pale or* (for Brunswick) ; 2, *Or, semé of hearts gules, a lion rampant azure* (for Luneburg) ; 3, *Gules, a horse courant argent* (for Westphalia) ; *and over all an inescutcheon gules charged with the golden crown of Charlemagne* (the augmentation or badge of the Arch Treasurer of the Holy Roman Empire).

George I, George II and George III until 1801 bore, *Quarterly,* 1, *England impaling Scotland ;* 2, *France ;* 3, *Ireland ;* 4, *Hanover* (Plate V) ; the shield encircled by the Garter ; crest, supporters, mantling and motto as the Stuart kings.

In 1801, following the Union with Ireland, the Royal Arms were re-marshalled, the occasion being taken to remove the arms of France. George III after 1801, George IV and William IV bore, *Quarterly,* 1 *and* 4, *England ;* 2, *Scotland ;* 3, *Ireland ; and over all an escutcheon of*

375. The Royal Arms, 1707–14

376. The Royal Arms, 1801–16

377. The Royal Arms, 1816–37

Hanover ; the Hanover escutcheon being ensigned with an Electoral Bonnet from 1801 to 1816, and with a Royal Crown from 1816 to 1837, consequent on Hanover becoming a kingdom (376 and 377).

Owing to the operation of the Salic Law, Queen Victoria did not succeed to the Kingdom of Hanover, and consequently at her accession the arms of Hanover were removed from the royal shield, and the Royal Arms became, *Quarterly,* 1 *and* 4, *England ;* 2, *Scotland ;* 3, *Ireland* (378). The crest, supporters and accessories remained unchanged.

The Prince Consort, Albert of Saxe-Coburg and Gotha, was empowered to quarter the Royal Arms, differenced with a label, with his own coat of Saxony, and bore : *Quarterly,* 1 *and* 4, *the Royal Arms of Queen Victoria with a label of three points argent charged on the middle point with a cross gules ;* 2 *and* 3, *Saxony (Barry of ten or and sable, a crown of rue in bend vert ;* the rue-crown is sometimes blazoned as a crancelin, or as *a bend enarched treflé*—443).

The children of Queen Victoria and the Prince Consort bore the Royal Arms with their distinctive labels, and with an inescutcheon of the arms of Saxony. All the labels were argent, that of the Prince of Wales being plain (Plate V), and the others charged with various devices.

Although the Sovereigns of the House of Windsor (this dynastic name was adopted by Royal Proclamation on 17th June 1917) have used various old royal badges only one or two new badges have been adopted, that for Wales (Plate XII) and the following badge for the House of

Plate XXI

(*See pp.* 82, 127, 154, 182, 188)

THE ARMS OF A PEER OF THE REALM

showing supporters, viscount's coronet, peer's helm, and crest of augmentation.

The achievement is that of the late Viscount Byng of Vimy. The crescents on the shield and sinister crest are marks of cadency, and the roses on the supporters are differencing marks, distinguishing the bearings from those of Byng, Earl of Strafford.

The colours of the 31st Regiment of Foot in the arms, and the crest of augmentation (on the dexter side), were granted to Field Marshal Sir John Byng, first Earl of Strafford, for the "signal intrepidity and heroic valour displayed by him in the action at Mouguerre, near Bayonne, 18 Dec. 1813", when he personally planted these colours on the enemy's lines.

PLATE XXI

THE ARMS OF A PEER OF THE REALM

378. The Royal Arms since 1837

Windsor, which was approved by King George VI on 28th July 1938 : *On a Mount Vert the Round Tower of Windsor Castle argent, masoned sable, flying thereon the Royal Standard, the whole within two branches of oak fructed or, and ensigned with the Imperial Crown.*

THE HOUSE OF SAXE-COBURG

The royal achievement of Edward VII was the same as that of Queen Victoria.

THE HOUSE OF WINDSOR

(See Plates I, V, VI and XII.)

The Royal Arms have remained unchanged since the accession of Queen Victoria and are now :

ARMS : *Quarterly, 1 and 4, England ; 2, Scotland ; 3, Ireland ;* the shield encircled with the Garter.

CREST : *upon the Royal Helm, the Crown proper, thereon a lion statant guardant or, crowned proper.*

MANTLING : *gold lined with ermine.*

SUPPORTERS : dexter, *a lion guardant or, crowned proper;* sinister, *a unicorn argent, armed, crined and unguled or, and gorged with a coronet composed of crosses paty and fleurs-de-lis, a chain affixed thereto passing between the forelegs and reflexed over the back, gold.*

MOTTO : *Dieu et mon Droit.*

BADGES : England—*the red and white rose united, slipped and leaved proper;* Scotland—*a thistle, slipped and leaved proper;* Ireland—1, *a shamrock leaf slipped vert;* 2, *a harp or, stringed argent;* the United Kingdom—1, *the rose, thistle and shamrock engrafted on the same stem, proper;* 2, *an escutcheon charged as the Union Flag.* All these badges are ensigned with the Royal Crown. Wales—*within a circular riband argent fimbriated gold, bearing the motto* Y DDRAIG GOCH DDYRY CYCHWYN (" The red dragon gives the lead ") *in letters vert, and ensigned with the Crown proper, an escutcheon per fess argent and vert and thereon a red dragon passant.* (This represents an honourable augmentation, in 1953, of the former badge of Wales, consisting of the red dragon alone.)

CREST OF SCOTLAND : *on the Crown proper, a lion sejant affronté gules crowned or, holding in the dexter paw a sword, and in the sinister a sceptre erect, also proper.*

CREST OF IRELAND : *on a wreath or and azure, a tower triple-towered of the first, from the portal a hart springing argent, attired and hoofed gold.*

ARMS OF THE THREE ROYAL DYNASTIES OF WALES : North Wales— *Quarterly or and gules, four lions passant guardant counterchanged;* South Wales—*Gules, a lion rampant within a bordure indented or;* Powys— *Argent, a lion rampant sable.*

ROYAL ARMS FOR USE ON THE GREAT SEAL FOR SCOTLAND : *Quarterly,* 1 *and* 4, *Scotland;* 2, *England;* 3, *Ireland;* the shield encircled by the Collar of the Thistle, with the badge of St. Andrew pendent therefrom. Upon the Royal Helm is the Crest of Scotland ; mantling, gold and ermine. Supporters, dexter, the unicorn as above, but regally crowned, and maintaining a banner of St. Andrew ; sinister, the lion as above, maintaining a banner of St. George. Mottoes : above the crest, *In defens*; below the shield, *Nemo me impune lacessit.* (The latter is sometimes omitted.) This design was approved in 1903.

H.R.H. THE PRINCE OF WALES bears the Royal Arms differenced by a label of three points argent and with an escutcheon of the arms of the Principality of Wales ensigned by the Heir Apparent's coronet (see page 185 and Plates V and XV). His shield is encircled with the

Garter. He also bears the Royal Crest and Supporters, all differenced by a label as in the arms and also by the substitution of his coronet for the crowns in the crest and the supporting lion. His motto is ICH DIEN. His badge as Heir Apparent is, *a plume of three ostrich feathers argent enfiling a coronet of crosses paty and fleurs-de-lis or, with the motto,* ICH DIEN (Plate XII, 7). In his full achievement this badge is placed below the shield together with the red dragon of Wales, differenced by a label as in the arms, and the arms of the Duchy of Cornwall : *Sable fifteen bezants,* the shield ensigned with the Heir Apparent's coronet.

Supporters were assigned to the arms of the Duchy by a Royal

378 *a.* Arms of the DUCHY OF CORNWALL

Warrant dated 21st June 1968. They are : on either side, *a Cornish Chough (proper) supporting an ostrich feather argent, penned or.* Beneath the shield is the motto HOUMOUT. (378 *a*). This motto was one used by the Black Prince and means " high minded," or " high spirited."

H.R.H. THE DUKE OF EDINBURGH has since 1949 borne, *Quarterly,* 1, *Or semé of hearts gules, three lions passant in pale azure crowned gold* (for Denmark) ; 2, *Azure, a cross argent* (for Greece) ; 3, *Argent, two pallets sable* (for Mountbatten) ; 4, *Argent, on a rock in base proper a castle triple-towered sable masoned silver, each tower topped by a vane gules* (for Edinburgh). (This replaced the arms which he bore from 1947 to 1949, viz. *Greece surmounted by an inescutcheon of the arms of Denmark* (see Chapter XXI) ; *and over all in the first quarter the arms of Princess Alice, daughter of Queen Victoria, viz. the Royal Arms differenced with a label of three points argent, the middle point charged with a rose gules and each of the others with an ermine spot.*) The shield is encircled by the Garter and ensigned with a princely coronet of crosses paty and fleurs-de-lis, above which is placed a barred helm affronté, and thereon the crest: *out of a ducal coronet or, a plume of five ostrich feathers alternately sable and argent.* The supporters are, dexter, *the figure of Hercules proper*, and sinister, *a lion queue fourché ducally crowned or, gorged with a naval coronet azure.* Motto: God is my help.

H.M. QUEEN ELIZABETH THE QUEEN MOTHER bears: *The Royal Arms*, impaling, *Quarterly*, 1 and 4, *Argent, a lion rampant azure, armed and langued gules, within a double tressure flory counter-flory of the second* (for Lyon); 2 *and* 3, *Ermine, three bows stringed palewise in fess proper* (for Bowes). The shield is encircled by the Garter and ensigned with the Royal Crown. Supporters, *a lion guardant or imperially crowned proper ;* sinister, *a lion per fess or and gules.* No crest or motto is used.

H.R.H. THE PRINCESS MARGARET, COUNTESS OF SNOWDON, bears on a lozenge *the Royal Arms with a label of three points argent charged on the middle point with a thistle proper and on each of the others with a rose gules surmounted of another argent* (379). The lozenge is ensigned with the coronet of her rank, encircled by the motto of the Royal Victorian Order, and flanked by the Royal Supporters differenced by labels as in the arms, the lion having a princely coronet instead of the Royal Crown. When married to the Earl of Snowdon their two achievements were shown side by side, that of Princess Margaret to the sinister.

H.R.H. THE LATE DUKE OF GLOUCESTER bore the Royal Arms with a label of three points argent, the centre point being charged with a lion of England gules, and each of the others with a cross of St. George (380). He bore the same label on crest and supporters, which are those

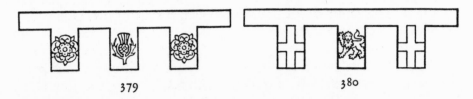

379   380

of the royal achievement except that a coronet of crosses paty and fleurs-de-lis replaced the Royal Crown in the crest, and the lion in the crest and the supporting lion wore similar coronets. His shield was encircled by the Garter. The mantling was gold lined with silver. He used no motto.

PLATE XXII

ECCLESIASTICAL HERALDRY

Plate XXII

ECCLESIASTICAL HERALDRY

(See Chapter XX, pp. 223–9; see also p. 139)

1. ARMS OF THE SEE OF DURHAM.
   The mitre of the Bishop of Durham is placed within a ducal crest-coronet, signifying that temporal or palatinate jurisdiction once rested in the bishops of this See. A sword and crozier may be placed in saltire behind the shield.

2. ARMS OF ARCHBISHOP LORD FISHER OF LAMBETH AS ARCHBISHOP OF CANTERBURY.
   The personal arms of Archbishop Fisher (*Argent a fesse wavy between three fleurs de lis sable*) are impaled by the arms of the See of Canterbury. Two croziers may be placed in saltire behind the shield.

3. ARMS OF CARDINAL WILLIAM GODFREY 7th ROMAN CATHOLIC ARCHBISHOP OF WESTMINSTER.
   The personal arms of the late Cardinal Godfrey (*Per fesse or and argent, two crosses formy in fesse gules, between in chief a rose of the last barbed and seeded proper, and in base a branch of olive vert*) are impaled by those of the See of Westminster. The double traversed cross symbolic of Archiepiscopal rank is placed in pale behind the shield, which is ensigned by a cardinal's hat. The motto beneath the shield is the Cardinal's personal motto. It should be noted that the arms of the Archdiocese are illegal, having been granted by Pope Leo XIII, who had no temporal authority in Great Britain (page 229).

4. ARMS OF THE SEE OF WORCESTER.
   Two croziers may be placed in saltire behind the shield.

H.R.H. The Late Duke of Windsor, formerly H.M. King Edward VIII, bore the royal achievement (without the motto), differenced with regard to the crowns as the Duke of Gloucester; and with a label argent charged on the middle point with an Imperial Crown proper (381) on shield, crest and supporters. The mantling is gold lined with ermine.

When he was Prince of Wales, he bore the Royal Arms with a label of three points argent, and in the centre of the shield an inescutcheon of the arms of the Principality of Wales, *Quarterly or and gules, four lions passant guardant counterchanged*, ensigned with the coronet of the Prince of Wales. Similar coronets were substituted for the crowns in the crest and on the dexter supporter, and crest and supporters were also differenced with the label argent. Below the shield was the motto, *Ich dien*.

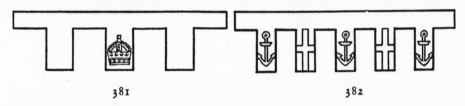

381   382

H.R.H. The Duke of Kent bears the Royal Arms, Crest and Supporters differenced with a label of five points argent, the first, third and fifth points each charged with an anchor azure, and the second and fourth with the cross of St. George (382). The shield is ensigned with a coronet of crosses paty and strawberry-leaves, and similar coronets replace the Royal Crown in the crest and supporters. The late Duke of Kent differenced the Royal Arms with a label of three points argent, each point charged with an anchor azure.

By a Royal Warrant dated 7th July, 1962, the following labels were assigned to other members of the Royal Family:

H.R.H. Prince Andrew. A label of three points argent, the centre point charged with an anchor azure.

H.R.H. Princess Anne. A label of three points argent the centre point charged with a heart and the other points with a St. George's cross gules.

H.R.H. The Late Prince William of Gloucester. A label of five points argent charged with three lions of England and two St. George's crosses gules alternately.

H.R.H. Prince Richard, Duke of Gloucester. A label of five

points argent charged with three St. George's crosses and two lions of England gules alternately.

In 1972, the Duke of Gloucester married Miss Birgitte Van Deurs. On 18th July 1973 the following arms were assigned to his wife by Royal Warrant: *azure, a lapwing proper, on a chief or, two pairs of ostrich feathers in saltire sable.* These arms are displayed in an escutcheon of pretence over the Duke's arms.

H.R.H. PRINCE MICHAEL OF KENT.   A label of five points argent charged with three St. George's crosses gules and two anchors azure alternately.

H.R.H. PRINCESS ALEXANDRA OF KENT, Hon. Mrs. A. Ogilvy.   A label of five points argent the centre point charged with a St. George's cross gules, the points on either side with an anchor azure and the exterior points with a heart gules.

HRH. The Princess of Wales. Marital arms for The Princess of Wales were assigned to her subsequent to her marriage to Prince Charles in 1981.

Royal Arms, or Arms of Dominion, are inseparable from the rank and office of royalty, and cannot be borne undifferenced by any person except the Sovereign.   In the case of the Sovereign's daughters, it was formerly held to be sufficient distinction for them to bear their parent's arms on a lozenge, or impaled with their husband's arms, but they now bear distinctive labels.   The Royal Arms may not be quartered without some difference.   In the persons of Sovereigns, all minor ranks and titles are merged in their royalty; consequently whatever arms they may previously have borne cease to be used at their accession, and no other arms can be quartered with the Royal Arms.   The arms of the Sovereign are not impaled with those of his or her consort.

To dispel any doubts as to when labels cease to be granted to members of the royal family, a Royal Warrant was issued on 24th February 1975. This lays down that the labels assigned to the grandchildren of a Sovereign, except the eldest son of the Prince of Wales, shall henceforth be heritable and borne as part of the arms together with ordinary marks of difference where these are appropriate.

The Warrant also laid down that the children of sons of a Sovereign and the eldest living son of the Prince of Wales shall be entitled to the style 'Royal Highness'.

383. SEE OF LLANDAFF   384. PROVINCE OF CANTERBURY

CHAPTER XX

OFFICIAL AND CORPORATE HERALDRY

AT an early period in the history of heraldry, shields of arms, in some cases originating in seals, were used by corporate bodies, ecclesiastical and civil, and were in due course recorded by the heralds. In modern cases there have been many grants of armorial bearings to official bodies, corporations and associations of all kinds. These bodies have many uses for heraldry, e.g. on seals and documents, badges of office, flags, the decoration of their buildings and the marking of their property. Corporate heraldry is in itself a large subject, and within the limits of a general handbook it is possible only to deal with it summarily and to give a few examples. A list of books on particular aspects will be found in the Bibliography.

ECCLESIASTICAL HERALDRY (Plate XXII)

Insignia, usually religious in character, were employed in the seals of Bishops before they began to use heraldic arms, and in some cases the arms subsequently devised repeat the emblems on the former seal.

223

Thus the device of Our Lord in the arms of the See of Chichester (165) appears on the seal of Bishop Sigefrid, 1180–1204.

The arms of several Sees contain the emblems of St. Peter and St. Paul. The See of London has borne two crossed swords, the emblem of St. Paul, since the 14th century, the earlier seals having included the figure of the Saint. The See of Peterborough displays St. Peter's keys, and Winchester a sword and two keys (236).

Ecclesiastical insignia, especially the mitre and the pastoral staff, are frequently found, e.g. the See of Llandaff bears, *Sable, two pastoral staves in saltire, or and argent ; on a chief azure, three gold mitres* (383). The arms of the Province of Canterbury are, *Azure, an Archiepiscopal staff in pale argent ensigned with a cross paty or, surmounted by a pall of the second, fimbriated and fringed gold, and charged with four crosses paty fitchy sable* (384).

385. Types of Mitre

Archbishops and Diocesan Bishops may impale their personal arms on the sinister side with those of their See. Other Bishops use only their personal arms. All Bishops ensign their shield with their mitre. They may also place two pastoral staves in saltire behind their shield. They do not use crests or supporters and, whilst it is unusual for a Bishop to use a motto, precedents suggest that it is not technically incorrect. Dr. John William Wand, 112th Bishop of London, used the motto *Virga Tua Consolatio Mea* and a motto was shown in the grant of arms made to Cardinal Godfrey in 1957 (Plate XXII, 3). In the grant of arms to the Bishopric of British Honduras, made in 1950, the motto *Hoy No Mañana* was inscribed beneath the arms. Mitres, when placed above shields, are always represented as gold, and may be

Plate XXIII

ARMS OF SCHOOLS AND COLLEGES

(See Chapter XX)

ETON COLLEGE, founded 1440 ; arms granted 1449. (*pp.* 87, 231)

STOWE SCHOOL, founded and arms granted 1923. (*p.* 231)

TONBRIDGE SCHOOL, founded 1553; arms granted 1923. (*pp.* 53. 231)

ROYAL HIGH SCHOOL, EDINBURGH, arms matriculated 1920. (*p.* 231)

AMPLEFORTH COLLEGE, revived 1802 ; arms granted 1912. (*p.* 231)

HAILEYBURY COLLEGE, incorporated 1864 ; arms granted 1920. (*p.* 231)

ETON

STOWE

TONBRIDGE

ROYAL
HIGH SCHOOL, EDINBURGH

AMPLEFORTH

HAILEYBURY

Plate XXIII

ARMS OF SCHOOLS AND COLLEGES

jewelled, or chased as jewelled. Two infulae, or ribbons fringed at the ends (also termed lables), depend from the mitre.

The Bishop of Durham, in token of his former jurisdiction as Count Palatine, shows his mitre rising from a ducal coronet, and may place a sword and pastoral staff in saltire behind his shield. Archbishops' mitres are not coroneted, though they are sometimes incorrectly shown in this way.

Many of the ancient religious houses had arms, and in some cases these have been preserved in the insignia of present-day institutions ; e.g. the Borough of Bridlington has arms which incorporate the three Gothic letters B which appeared in the shield of the former priory ; the arms of Reading University include the three escallops of St. James which were the arms of Reading Abbey.

Anglican clergy, not of episcopal rank, unlike the Roman clergy, have always borne arms in the same way as laymen, that is with shield, helmet, crest and motto. Recently, particularly in High Church circles, there has been a movement to dispense with helms and crests and replace them with ecclesiastical hats like those used in the Roman Catholic Church (*see below*). This mild agitation culminated in the Archbishop of Canterbury writing to the Earl Marshal, to say that in his view it would be proper and acceptable that those clergy of the Anglican Communion, who desired to ensign their arms with an approved design of ecclesiastical hat, should be permitted to do so. In response to this letter the Earl Marshal issued a Warrant on 21st December 1976 permitting the Officers of Arms to marshal the arms of those clergy of the Anglican Communion who wished to use hats in place of crests to do this and a list of appropriate hats was annexed to the Warrant. The hats authorized are as follows:

DEAN. A black hat having three red tassels pendent from purple cords on either side.

ARCHDEACONS. A black hat having three purple tassels pendent from purple cords on either side.

CANONS, HONORARY CANONS EMERITUS AND PREBENDARIES. A black hat having three red tassels pendent from black cords on either side.

PRIESTS. A black hat having one black tassel pendent from a black and white cord on either side.

DOCTORS OF DIVINITY. The hat appropriate to their degree, the cord, from which the tassel or tassels depend, being interlaced with a skein of red.

MEMBERS OF THE SOVEREIGN'S ECCLESIASTICAL HOUSEHOLD. The hat appropriate to their degree charged on the front of the crown with the Tudor Rose (i.e. a white rose on a red rose) proper.

DEACONS. A black hat without either cords or tassels.

The methods of marshalling ecclesiastical arms referred to in the preceding paragraphs refer to the post-Reformation English Church. During the years between the Reformation and the restoration of the Roman Catholic Hierarchy in 1850, the customs regarding the use of arms by dignitaries of the Roman Church have evolved along somewhat different lines, notably by the use of a variety of different ecclesiastical hats to signify rank.

The use of a red hat over the arms of a Cardinal and a black hat over those of a Protonotary Apostolic are known to English heraldry and are contained in an early Tudor manuscript in the College of Arms.[1] The Cardinal's hat is shown as a red hat with six tassels pendent on either side and that of the Protonotary as a black hat with three tassels on either side. Though in the early 16th century it is doubtful whether the number of tassels was significant, it later became so and today many hats are used of diverse colours and sporting a varying number of tassels, the combination of colours and tassels indicating the rank of the bearer of the arms.

Although most of the ecclesiastical hats used in heraldry have not received the explicit approval of the Apostolic See, their use has been sanctioned by custom and has not been opposed by the Vatican; the same is true of the other ornaments used by ecclesiastics. The use of insignia varies to some extent from country to country, but generally speaking the hat has replaced the mitre in the arms of bishops and the cross the croziers.

Since the last war, there has been a number of grants of arms made to Roman Catholic prelates and clergy. The first grant was to Archbishop Godfrey, just before he was transferred from Liverpool to Westminster. In the letters patent the arms were ensigned by a green hat with ten tassels on either side and, behind the shield, was the double-traversed cross, appropriate to an archbishop. The insignia

[1] College of Arms ms. L. 10.

did not form part of the actual grant. However, the English Kings of Arms later felt that they had no real authority for including such insignia, as they had no official knowledge of what should be used. Indeed, as has been stated, custom slightly varies from country to country. In the circumstances, it seemed sensible to discover what customs were generally followed in England and then, in consultation with the ecclesiastical authorities, draw up a list of appropriate insignia and embody it in an Earl Marshal's Warrant. This was done and Cardinal Heenan, Archbishop of Westminster, approved the insignia chosen. Then, by an Earl Marshal's Warrant dated 17th July 1967, insignia appropriate for use in connection with the personal armorial ensigns of prelates and other clergy of the Roman Catholic Church was formally laid down. It is as follows :

CARDINALS. Above the arms is placed a red hat, having fifteen tassels interwoven with gold thread on either side (Plate XXII, 3). The tradition is that the scarlet hat was instituted by Pope Innocent IV (1243–54) at the time of the Council of Lyons, but the number of tassels was not finally fixed until a degree of the Sacred Congregation of Ceremonial in 1832. Pope Paul VI announced in April 1969 that he would no longer present the hat to Cardinals, but, unless the present Earl Marshal's Warrant is rescinded or altered, the hat will, presumably, still be used symbolically in the arms of Cardinals.

ARCHBISHOPS. Above the arms is placed a mitre (*mitra pretiosa*, 385) and/or a green hat, having ten tassels pendent on either side. Behind the arms is placed a double-traversed cross in pale (Plate XXII, 3). Patriarchs and Primates, of whom there is none in this country, normally use the same hat as a Cardinal, but it is green not red. They also use the double-traversed cross. Originally, a plain cross on staff, like that shown in the arms of the Province of Canterbury (384) was carried immediately in front of the Pope and his legates. In 1215 this privilege was extended to Patriarchs and in the next century to Archbishops. In the 15th century it became customary for these dignitaries to use a double-traversed cross, the top traverse representing the legend placed by Pontius Pilate over Christ's Cross, to distinguish them from Bishops who had started to use the single cross. Some writers assert that when the Archbishops used the double-traversed cross, Patriarchs assumed a triple-traversed cross, but there seems to be no foundation for this idea.

Diocesan and Titular Bishops and Abbots Nullius Dioceseos. Above the arms is placed a mitre (*mitra pretiosa*, 385) and/or a green hat having twelve tassels pendent on either side (385 *a*). Behind the arms is placed either a single-traversed cross, or a crozier, either in pale or in bend. Although there are no Abbots Nullius Dioceseos (Abbots with episcopal jurisdiction) in England, there are some in the Commonwealth, who come under the jurisdiction of the Kings of Arms.

385 *a*. Ecclesiastical Hat with twelve tassels

4. Abbots

Abbots. Above the arms is placed a mitre (*mitra simplex*, 385 *b*) or a black hat having six tassels pendent on either side. Behind the arms is placed a crozier either in pale or in bend. Archbishop Bruno Bernard Heim in his authoritative work on ecclesiastical heraldry, *Heraldry in the Catholic Church* (1978), states that Abbots should use the same hat as Bishops, but there has been a definite ruling by the Vatican authorities that the hat should be that described above and that if a mitre is used, it should be the *mitra simplex* (i.e. the plain white mitre) and not the precious mitre used by higher dignitaries. On the continent abbots often show a short veil fixed beneath the crook of their crozier, but the Earl Marshal's Warrant does not sanction this use.

385 *b*. Mitra simplex

Protonotaries Apostolic, and Vicars, Prefects and Administrators Apostolic. Above the arms is placed a crimson hat, having six tassels pendent on either side.

Religious Superiors General or Provincial and Honorary or Titular Protonotaries Apostolic. Above the arms is placed a black hat having six tassels pendent on either side.

Domestic Prelates to the Pope. Above the arms is placed a violet hat having six tassels pendent on either side.

Privy Chamberlains and Privy Chaplains to the Pope. Above the arms is placed a black hat with six violet tassels pendent on either side.

PLATE XXIV

CORPORATION AND COMPANY ARMS

Plate XXIV

CORPORATION AND COMPANY ARMS

(See Chapter XX)

1. THE BRITISH BROADCASTING CORPORATION, granted 1927. (*p.* 233)
2. THE CORPORATION OF LLOYD'S, granted 1926. (*pp.* 82, 98, 234)
3. THE AUCTIONEERS' AND ESTATE AGENTS' INSTITUTE, granted 1927. (*p.* 234)
4. THE WORSHIPFUL COMPANY OF HABERDASHERS OF LONDON, granted 1503 and confirmed in 1570 when Robert Cooke, Clarenceux, granted the Company a crest and supporters. (*p.* 238)

CANONS. Above the arms is placed a black hat having three tassels pendent on either side.

PRIESTS. Above the arms is placed a black hat having one tassel pendent on either side.

It should be noted that if any of the prelates or clergy listed above are Cardinals of the Roman Catholic Church, then they substitute the Cardinal's hat for that which they would otherwise use.

The clergy of the Church of England, other than Bishops, generally use crests, but the Roman clergy substitute the appropriate hat for the crest. In Great Britain the shield is generally employed but on the continent of Europe and elsewhere the arms of ecclesiastics are frequently shown in ovals and cartouches of various shapes. By papal decree the clergy may not embellish their arms with the insignia of temporal rank. An example may be found in the arms of the late Lord Vaux of Harrowden, a Benedictine Monk, whose arms are illustrated in Debrett's *Peerage* without crest or coronet.

By Letters Apostolic (*Universalis Ecclesiae*) of Pope Pius IX dated 29th September 1850, the Roman Catholic Hierarchy in England was restored, that in Scotland being re-established in 1878. Although the country was divided up into dioceses administered by Bishops who distinguished themselves by taking territorial titles, these titles were and still are illegal, being borne contrary to certain provisions contained in the Catholic Emancipation Act 1829, and Roman Catholic Bishops do not have the legal status enjoyed by Anglican Bishops of being corporations sole. For these reasons the Kings of Arms cannot grant arms of office to the Roman Catholic Bishops. The result of this impasse has been that arms have been assumed or even, as in the case of the Archbishopric of Westminster, granted by the Vatican, for a Bishop needs to use a seal and such seals are, by tradition, armorial.

The result of these assumptions of arms has in many cases been most unfortunate. The arms of the Metropolitan See of Westminster and those of Canterbury are not distinguishable when rendered in monochrome (Plate XXII, 2 and 3) whilst the Roman Catholic Archbishopric of Southwark used to use the arms of St. George undifferenced.

UNIVERSITIES AND COLLEGES

The arms of Oxford University (217) have been in use since the middle of the 15th century. Cambridge University was granted arms in 1573 (386). The latter are blazoned, *Gules, on a cross ermine between four lions passant guardant or, a closed book of the first, edged, clasped and garnished gold.*

Most of the Colleges of these two Universities have been granted arms, or have had their arms recorded by the heralds, and in many cases such arms are based on those of the founders. Christ's and St. John's Colleges, Cambridge, founded by the Lady Margaret Beaufort, bear *France Modern and England quarterly within a bordure compony argent and azure* (285). King's College, Cambridge, founded by Henry VI, bears, *Sable, three roses argent, on a chief per pale azure and gules a fleur-de-lis and a lion passant guardant or;* these arms clearly indicate the link between the foundation and Eton College (see the next section).

In some cases, colleges bear the arms of their founders without difference. Thus Balliol College, Oxford, founded about 1265 by Devorguilla and her husband, John Balliol of Barnard Castle, bears, *Azure, a lion rampant argent crowned or* (for Devorguilla) impaling *Gules an orle argent* (for Balliol) (387). A later instance is provided by Sidney

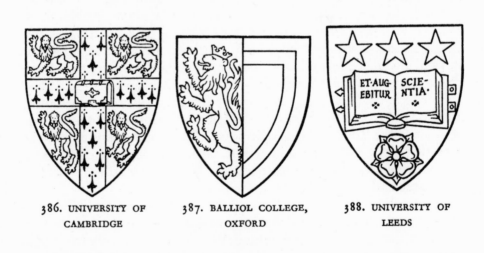

386. UNIVERSITY OF   387. BALLIOL COLLEGE,   388. UNIVERSITY OF
CAMBRIDGE   OXFORD   LEEDS

Sussex College, Cambridge, founded in 1595 by the Lady Frances Sidney, Countess of Sussex, which bears, *Argent, a bend engrailed sable* (for Radcliffe, Earl of Sussex) impaling *Or, a pheon azure* (for Sidney).

A number of universities and colleges of later foundation has

obtained grants of arms, and these often contain charges from the arms
of the cities and counties with which the foundations are connected.
Thus Leeds University displays molets from the shield of the City of
Leeds and a white rose for Yorkshire : *Vert, a book proper edged and
clasped or and inscribed with the words ET AUGEBITUR SCIENTIA,
between in chief three silver molets and in base a rose argent seeded
proper* (388).

Public Schools (Plate XXIII)

Eton College was granted arms by its founder, Henry VI, in 1449.
The arms are, *Sable, three lilies slipped and leafed argent ; on a chief per pale
azure and gules a fleur-de-lis and a lion passant guardant or.*　The lilies refer
to the dedication of the College to the Virgin Mary.

Plate XXIII also shows the arms granted in recent times to the following schools :

Stowe School, founded and arms granted in 1923 ; the arms contain
charges from the arms of families connected with Stowe, namely Bruce,
Chandos, Grenville and Temple.

Tonbridge School, founded 1553, arms granted 1923 ; the quartered
arms of the founder, Sir Andrew Judd, are differenced and become an
indivisible coat by the addition of the narrow gold fillet cross.

Royal High School, Edinburgh, arms matriculated in the Lyon
Office, 1920 ; the arms are related to those of the City of Edinburgh.

Ampleforth College, revived 1802, arms granted in 1912 ; the shield
includes the keys of St. Peter and the arms of Edward the Confessor
in allusion to the fact that the Benedictine Community by which the
College is governed claim succession from Westminster Abbey.

Haileybury College, arms granted in 1920 ; the charges refer to the
words inscribed in the book.

The College of Arms and Lyon Office of Arms

The College of Arms, or Heralds' College, in London, bears for arms,
*Argent, a cross of St. George between four doves, their dexter wings elevated
and inverted, azure* (423).　Crest : *From a crest-coronet or, a dove rising
azure.*　Supporters : *Two lions rampant guardant argent, ducally gorged or.*
These arms may have been derived from those used by John Wrythe

389. GARTER
KING OF ARMS

390. LYON
KING OF ARMS

391. CLARENCEUX
KING OF ARMS

who was Garter at the time of the foundation of the College of Arms in 1484. On the other hand the converse could be true. The dove is a traditional symbol of a herald's office.

The Heralds' Office, or Lyon Office, of Scotland: *Argent, a lion sejant affronté gules, holding in his dexter paw a thistle slipped vert, and in the sinister an escutcheon gules; on a chief azure, the cross of St. Andrew.* This is also the official coat of Lyon King of Arms (390).

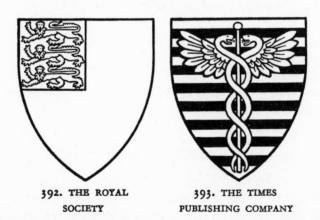

392. THE ROYAL
SOCIETY

393. THE TIMES
PUBLISHING COMPANY

Garter, Norroy, and Clarenceux Kings of Arms have official arms, all *Argent, the cross of St. George* with various chiefs, viz. for Garter,

Plate XXV

ARMS OF A BARONET OF THE UNITED KINGDOM:

MEREDITH OF MONTREAL, CANADA

(Created 1916, *extinct* 1929)

(See pp. 63, 201)

Arms : Argent, a lion rampant sable collared and with a chain reflexed over the back gold ; on a chief of the second two maple leaves or.

Crest : A demi-lion sable, collared and chained as in the arms, holding in the dexter paw a sprig of maple gold.

Note the badge of a Baronet at the centre chief of the shield, and the helm open and affronté befitting this rank.

PLATE XXV

ARMS OF A BARONET (U.K.)

394. THE HERALDRY SOCIETY

on a chief azure, a ducal coronet enfiled by the Garter between a lion of England and a fleur-de-lis, all or (389) ; for Norroy, *on a chief per pale azure and gules, a lion of England crowned between a fleur-de-lis and a key erect, all or ;* for Clarenceux, *on a chief gules a lion of England crowned or* (391). Ulster King of Arms bears, *Or, a cross gules, on a chief of the last a lion of England between a harp and a portcullis, both gold.* The offices of Norroy and Ulster have now been joined to make one office of Norroy and Ulster, for which office new arms have been assigned (page 300).

PUBLIC INSTITUTIONS

As instances of the armorial bearings of important institutions of a national character and of various types, granted at different periods, the following are selected from many :

The Royal Society, incorporated 1663 : *Argent, a quarter of England*—a rare example of the coat of England being granted in its entirety and without difference (392).

The British Broadcasting Corporation, granted in 1927 (Plate XXIV, 1) ; the gold band round the globe represents broadcast transmissions ; the thunderbolt stands for electrical activity ; the swift-flighted eagles have bugle-horns as emblems of proclamation.

395. CITY OF CANTERBURY   396. BOROUGH OF BURY   397. STIRLING COUNTY
                                   (LANCS.)   COUNCIL

The Corporation of Lloyd's, granted in 1926 (Plate XXIV, 2); the shield combines the arms of the City of London with a fouled anchor; and the ship in the crest is H.M.S. *La Lutine*, which was wrecked in 1799; her bell hangs at Lloyd's, and is rung before important announcements, especially about overdue vessels; one stroke for bad news and two for good.

The Auctioneers' and Estate Agents' Institute, granted in 1927 (Plate XXIV, 3); emblems of land and property, and the auctioner's gavel.

The Times Publishing Company, granted in 1929—Arms: *Argent eight barrulets sable, over all a caduceus in pale or.* The shield (393) represents a page of print, and the staff of Mercury refers to the news-bearing function of *The Times* newspaper.

The Heraldry Society, granted in 1957—Arms: *Quarterly azure and gules, a lion's face crowned with an ancient crown or within a tressure flory on the outer edge of the same;* with crest, supporters and motto (394), and a badge which is displayed on the mantling.

Civic Heraldry

In the 14th and 15th centuries several English cities and towns placed in their seals shields of arms which were in due course recorded by the Heralds. From the 16th century onwards, the Kings of Arms have granted armorial bearings to the corporations of cities and towns. The Local Government Act, 1888, introduced a plethora of new authorities, County, Urban and Rural District Councils, over 500 of which were granted arms. These and all City and Borough Councils were abolished by the Local Government Act 1972 (page 237), resulting in a great many new grants being made. Civic heraldry is thus largely of modern growth, though firmly rooted in antiquity and tradition.

Early civic arms fall into four main groups according to the nature of the charges that predominate, namely royal and seignorial emblems, symbols of national or local patron saints, castles, and ships or other tokens of maritime interests. Modern civic heraldry is more complex, reflecting a wider range of interests, and including charges referring to industries, national or local history, or to some special feature or characteristic of the town or county. Examples of these various classes of civic arms are given below, and others occur elsewhere in this book.

London (City), arms dating from the middle of the 14th century: *Argent, the cross of St. George, and in the canton the sword of St. Paul, gules.* Crest: *on a wreath argent and gules a dragon's sinister wing argent charged on the underside with a cross gules.* Supporters: *two dragons argent charged on the underside of the wings with a cross gules.* Motto: *Domine dirige nos.* The crest has been in use since the sixteenth century, and the supporters since early in the seventeenth century, and they were confirmed in 1957. The crest is placed on a helm of the type used by a peer.

Westminster, arms granted in 1601: *Azure, a portcullis or ; on a chief gold, a pale bearing the arms of Edward the Confessor between two Tudor roses.*

Canterbury, ancient arms: *Argent, three Cornish choughs proper and on a chief gules a lion of England or* (395); the choughs are from the arms attributed to St. Thomas Becket.

York, ancient arms: *Argent, on a cross of St. George gules five lions of England or.*

Winchester, ancient arms: *Gules, five castles in saltire argent, the middle one supported by two lions of England or.*

Edinburgh, arms granted in 1732: *Argent, on a rock in base proper, a castle triple-towered sable, masoned of the first, topped with three fans gules, windows and portcullis closed of the last.*

Bristol, arms recorded 1623: *Gules, on the sinister side, on a mount in base vert, a castle with two towers domed argent, on each dome a banner of St. George ; in the dexter base water and thereon a ship of three masts or, sailing from a port in the dexter tower of the castle, two masts being visible and a sail argent set on the foremast.*

Glouce&ter (City): *Or, three chevrons gules between ten torteaux;* the chevrons of the Clare Earls of Glouce&ter, and torteaux from the arms of the See of Worce&ter.

Leeds, arms recorded 1662: *Azure, a fleece or, on a chief sable three molets argent.*

Bury (Lancs.), arms granted 1877: *Quarterly argent and azure, a cross double parted and fretty counterchanged, in the fir&t quarter an anvil sable, in the second a fleece or, in the third two shuttles in saltire proper, and in the fourth three culms of the papyrus plant growing on a mound also proper* (396); dire&t references to local indu&tries. Emblems of indu&try of all kinds, of agriculture and of transport, abound in civic heraldry, and as some indication of their variety the following may be mentioned: garbs, borne by numerous authorities; lozenges sable (i.e. " black diamonds " for coal), picks, spades and miners' lamps, borne by many authorities in the mining areas; a chain (Stourbridge); a padlock (Wolverhampton); a needle and salmon-fly (Redditch); cannon (Woolwich); a railway locomotive (Swindon); an aeroplane volant (Beddington and Wallington).

Kent County Council, arms granted 1933 but used earlier: *Gules, a horse forcene argent*[1]; the arms attributed to the ancient Kingdom of Kent. Similarly Essex C.C. and Middlesex C.C. bear in their arms the seaxes, or notched swords, regarded as the device of the Ea&t and Middle Saxon Kingdoms.

County Councils may be granted arms *ensigned by a mural crown* in&tead of the usual helmet, cre&t and mantling. The arms granted to the London County Council in 1914 are shown in this way as are those of the County Councils of Monmouth, Durham and Cambridgeshire and Isle of Ely.

Stirling County Council, arms matriculated 1890: *Azure, on a saltire between two caltraps in pale and two spur-rowels in fess argent, a lion rampant gules* (397); the lion of Scotland on the saltire of St. Andrew with charges alluding to the Battle of Bannockburn.

The arms of many Scottish local authorities contain references to the great families and clans with which the hi&tory of the locality is closely conne&ted.

[1] Although the horse is blazoned *forcene* in the grant of arms, the illu&tration in the margin shows it to be rampant. The two terms are often confused, but &tri&tly *forcene* should only be used when the horse is rearing.

Plate XXVI

ARMS OF THE GOVERNMENTS OF STATES

(See Chapter XXI)

1. AUSTRALIA (*p.* 241).
2. CANADA (*p.* 240).
3. NEW ZEALAND (*p.* 241).
4. TANGANYIKA (*p.* 242).
5. SIERRA LEONE (*p.* 243).

1

2

3

4

5

Plate XXVI

ARMS OF THE GOVERNMENTS OF STATES

Some of the foregoing authorities, and many others, have also crests and supporters; the latter may be granted to county and district councils and municipal corporations.

The whole history of civic heraldry was re-written when the Local Government Act 1972 became law on 1st April 1974. Under terms of this Act every county council was reconstituted and Urban and Rural District Councils were abolished, as were City and Borough Councils. New District Councils were introduced and former Borough Councils were superseded by Parish Councils. In essence all existing local authorities were abolished, their arms becoming historic. Literally hundreds of arms which if the truth were known, many had long wished in *hades*, went to *limbo* instead. The sad thing was that among the coats loaded with fleeces, cog-wheels, red and white roses, shuttles and similar recurrent symbols, which cluttered up the arena of municipal heraldry, many a noble and ancient coat was put on the shelf.

Fortunately it was appreciated that many local authorities whose status had changed but which in most ways were not all that different from their predecessors, might want to bear the same arms. It was therefore enacted that arms could be transferred from an old to a new authority by Order in Council for a fee (now £120). Garter King of Arms was instructed to advise the Privy Council as to when such transfers may properly be made. In doing this he takes into consideration a number of factors, such as the name of the new authority being the same as the old, the boundaries being more or less coterminous, the population roughly the same and so forth.

Since the Act came into force a number of Orders in Council has been made transferring arms from well over one hundred old authorities to new ones.

In some cases transfers, which were not straightforward, have been made by Royal Licence. Thus the new District of Huntingdon has been assigned the old arms of the County of Huntingdonshire which became historic when Huntingdonshire merged with the Isle of Ely.

MERCHANT COMPANIES AND GUILDS

The use of armorial bearings by associations of merchants and craftsmen dates from the fifteenth century. Individual merchants frequently adopted devices, termed merchants' marks, consisting of a monogram of their initials, or the letters forming their name, under a sign of the cross (which may also be intended to represent the mast and yard of a ship). These marks, which may be regarded as the forerunners of the

398. MERCHANTS' MARKS

trademarks of our day, were often borne in shields, and were sometimes quartered by the merchant with the arms of the company to which he belonged. This practice was regarded with disfavour by the Heralds, since it appeared to claim for the merchant's mark the status of arms, and it probably induced them to extend the granting of armorial bearings to the merchant class.

The following are examples of the arms of merchant companies and guilds:

The Merchants of the Staple of Calais, ancient arms : *Barry undy of six argent and azure, on a chief gules a lion of England or ;* crest, *a ram argent armed or ;* the field of the shield apparently alludes to sea travel, and the crest to the wool trade.

The Grocers' Company of London, arms granted 1531 : *Argent, a chevron gules between nine cloves sable ;* used by Oundle School, a foundation of the Company.

The Fishmongers' Company of London, arms granted 1536 : *Azure, three dolphins naiant in pale argent finned or, between two pairs of lucies in saltire proper, over the nose of each lucy a ducal coronet gold ; on a chief gules three pairs of keys in saltire wards outward or ;* the keys are the emblem of St. Peter.

The Haberdashers' Company of London—see Plate XXIV.

The Parish Clerks' Company of London were first granted arms by Walter Bellenger, Ireland King of Arms. Sir Thomas Holme, Clarenceux King of Arms, whose jurisdiction had been encroached upon, regranted the arms in 1482. In this Patent he states: "I nevertheles seing the un-lauful and insufficient graunt have alterly adnulled and dampened the same and wol yat it be frustrate and void and of noon effect". He granted the Company: *Azure, in base a fleur-de-lis or, on a chief gules a leopard's face gold, over all two holy-water sprinklers in saltire of gold and silver.*

Then in 1582 the Company were granted: *Azure a fleur-de-lis or, on a chief gules a leopard's face between two prick-song books gold, laced vert.* The reason for this new grant was because the old arms, containing holy-water sprinklers, were considered to be "over muche charged with certayne superstition".

COMMERCIAL COMPANIES

Since the last war, arms have been granted with increasing regularity, to purely commercial companies. Such bodies must be pre-eminent in their field and show every sign of perpetual succession.

Among the first such companies to be granted arms were the British Oxygen Company Ltd (1961) and Vickers Ltd (1963) (398 *a*). More recent grants have been made to the Savoy Hotel Ltd (1966), Marks and Spencer Ltd (1968) and Standard Telephones and Cables, P.L.C. (1982) (398 *b*).

398*a*. Arms of Vickers Ltd.

398*b*. Illustrated by kind permission of Standard Telephones & Cables PLC

399. TASMANIA

CHAPTER XXI

COMMONWEALTH AND FOREIGN HERALDRY

THE history, development and resources of the countries which compose the Commonwealth and the colonial possessions of the Crown, are illustrated most interestingly in their heraldry. The armorial bearings of the governments of the dominions and colonies have for the most part been assigned to them by Royal Warrant. (While for convenience one may refer to the arms of a dominion or colony, strictly the arms appertain to the government and not to the territory in general.)

The arms of Canada (Plate XXVI, 2) are traditional in character, being based on the Royal Arms. The shield contains the coats of England, Scotland, Ireland and France quarterly, with a sprig of three maple leaves proper on argent in the base. The arms thus contain emblems of Canada and of the four countries from which her first European settlers came. In the crest, the crowned lion statant guardant holds a red maple leaf which is symbolic of the sacrifices made by Canadians in the wars for civilization. The torse is argent and gules and the mantling, though shown as gules lined argent, is blazoned argent lined gules in the Royal Proclamation assigning the arms. Above the crest is placed the Royal

240

Plate XXVII

BANNERS AND STANDARDS

Plate XXVII

BANNERS AND STANDARDS

(See Chapter XXII)

1. Banner of Sir John Botetourt, temp. Edward I ; from the Roll of Caerlaverock.

2. Banner of King Richard II, after the representation on the tomb of his banner-bearer, Sir Simon de Felbrigge. *(p. 252)*

3. Banner of Sir Ralph de Monthermer, as Earl of Gloucester ; from the Roll of Caerlaverock. (He held the earldom, and displayed the banner of Clare associated therewith, during the minority of Gilbert de Clare, who succeeded as Earl of Gloucester in 1307.)

4. A modern standard : the King's Standard of the Royal Horse Guards (The Blues : *p.* 256).

5. Standard of Sir Henry de Stafford, c. 1475.

Crown. The supporting lion (uncrowned) and unicorn respectively maintain banners of the Union Flag and France. In the compartment are roses, thistles, shamrocks and lilies. The motto, in letters of gold on a blue scroll, is taken from the Latin version of Psalm lxxii. 8, "From sea to sea." This achievement was assigned by Royal Proclamation in 1921, replacing former arms consisting of the quartered coats of Ontario, Quebec, Nova Scotia and New Brunswick. The several provinces in the Dominion have separate armorial bearings. In the original grant the maple leaves in the base of the shield are blazoned *proper* and shown green. Recently the Canadian Government has altered the tincture of the leaves to red, like the maple leaf which features in the new National Flag of Canada. This flag, which was approved by Royal Proclamation on 28th January 1965, introduces a new charge to armory, namely a *Canadian pale*, which is about half as wide again as an ordinary pale. The flag is officially blazoned as follows: *Gules on a Canadian pale argent a maple leaf of the first* (400).

The Commonwealth of Australia has armorial bearings (Plate XXVI, 1), assigned in 1912 in place of earlier arms. The shield is, *Quarterly of six ; 1, Argent, a cross gules charged with a lion passant guardant between on each limb a molet of eight points or ; 2, Azure, five molets, one of eight, two of seven, one of six and one of five points of the first (representing the Constellation of the Southern Cross) and in Chief an Imperial Crown proper ; 3, Argent, a Maltese cross azure surmounted by an Imperial Crown proper ; 4, Or, on a perch wreathed vert and gules an Australian piping shrike displayed proper ; 5, Or, a swan naiant to the sinister sable ; 6, Argent, a lion passant gules ; the whole within a bordure ermine.* Crest : *on a wreath or and azure, a seven-pointed star or.* Supporters : *dexter, a kangaroo, sinister, an emu, both proper.* The quarters represent New South Wales, Victoria, Queensland, South Australia, Western Australia and Tasmania. The bordure makes them indivisible, and they are not intended to be used separately. The supporters are sometimes shown standing in a compartment adorned with golden wattle.

The arms of Tasmania (399), granted in 1917, are supported by Tasmanian tigers. The thunderbolt alludes to the harnessing of water power, and the other emblems represent the products of the island.

New Zealand has armorial bearings (Plate XXVI, 3), granted in 1911 The arms are, *Quarterly azure and gules, on a pale argent three lymphads sable, between in the first quarter four molets in cross gules, fimbriated argent, in*

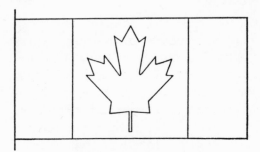

400. NATIONAL FLAG OF CANADA

401. KENYA

the second a fleece, in the third a garb, and in the fourth two hammers saltire-wise all or. Above the shield is the Royal Crown, which has been used, with royal approbation, in place of the crest of a demi-lion holding a Union Flag, since 1956. Supporters: *dexter, a female figure proper vested argent, holding in the dexter hand a flagstaff proper and thereon a banner azure with a canton of the Union and in the fly four stars in cross gules, fimbriated argent as in the first quarter of the arms; sinister, a native habited all proper. Beneath the shield the name NEW ZEALAND appears on a scroll.* This has replaced the motto which was *Onward.*

The arms assigned to Tanganyika in 1961 (Plate XXVI, 4) created a precedent for the use of a native shield. The arms are: *Per fess vert and barry wavy argent and azure, a chief gules, on the vert a bar sable, fimbriated or, overall a torch enflamed and enfiled of four interlaced annulets gold, and upon a compartment representing Mount Kilimanjaro.* Supporters: *dexter, a Tanganyikan man proper habited vert, supporting in the exterior hand an elephant's tusk and at the feet a cotton bush leaved and fructed also proper; sinister, a Tanganyikan woman likewise proper habited vert, and with a head cloth gold, supporting with the exterior hand an elephant's tusk and at the feet a coffee bush leaved and fructed also proper.* Motto: *Uhuru Na Umoja.* No arms have so far been assigned to the new state of Tanzania.

In 1962 the precedent of using a native shield was followed when Uganda was granted arms. They are: *Sable, upon the fess point a sun in splendour and in base a Uganda drum gold, the skin and guy ropes argent, a chief barry wavy of six azure and argent; behind the shield two Uganda spears of estate in saltire proper.* Supporters: *dexter, a male Uganda kob: sinister, a crested crane, both proper and standing on a compartment representing*

402. CEYLON

INDVS·VTERQVE SERVIET·VNI

403. JAMAICA

a grassy mount down the centre of which flows a river, between in dexter a sprig of coffee and in sinister a sprig of cotton, both leaved and fructed proper. Motto: *For God and My Country.*

Another example of the use of the native shield is afforded by the arms granted to Kenya in 1963 (401), namely: *Per fess sable and vert, on a fess gules fimbriated argent, a cock grasping in the dexter claw an axe also argent.* Supporters: *on either side a lion or, grasping in the interior forepaw a spear of estate, the hafts of the spears crossed in saltire behind the shield, the whole upon a compartment representing Mount Kenya proper.* Motto: *Harambee.*

Arms were granted to Sierra Leone in 1960 (Plate XXVI, 5). The arms are: *Vert, on a base barry wavy of four argent and azure, a lion passant or, on a chief dancetty of three points also argent, as many torches sable, enflamed proper.* Supporters: *on either side a lion or, supporting between the fore-legs an oil palm proper.* Motto: *Unity, Freedom, Justice.*

Arms were granted to the Colony of Ceylon in 1906, but some years after Ceylon's status within the Commonwealth had changed, new arms were granted in 1954 (402). These arms are: *The Ceylon lion in the centre of a circular design having a lotus petal border ensigned with a representation of the Ceylon crown and at the base, upon a scroll, the word " Lanka " in three languages.*

The arms of the Federation of Rhodesia and Nyasaland, granted in 1954, were: *Per fess azure and sable, in chief a sun rising or, and in base six palets wavy argent, over all a fess dovetailed counter-dovetailed of the last, thereon a lion passant gules.* Crest: *on a wreath or and azure an eagle reguardant, wings extended or, perched upon and grasping in the talons a fish argent.*

404. FEDERATION OF RHODESIA
AND NYASALAND

405. MALAWI

Supporters : *dexter, a sable antelope, and siniſter, a leopard, both proper.*

Motto : *Magni esse mereamur* (404).

When the independent state of Malawi was established similar arms to those of the Federation of Rhodesia and Nyasaland were granted, namely : *Per fess barry wavy azure and argent, and sable, over all a fess gules, thereon a lion passant and in base a sun rising or.* Creſt : *On a wreath or and gules, on water barry wavy argent and azure, and in front of a sun rising or, a fish eagle rising proper.* Supporters : *dexter, a lion ; siniſter, a leopard, both guardant proper and upon a compartment representing the Mlanje mountain.* Motto : *Unity and Freedom* (405).

It will have been observed that in grants to Commonwealth countries many of the usual heraldic conventions are not followed. Thus Canada has a royal helm, Uganda spears of eſtate behind an African war shield and in most grants the compartment and motto are included in the

406. MALTA

PLATE XXVIII

A GRANT OF ARMS

Plate XXVIII

LETTERS PATENT GRANTING ARMORIAL BEARINGS

In these Letters Patent Edward Harold Cole is granted new arms in substitution for those previously granted to his father, together with a badge and arms for the family of his late mother, Ellen Cole, daughter and co-heir of Daniel Perry. The arms granted for Cole are depicted in the margin and those for Perry, together with the badge, in the body of the Patent. Pendent from the document are the seals of the granting Kings of Arms, Garter, and because the grantee resided south of the River Trent, Clarenceux. The patent is headed with the arms of (from left to right) the Duke of Norfolk, the Earl Marshal, for without his Warrant the Kings of Arms may not grant ; the Royal Arms, because the power of granting arms is specifically bestowed upon the Kings of Arms by the Crown and the arms of the College of Arms where the Letters Patent are prepared and recorded.

As one of the principal uses of a badge is for display on a standard, this is painted over the arms. The actual form of the standard is not laid down in the grant, but when a badge is granted a standard may, if the grantee wishes, be shown on the Patent. The decorated margins of the Patent are in the best traditions of heraldic illumination.

406 *a*. Arms of GUYANA

blazon. The arms assigned to Malta in 1964, when she achieved her independence, contain several interesting features (406). They replace the arms borne by Malta as a colony and are blazoned : *Per pale argent and gules, in dexter chief a representation of the George Cross proper, fimbriated gules* (the island of Malta was awarded the George Cross in the Second World War). Crest: *upon a representation of the royal helmet, mantled gules doubled argent, on a wreath of the colours a mural crown with a sally port, the battlements turreted of eight octagonal turrets or.* Supporters : *on either side a dolphin, the dexter supporting with the fins an olive branch and the sinister likewise supporting a palm branch all proper, and upon a compartment of water barry wavy issuing therefrom a rocky mount proper, charged with a maltese cross argent.* Motto: *Virtute et Constantia.*

By a Warrant dated 21st January 1966, the following armorial bearings were assigned to Guyana (formerly the colony of British Guiana) : *Argent in fess three barrulets wavy azure, in chief a Victoria Regia Lily leaf and two flowers conjoined on one stem, the flower to the dexter open the other opening, and in base a Canje pheasant proper.* Crest: *On a wreath of the colours, between two diamonds, a Cacique's crown proper.* Supporters: *On either side a jaguar, the dexter holding a pick, the sinister a sugar cane and a plant of rice all proper.* The royal helm is used (406 *a*).

Interesting features of the arms of other British possessions include a representation of the wreck of the *Sea Venture* (1609) in the shield of Bermuda, and the dodo and sambur deer which support the arms of Mauritius. In several cases, natives of the countries act as supporters. An historic example of the arms of a British possession, granted as long ago as 1661, are those of Jamaica (403) : *Argent, a cross gules charged with five pineapples or.* The crest is a crocodile on a log and the supporters are a West Indian native woman holding a basket of fruit and a West Indian man with a bow in his exterior hand. As there was some doubt as to the proper blazon of these arms they were confirmed in 1957, the royal helmet and mantling being allowed. The old motto, *Indus Uterque Serviet,* was altered to *Out of Many, One People* at the request of the Jamaican Legislature in 1962.

In many cases the arms granted to colonies are based upon Seals and are purely pictorial. The arms granted to Trinidad and Tobago in 1958 are an example, being based upon the flag and badge of the colony. The arms are blazoned : *A seascape having a mountain in the middle distance, a jetty and shipping on the water proper.* If this coat had not been granted few would have described it as real heraldry. In fact the Legislature of Trinidad and Tobago petitioned for an alteration of arms, and a substitute and far more heraldic coat was granted in 1962, namely : *Per chevron enhanced sable and gules, a chevronel enhanced argent, between in chief two humming birds respectant gold, and in base three ships of the fleet of Christopher Columbus also gold, the sails set proper.* A crest, on a royal helm, supporters, a compartment and a motto were also granted.

The arms granted to the British Virgin Islands in 1960 form a rather pleasing canting coat. They are blazoned *Vert, a virgin proper, vested argent, sandalled or, holding in the dexter hand by the chain an ancient lamp gold, enflamed also proper, between eleven like lamps, five in pale to the dexter and six in pale to the sinister.* Motto : *Vigilate.*

A new colony, the British Antarctic Territory, formerly the Dependencies of the Falkland Islands, was assigned the same arms as were granted to the Dependencies in 1952, namely *Per fess wavy, barry wavy of six argent and azure, and argent, on a pile gules, a torch enflamed proper.* Supporters : *dexter, a lion or ; sinister, an emperor penguin proper.* Motto : *Research and Discovery.* In addition the following crest was granted : *on a wreath of the colours, a representation of the research ship " Discovery," with sails furled and flying the blue ensign at the mizzen peak* (407).

In the grant of arms to The Gambia in 1964 no compartment was granted or shown in the painting annexed to the royal warrant. The result is a very pleasant simple coat (408). It is blazoned *Azure a Locar axe and a Mandinka hoe in saltire or, a bordure parted per bordure vert and argent.* Crest : *on a wreath of the colours, issuant from a mount vert, an oil palm nut tree fructed proper.* Supporters : *on either side a lion guardant*

407. BRITISH ANTARCTIC
TERRITORY

408. THE GAMBIA

409. MID-WESTERN
NIGERIA

proper, the dexter supporting a Locar axe and the sinister a Mandinka hoe both or. The motto does not form part of the grant.

In 1960 the Federation of Nigeria became a fully independent state within the Commonwealth. The very simple and dramatic arms assigned to the Federation are blazoned: *Sable a pall wavy argent.* Crest: *on a wreath argent and vert, an eagle, wings displayed and inverted gules.* Supporters: *on either side a white horse proper.* Motto: *Unity and Faith.* The Federation consists of four regions, the Northern, Eastern, Western and Mid-Western. The first three were granted arms by Royal Warrant in the usual form, but the newest region, the Mid-Western, adopted arms by proclamation of the Governor in 1964. The proclamation recites that: "Whereas in divers times and places it has been the custom of Rulers to adopt arms or Ensigns Armorial for the greater honour and distinction of their States," so in this instance, at the request of the Premier of Mid-Western Nigeria the Governor has thought fit to appoint and declare that the arms of the Governor and State shall be as follows: *Per fess vert and or, a Benin Royal Sword (Ada) and a Canoe paddle (Uguoko) in saltire proper.* Crest: *on a wreath of the colours, a bunch of palm nuts proper.* Supporters: *dexter, a lion guardant; sinister, a horse, each supporting an elephant's tusk argent* (409).

The arms of Northern Ireland (410) contain a red cross surmounted by a six-pointed star (representing the six counties) ensigned with the Crown and charged with the red hand of Ulster. The supporters are a red lion maintaining a blue banner charged with the crowned harp of Ireland in gold, and an Irish elk supporting a banner of Ulster (a red cross on a gold field).

410. NORTHERN IRELAND　　　　411. REPUBLIC OF IRELAND

The arms of the Republic of Ireland (411) are, *Quarterly ; 1, Vert, a gold harp with silver strings*, for Leinster ; *2, Per pale argent and azure, on the dexter side a dimidiated eagle displayed sable, and on the sinister conjoined therewith at the shoulder a sinister arm embowed in a sleeve argent, the hand grasping a sword erect proper*, for Connaught ; *3, Or, a cross gules, an inescutcheon argent charged with a dexter hand couped at the wrist also gules*, for Ulster ; *4, Azure, three antique crowns or*, for Munster.

In America, national and state insignia are not strictly bound by heraldic conventions, though some are armorial in character. The shield of the United States of America is, *Argent, six pallets gules, a chief azure*. This is placed on the breast of the American (or bald) eagle displayed proper, which grasps in the dexter talon an olive branch proper, and in the sinister a bundle of 13 arrows argent. The eagle holds in its beak a ribbon on which is the motto, *E pluribus unum*. Above its head is a circle of cloud enclosing a field azure containing

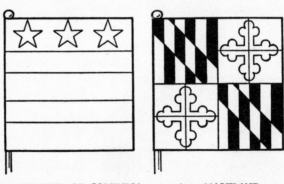

412. DISTRICT OF COLUMBIA　　　413. MARYLAND

13 stars argent arranged in the form of a six-pointed star. The number of stars, as the number of palar divisions of the shield, represents the 13 original States. It will be observed that the arms on the shield differ from the banner of the United States, which is *Gules, six barrulets argent, a canton azure charged with 50 stars argent, in five rows of six and four rows of five.* It has been suggested that the " stars and stripes " design was based on the arms of George Washington, *Argent, two bars and in chief three molets gules,* but there is no proof of this.

The Washington arms, however, form the flag of the District of Columbia (412). Every State in the Union has its own flag, and a few of these are on traditional heraldic lines, e.g. :

Alabama : *Argent, a saltire gules.*

Louisiana : *Azure, a pelican in its piety proper.*

Maryland : *Quarterly, 1 and 4, Paly of six or and sable, a bend counterchanged ; 2 and 3, Quarterly argent and gules, a cross botonny counterchanged* (413). These were the arms of Calvert, Lord Baltimore.

Among the countries of Europe now using heraldic insignia, Denmark is of the most interest to us because her arms are marshalled in part (and formerly in full) by the Duke of Edinburgh (see p. 219), and were also borne by Queen Alexandra. They also figured in our Royal Arms at an earlier period, through the marriage of James I with Anne of Denmark, though at that time they took a slightly different form. The arms of Denmark (414), as formerly borne on an escutcheon by H.R.H. the Duke of Edinburgh, are : *Quarterly, a cross paty throughout argent fimbriated gules ; the first quarter Or semé of hearts gules, three lions passant in pale azure crowned or* (for Denmark) ; *the second Or, two lions passant in pale azure* (for Sleswick) ; *the third, per fess, the chief Azure, three crowns or* (Sweden, for Scandinavia), *the base of three coats, viz. dexter, Gules, a stockfish erect argent crowned or* (for Iceland), *sinister chief Azure a ram passant argent* (for the Faroe Islands), *sinister base Azure a bear sejant erect argent* (for Greenland) ; *the fourth per fess, the chief Or ten hearts gules and in chief a lion passant azure* (for Gothland), *the base Gules a wyvern passant crowned or* (for Vandalia) ; *over all an escutcheon quarterly : 1, Gules, an escutcheon per fess argent and gules between three nettle leaves and three nails in pairle proper* (for Holstein) ; *2, Gules, a swan argent beaked sable, gorged with a coronet proper* (for Stormerk) ; *3, Azure, a chevalier armed at all points brandishing his sword, his charger argent, trappings or* (for Ditzmers) ; *4, Gules, a horse's head couped or* (for Lauenburg) ; *and surtout in the*

414. DENMARK

centre of the escutcheon an inescutcheon bearing Or, two bars gules (for Olden-
burg) *impaling Azure, a cross paty or* (for Dalmenhurst).

The foregoing are the arms of Denmark as borne by King Christian
IX, from whom the Duke of Edinburgh is descended. In the mean-
time the Danish royal arms have been revised, and in their present
form they do not include the stockfish for Iceland, the quarterings for
the Faroe Islands and Greenland being impaled in the lower half of
the third quarter of the shield.

Many of the arms detailed in this Chapter are now historic. The
constitutional composition of the Commonwealth is so fluid that old
arms are shed and new ones assigned very frequently. The subject now
argues a separate volume being devoted to it. However, the examples
given illustrate the differences which exist between Commonwealth and
ordinary corporate heraldry.

415. Standard of HENRY BOLINGBROKE

CHAPTER XXII

FLAGS

FROM a very early period devices have been emblazoned on flags of various kinds. The Bayeux Tapestry has preserved for us some of the earliest examples of flags used in this country. These are for the most

416. Banner of
NEVILLE with
Supporter

part small, and generally terminate in three points. They bear simple devices, such as a pale, or a pale and three bars, or some form of cross with a group of roundels. The standard of the English at Hastings was a dragon (of the type now termed a wyvern), and this appears to have been a cut-out figure rather than something painted or worked on a flag. This was retained among their ensigns of war by the early Norman kings. In the 12th and 13th centuries, car standards were used, which were so large that they had to be mounted on a wagon, by which they were also conveyed from place to place.

Military and national ensigns became systematic as a result of the Crusades, and in the 13th and 14th centuries three principal varieties of ensign were in use, namely the pennon, the banner and the standard.

The PENNON was the personal ensign of the knight who bore it.

251

It was small, pointed or swallow-tailed at the fly, and was borne immediately below the lance-head. It was charged with the badge or other armorial device of the bearer, and sometimes was richly fringed with gold. It might repeat the charge on the shield; in the brass to Sir John D'Abernoun, at Stoke Dabernon, 1277, there is a chevron on both shield and pennon, that on the pennon being so placed that the point of the chevron would be upwards when the lance was levelled.

The BANNER was square or oblong (the depth greater than the breadth), and was charged with the arms of its owner and with no other device. It was borne by Knights Bannerets, who ranked higher than other Knights, and also by Barons, Princes and the Sovereign. A pennon with its points torn off would become a little banner, and this was the ceremonial observed when a knight, in reward for his gallantry, was advanced to the rank of banneret on the field of battle by the Sovereign in person. However, the display of arms on a banner does not seem to have been strictly confined to bannerets.

The first Royal Banner of which we have a blazon is that of Edward I at the siege of Caerlaverock, 1300, which the Chronicler thus describes : " On his banner were three leopards courant, of fine gold set on red ; fierce were they, haughty and cruel, to signify that like them the King is dreadful to his enemies. For his bite is slight to none who inflame his anger ; and yet, towards such as seek his friendship or submit to his power, his kindness is soon rekindled."

The brass to Sir Simon de Felbrigge has preserved an example of the Royal Banner of Richard II, to whom Sir Simon was banner-bearer. It shows the Royal Arms, *Quarterly France Ancient and England*, impaled with those of the Confessor (Plate XXVII, 2).

The banner was the ensign of the banneret himself and of his own followers and retainers, and also of any military division under his command. Persons of high rank appear sometimes to have displayed banners bearing insignia altogether different from their shields of arms. Thus Simon de Montfort, Earl of Leicester (temp. Henry III), bears on his shield, *Gules a lion rampant, queue fourché, argent*, and as his banner, *Per pale indented argent and gules*, this referring to the honour of Hinckley.

In the Middle Ages banners were used at sea as well as on land, and it was customary to emblazon the sails of a ship with armorial insignia. The illustration (417) shows the sail, *Quarterly Newburgh and Beauchamp*, of the Earl of Warwick's ship.

417. Sail of the
EARL OF WARWICK's ship

418. Seal of JOHN, EARL OF HUNTINGDON,
Admiral of England, 1436

Another example is provided by the seal of John Holland, Earl of Huntingdon, Admiral of England, Ireland and Aquitaine, 1436. Here the sail bears the arms, *England with a bordure of France*. The ship has a nautical pennon of ample size at the mast-head (418).

Towards the close of the Plantagenet period, and in Tudor times, banners were frequently used for the display of the quarterings (sometimes numerous) to which the bearer was entitled, and they were represented with one or both supporters holding the staves, and were sometimes ensigned with coronets.

Arms are still displayed upon banners. The Royal Banner (now commonly misnamed " Royal Standard ") flies over the place where the Sovereign is in residence. Armorial banners are seen flying over Colleges of Oxford and Cambridge on occasions, and some armigerous bodies consistently fly a banner of their arms over their premises. Many municipal corporations and other local authorities possess banners, and any armigerous person may have one, though its private use is not now common. Quarterings (but not impalements), marks of cadency, and differences are included on banners as on shields of arms. Crests, badges, and supporters and other accessories have no place on a banner, though in the 17th century complete achievements were sometimes displayed on banners.

The STANDARD, in use in the reign of Edward III and in especial favour in Tudor times, was a narrow and tapering (sometimes swallow-tailed) flag, always of considerable length, and the higher the rank of its owner the longer it was. It appears to have been used solely for the purpose of pageantry, and particularly for the display of badges and livery colours. Early standards were usually divided along their length into two tinctures, and were charged with various devices without regard to any special rule. Edward III had a standard displaying St. George and the Dragon, and another with the Royal Arms against the staff and the tail party azure and gules and charged with gold fleurs-de-lis and lions. The Earl of Warwick placed the cross of St. George at the head of his standard, and the fly was semé of his badge of the bear and ragged staff. Henry of Bolingbroke had a swallow-tailed standard with St. George's cross at the head, the fly argent and azure (the Lancastrian colours), and charged with the white swan of Bohun, red roses of Lancaster, gold stocks of trees for Woodstock, and the fox's brush (415).

Mottoes were sometimes introduced bendwise across standards. In a Book of Standards, c. 1532, at the College of Arms, an example of Edward IV shows the cross of St. George and the fly per fess azure and gules, fringed argent and vert, bearing a lion passant guardant argent royally crowned, the motto *Dieu et mon Droyt*, and six white and six red roses, all irradiated. Another standard of Edward IV is semé of white roses, and a third has one large white rose en soleil and eight small ones. Henry V displayed his chained antelope on a standard argent and azure semé of roses gules.

Except when they bore royal devices, the English standards of the Tudor period always had the cross of St. George at their head; then came the device, badge or crest of its owner, with his motto. They did not bear the coat of arms. Today, however, the standards, which with badges may be granted to any armigerous persons, display the bearer's arms next to the staff, and his badge (sometimes accompanied by his crest) on the fly, which may be of one tincture or party, and is crossed diagonally by the motto (Plate XII, 10). A modern instance is the standard of the Borough of Hertford, depicted on the grant of a badge made in 1925. This bears at the head the arms, *Argent, in base three bars azure and in chief a stag lodged proper;* the fly is white crossed by two

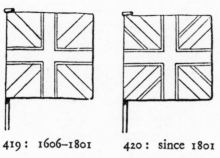

419 : 1606–1801   420 : since 1801

THE UNION FLAG

diagonal bands of blue, and thereon in gold letters, *Pro Hertfordae :*
Honore ; in each of the three divisions made by the motto is the badge :
within a chaplet of roses gules, a stag's head affronté proper, between the attires
an escutcheon or charged with three chevronels gules ; the standard is fringed
with white and blue.

The NATIONAL BANNERS of England, Scotland and Ireland bear
respectively the cross of St. George and the saltires of St. Andrew and
St. Patrick. The cross of St. George and the saltire of St. Andrew
were combined in 1606 to form the first " Union Jack," which was
declared to be the National Ensign of Great Britain by James I (419).
This was superseded in 1801, on the Union with Ireland, by the second
Union Flag, in which the saltire of St. Patrick was incorporated with
the other two devices (420). From the heraldic viewpoint the flag is
interesting because it represents a return to the earlier practice of compounding insignia, rendered possible in this case by the simplicity of the
three components. The result is far more effective and distinctive than
would have been obtained had the cross of St. George and the saltires
of St. Andrew and St. Patrick been quartered together, as the coats of
England, Scotland and Ireland are quartered in the Royal Arms. It
should be noted that the white fimbriation of the red cross represents
the argent field of the banner of St. George ; the blue field and the
broad sections of the white diagonals constitute the banner of St.
Andrew ; and the narrow white diagonals represent the white field of
St. Patrick's saltire. As St. Andrew's insignia take precedence of those
of St. Patrick, the flag must be so flown that at the corner nearest the
head of the staff the broad white stripe is above the narrow one.

There were formerly three ensigns—the red, the white and the blue

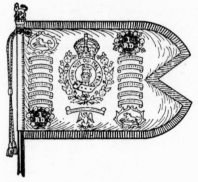

421. Guidon

—originally charged in the canton with the cross of St. George on white, and later with the combined crosses of the Union. These were formerly the insignia of the three squadrons of the Royal Navy, but in the course of time their form and function have changed. There are now five ensigns :

THE WHITE ENSIGN : the Cross of St. George with the Union in the canton—distinctive of the Royal Navy.

THE ROYAL AIR FORCE ENSIGN : Air Force blue, a canton of the Union, and on the fly the red, white and blue target which is the distinguishing mark of R.A.F. aircraft.

THE BLUE ENSIGN : blue with a canton of the Union ; distinctive of the public offices, the Consular Service, the Colonial Governments and their ships, etc.

THE RED ENSIGN : red with a canton of the Union ; the national colours for all ships belonging to any British subject.

THE CIVIL AIR ENSIGN : Air Force blue charged with a dark blue cross edged with white and having the Union in the canton ; this may be flown by any British aircraft registered in the United Kingdom, and at licensed aerodromes, etc., in the United Kingdom.

MILITARY FLAGS in use today consist of standards, guidons and colours. Military standards (Plate XXVII) approximate to the banner of heraldry, being nearly square ; these are carried by the Household Cavalry and the Dragoon Guard Regiments. They are crimson and in the case of the Life Guards and the Royal Horse Guards they bear the Royal Achievement, the Dragoon Guards bearing various other devices.

The guidon (421), borne by the Dragoon Regiments, is also crimson and has a slit in the fly. All battalions of the Foot Guards and the Infantry of the Line have a " pair of colours "—the Sovereign's Colour and the Regimental Colour. In the Brigade of Guards all the Sovereign's Colours are crimson and bear battle honours ; the Regimental Colours take the form of the flag of the Union, also charged with battle honours ; in addition, each company has a badge and a company colour. In the case of the Infantry of the Line, the Sovereign's Colour is the Union Flag ; the colour of the Regimental Colour follows that of the facings of the Regiment. Both bear battle honours (Plate XIII).

ECCLESIASTICAL FLAGS : The flags, gonfanons, banners and so forth used in connection with religious services and soldarities are not properly heraldic nor are the banners of attributed arms of saints which are flown from some churches. There is, however, a proper flag for use by Anglican Churches. It was approved in 1938 by a Warrant of the Earl Marshal, in the terms following : " The Banner or Flag proper to be flown upon any Church within the Provinces of Canterbury and York to be the Cross of St. George and in the first quarter an escutcheon of the Arms of the See in which such Church is ecclesiastically situate." For example : the proper flag to be flown in the diocese of Rochester is the flag of St. George with, in the canton, a shield of the arms : *Argent on a saltire gules an escallop or* (421 *a*).

NEW FLAGS

A new chapter in the history of flags was written in 1960 when the Queen adopted a personal flag, just before her visit to India and Pakistan. Although there was officially no connection between the adoption

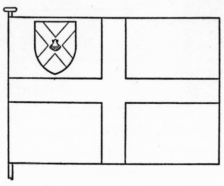

421 *a*. DIOCESE OF ROCHESTER

of this flag and the visit, clearly this flag was intended for use in place of the Royal Banner, when its use might give the wrong impression. It was never intended that the personal flag should supplant the Royal Banner, but whereas the Royal Banner is associated with the United Kingdom, the new flag is entirely personal to the Queen, and is not associated with any one country of the Commonwealth, of which the Queen is the Head.

The flag consists of the Queen's initial E ensigned with a Royal Crown (symbolic of her personal dignity) within a chaplet of gold roses on a square blue flag fringed with gold (421 *b*).

For visits to other Commonwealth Countries the Queen has adopted a special flag consisting of the arms of the Government of the country in question with the central motif on her personal flag over all. For example the Queen's personal flag for use in Jamaica consists of a banner of the arms of Jamaica (403) with the motif from her personal flag in the fess point (421 *c*).

By a Royal Warrant dated 21st May 1968 the Queen assigned to the Prince of Wales a personal flag for use in Wales. The Warrant states that it is " to be flown and used in Wales by His Royal Highness upon all occasions." The flag is blazoned *Quarterly or and gules, four lions passant guardant counterchanged* (the arms of the Principality) *over all an inescutcheon vert charged with the coronet of the Prince of Wales* (421 *d*).

The Welsh Flag, as distinct from the Prince's Flag, shows the Welsh

421 *b*. THE QUEEN's Personal
Flag

421 *c*. THE QUEEN's Personal Flag for use in
Jamaica

421 *d.* PRINCE OF WALES' Personal Flag for use in Wales

dragon in red on a field *per fess vert and argent.* This flag was approved by the Queen in 1959. In a reply to a Parliamentary Question on 23rd February 1959 the Minister of Housing and Local Government and Minister for Welsh Affairs (Mr. Henry Brooke, later Lord Brooke of Cumnor) stated : " I now have it in command from the Queen to say that Her Majesty has been pleased to direct that in future only the Red Dragon on a green and white flag and not the flag carrying the augmented Royal Badge " (see page 218 ; the flag referred to was approved in 1953 but it never became popular) " shall be flown on Government buildings in Wales and, where appropriate, in London . . . the augmented Royal Badge will, of course, continue in use for other purposes."

The subject of flags in general is too large in itself to be dealt with in a book primarily devoted to heraldry. The reader is referred to *Flags of the World*, edited by E. M. C. Barraclough and William Crampton (Frederick Warne and Co., 1978).

The College of Arms will also take note of other, not strictly heraldic flags, by entering them in a series of records entitled *Miscellaneous Enrollments* (not to be confused with *Miscellaneous Collections*, which are not official records). For example, the flag of the Royal British Legion and the car pennant of the Master Gunner within the Tower of London have both been put on permanent record.

422. THE DUKE OF NORFOLK,
EARL MARSHAL OF ENGLAND:
Shield at the College of Arms

423. COLLEGE OF ARMS

CHAPTER XXIII

THE HERALDS AND THEIR FUNCTIONS

BECAUSE the medieval heralds were entrusted with the task of bearing messages between Sovereigns and Princes, and especially between opposed armies, they have come to be regarded (in Boutell's words) as " officially the descendants and representatives of the Royal Messengers and Ambassadors of Antiquity." It has, however, been shown [1] that the carrying of messages was not the original function of the heralds in the Middle Ages. Heralds are first found in the 12th century as officers connected with tournaments. They proclaimed and conducted the event; and to be able to identify and announce the champions they had to have a wide knowledge of armorial devices. Out of these duties their later functions developed. From carrying word of a forthcoming joust, it was but a step to carrying a message of defiance or statecraft. The conduct of tournaments led naturally to the

[1] A. R. Wagner, Richmond Herald: *Heralds and Heraldry in the Middle Ages.*

marshalling of State ceremonies and pageantry. As men well-versed in armory, they were entrusted with the task of registering and compiling records of heraldic arms, and inevitably they had to concern themselves with genealogy in connection with cadency and the marshalling of arms.

The early heralds were "free-lances," employed for a particular occasion; but by the 14th century, kings and the great nobles had heralds in their permanent service, and gave them their own names, or those of their castles or badges, like Chandos, Windsor and Falcon—a custom which survives in the titles of the present-day heralds and pursuivants. As the heralds developed a sense of professional standing and dignity, different grades appeared among them; the assistant, aspiring to the office of herald, being termed pursuivant, while the senior herald was styled King of Heralds or King of Arms. In the fifteenth century we hear of chapters of heralds being held. The Kings of Arms were usually charged with the supervision of a province or march, e.g. Norroy, Herald-King of the North, and Clarenceux in the South of England. With the decline of feudalism the employment of heralds by nobles came to an end, and heralds are found only in the Royal service.

Since disputes concerning armorial matters were dealt with in the Court of Chivalry, over which the Constable and Marshal presided, the heralds acquired a standing in this court, and in due course the Marshal (styled Earl Marshal since 1386) became recognized as the Officer of State to whom the heralds were responsible. In Scotland, however, the Lyon King of Arms became independent of the Constable and Marshal at an early date, and he held his office immediately of the Sovereign, with judicial powers and status which he still possesses, constituting the Court of the Lord Lyon as a Court of Law.

The Court of Chivalry still exists. After an interval of 223 years it sat in 1954, when Lord Goddard, as Surrogate for the Earl Marshal, held that the Court still has jurisdiction to deal with complaints relating to the usurpation of armorial bearings. The present surrogate is Mr G. D. Squibb, Q.C., Norfolk Herald Extraordinary, who was appointed on 1st December 1976.

In England the Sovereign's authority in armorial matters was clearly exhibited in 1418, when Henry V issued a writ to the Sheriffs of certain counties proclaiming that no man should assume a coat of arms unless he possessed or ought to possess one in right of his ancestors or by the gift of some person competent to grant it, excepting from this prohibition those who had fought at Agincourt.

In 1415 a principal King of Arms was appointed with the title of Garter, associated particularly with the Order of the Garter but empowered also to exercise a general supervision over the other Herald Kings. In 1484 the Kings, Heralds and Pursuivants, while remaining officers of the Royal Household, were incorporated by Charter, and granted a messuage with its appurtenances, called "Coldearber" in the Parish of All Saints the Less in the City of London.

It was the duty of the Kings of Arms to survey and record the bearings and descent of the armigerous persons in their provinces and to correct arms irregularly used. In due course they began to devise arms for other persons of sufficient standing to bear them, and early in the 15th century they were definitely granting arms. At first their authority to do so was somewhat nebulous, but from early in the 16th century their patents of appointment have specifically conferred on them the power to grant arms.

Occasionally in the 15th century, and with some regularity in the following two centuries, the heralds made periodical circuits of various parts of the country, under the authority of Royal Commissions, to inquire into all matters connected with the bearing of arms, the use of styles of worship, to correct arms unlawfully borne or usurped, to collect information, and to draw up authoritative records. The Officer of Arms conducting a Visitation was empowered "to put down or otherwise deface at his discretion" all unlawful arms, crests, cognizances, and devices, "in plate, jewels, paper, parchment, windows, gravestones and monuments or elsewhere wheresoever they be set or placed." He was also to make infamous by proclamation any person who unlawfully and without just authority had "usurped and taken upon him any name or title of honour or dignity as esquire, gentleman or other." A person summoned to appear before an Officer of Arms might satisfy him that the arms he bore were lawfully his, by grant to or ancient usage by an ancestor, or if he could not do this he might either have the arms rectified and recorded or he might disclaim all pretence and title thereto in the future.

There is evidence that some local visitations took place in the 15th century, but from 1530 they were held at intervals of about thirty years. The latest Commission of Visitation bears the date 13th May, 1686. Most records compiled on these occasions are preserved at the College of Arms, and a large proportion of hereditary armorial bearings is borne on their authority.

In 1555, the former London house of the Earls of Derby, between St. Paul's and the River Thames, was assigned to the Heralds by Charter, " to the end that the Officers of the College might be enabled to assemble together and consult and agree amongst themselves, for the good of their faculty, and that the Records and Rolls might be more safely and conveniently deposited." The house was destroyed in the Great Fire of 1666, but the records were saved. The present building (in Queen Victoria Street) was erected on the site of the former house.

The present establishment of the College of Arms (or Heralds' College) consists, under the Earl Marshal (the Duke of Norfolk, who is not himself a member of the corporation), of three Kings of Arms—Garter, Clarenceux, and Norroy and Ulster ; six Heralds—Lancaster, Somerset, Chester, Richmond, Windsor and York ; and four Pursuivants—Rouge Dragon, Rouge Croix, Portcullis and Bluemantle. From time to time officers of arms who are not members of the corporation of the College of Arms are appointed by warrant under the Queen's sign manual. The duties of these officers, styled "extraordinary," are purely ceremonial and the appointments are generally made *honoris causa*. Frequently such officers are appointed at the time of a coronation and in many cases people so appointed become officer-in ordinary when vacancies occur. Since the last coronation the policy would appear to be to appoint people to the extraordinary offices of Norfolk and Arundel Heralds and Fitzalan Pursuivant when such offices become vacant. The titles of extraordinary officers are generally taken from those of the Earl Marshal. Badges were assigned to the three extraordinary offices mentioned above in 1959. Norfolk Herald was assigned two white ostrich feathers in saltire, each charged with a gold chain laid along the quill ; Arundel was granted a white horse holding a sprig of oak in its mouth (the Duke of Norfolk's sinister supporter), and Fitzalan's badge is an old badge of the family of that name, a sprig of green oak bearing two golden acorns.

In 1963 an appointment was made to the office of Wales Herald Extraordinary. This title had not been employed since the end of the 14th century. A badge for Wales Herald has been approved by the

Queen and was recorded at the College of Arms on 13th October 1967 (423 *a*).

In Scotland, the office of the Lord Lyon King of Arms is at H.M. Register House at Edinburgh. There are three Heralds—Marchmont, Rothesay and Albany; and three Pursuivants—Ormond, Unicorn and Carrick.

The heraldic authority in Northern Ireland was Ulster King of Arms, but since the death of the last holder of this office it has been united to that of Norroy. In the Republic of Ireland, the heraldic functions formerly carried out by Ulster are exercised by an officer designated as " Chief Herald of Ireland."

The Right to bear Arms

Ancient heraldic writings and usages are sometimes quoted in support of the view that it is still legal and permissible for a man to assume armorial bearings at will, as was undoubtedly the case in the early days of heraldry. This view deliberately overlooks the facts (summarized above) that more than 500 years ago the Crown assumed the full control of armorial bearings, and has ever since exercised it through Officers of Arms appointed for the purpose.

423 *a*. Badge of WALES HERALD EXTRAORDINARY

Since at latest 1418, it has been impossible to acquire a legal title to armorial bearings by any other method than inheritance according to the laws of arms, or a grant or confirmation of arms from the duly constituted authorities. To bear arms by inheritance, one must be able to prove, to the satisfaction of the Officers of Arms, legitimate male descent from some person who received a grant of arms, or to whom the right to bear arms was at some time confirmed. Conjectural descent is inadmissible. A person who bears a device of heraldic appearance invented by himself or an ancestor, and neither granted nor confirmed by the Kings of Arms, is in fact not armigerous, and the device is not a legal coat of arms. A man who makes use of a genuine coat of arms to which he cannot prove a right according to the laws of arms (even though it be that of a family from which he is descended other than in the legitimate male line) is not in fact a gentleman of coat armour. He can, of course, petition the Earl Marshal for his Warrant to the Kings of Arms to grant him armorial ensigns.

In Scotland the ancient Laws of Arms have been reinforced by statutory provisions establishing the Public Register of All Arms and Bearings, with penalties for the use of unregistered arms or infringement of the rights of registered proprietors. Arms are treated as incorporeal heritable property, held of the Crown in strict entail. They descend of right only to the heir male. Younger sons have no right to bear the arms of their father until they have been re-matriculated with such marks of cadency as the Lord Lyon may determine. The coat thus differenced again descends to the heir male, and his younger brothers must again re-matriculate it with further difference.

In Northern Ireland, arms descend to all legitimate male descendants, and to establish the right to bear arms a man must show descent in the legitimate male line from someone to whom arms have been granted or confirmed. Owing to the infrequency of Visitations in Ireland, and consequent incompleteness of records, Ulster King of Arms had power to grant certificates of confirmations of arms to persons who proved to his satisfaction that their ancestors in the male line had borne the same arms for at least three generations or before 1800. In the Republic of Ireland, the Chief Herald works on the same principles.

424. SHAKESPEARE

GRANTS OF ARMS

All grants and confirmations of arms are formally and regularly recorded, with a full emblazonment of the insignia, at the College or Offices of Arms. Confirmation is the procedure adopted in the case of a claim to bear arms by some uncertain right and title, which is duly set forth and approved, and thereafter legalized by the Crown.

In the 16th and 17th centuries grants were couched in extravagant terms characteristic of the times. An interesting example is the grant to

John Shakespeare, William Shakespeare's father, in 1596. Two draft copies of the original grant are preserved at the College of Arms. The following transcript is made from the later, words in brackets having been supplied from the earlier copy :

TO ALL and singuler Noble and Gentelmen of what estate [or] degree bearing arms to whom these presentes shall come, William Dethick alias Garter principall King of Armes sendethe greetinges. Know yee that, whereas by the authoritie and auncyent pryveleges perteyning to my office from the Quenes most excellent Mat^e and by her highnesse most noble and victorious progenitors, I am to take generall notice and record and to make declaration and testemonie for all causes of arms and matters of Gentrie thoroughe out all her Majestes Kingdoms, Domynions, Principalites, Isles, and Provinces, To th'end that, as manie gentelmen, by theyre auncyent names of families, kyndredes and descentes, have and enjoye certeyne enseignes and cotes of arms, So it is verie expedient in all ages that some men for theyr valeant factes, magnanimite, vertu, dignites, and desertes, may use and beare suche tokens of honour and worthinesse, whereby theyre name and good fame may be the better knowen and divulged, and theyre children and posterite in all vertu (to the service of theyre Prynce and Contrie) encouraged. Wherefore being solicited and by credible report informed that John Shakespeare of Stratford uppon Avon in the counte of Warwik, whose parentes and late antecessors [1] were for theyre faithefull and va[leant service advaunced and rewarded by the most prudent] prince King Henry the Seventh of [famous memorie, sythence which tyme they have continewed at] those partes, being of good reputacion [and credit ; and that the] said John hathe maryed [Mary, daughter and one of the heyrs of Robert Arden, of Wilmcote, in the said] counte, esquire. [2] In consideration whereof, and for the encouragement of his posterite, to whom such Blazon [or Atchevement] by the auncyent custome of the lawes of armes maie descend, I the said Garter King of Armes have assigned, graunted and by these presentes confirmed this shield or cote of arms, viz. Gould, on a bend sables a speare of the first, steeled argent ; and for his crest or cognizance a falcon, his winges displayed, argent, standing on a wrethe of his coullors, supporting a speare gould, steeled as aforesaid, sett upon a helmett with mantelles and tasselles as hath ben accustomed and dothe more playnely appeare depicted on this margent. Signefieng hereby, and by the authorite of my office aforesaid ratifieng, that it shalbe lawfull for the sayd John Shakespeare gent. and for his cheldren, yssue and posterite (at all tymes and places convenient) to bear and make demonstracion of the said Blazon or Atche ˜ement uppon theyre Shieldes, Targets, Escucheons, Cotes of arms, Pennons, Guydons, Ringes, Edefices, Buyldinges, Utensiles, Lyveries, Tombes or Monumentes, or otherwise, for all lawfull warrlyke factes or

---

[1] *Above the word* antecessors *is written* Grandfather.
[2] Gent. *was first written, and it is altered to* esquire.

civile use and exercises, according to the lawes of armes, without let or interruption of any other person or persons for use or bearing the same. In witnesse and perpetuall remembrance hereof I have hereunto subscribed my name, and fastened the seale of my office endorzed with the signett of my armes, At the Office of Armes, London, the xx. daye of October, the xxxviij. yeare of the reigne of our Soveraigne Lady Elizabeth, by the grace of God Quene of England, France, and Ireland, Defender of the Faythe, etc. 1596.

The following is an example of a confirmation or record of arms, dated 1606 :

Theis are the auncient Armes and Creast, belonging to the name and famely of Leechforde in the County of Surrey, descended from the Leechfords in Buckinghamshire. Which at the request of Sr Richard Leechforde of Shelwood in the County of Surrey Knight, I Will'm Segar Garter Principall King of Armes have blasoned, and sett forth in coullors, according as they are here depicted in the margent. Viz. [here follows a written blazon] Testifying hereby the saide armoryes to belong vnto the saide Sr Richard Leechford and to his yssue, to vse, beare, and shewe forth at all tymes, and in all places, at their free lib'ty and pleasure. In Witnes wherof . . . etc.

Arms are normally granted to a man and to his descendants but, by arrangement with the Kings of Arms this limitation may be extended to include the other descendants of the grantee's father, of his grandfather and, in certain circumstances, of even more distant ancestors. The procedure is for the applicant for arms to ask one of the Officers of Arms to act for him. Provided the applicant is a worthy person, the herald acting for him will prepare a Memorial or petition to the Earl Marshal. This memorial, which the applicant signs, prays the Earl Marshal to direct his warrant to the Kings of Arms for their granting and assigning him arms. It is important to appreciate that the prayer is not for any particular coat of arms, but such arms as the Kings of Arms shall think fit and proper to grant. This means that whilst, in accordance with ancient practice, the wishes of the grantee are always considered, this is an act of grace on the part of the Kings of Arms. When a design has been agreed upon, it will be submitted to the Kings of Arms who, if they find it unique and heraldically acceptable, will agree to grant. The Letters Patent are then prepared, enrolled in the records of the College and handed to the grantee. The same procedure is adopted in the case of corporations, the chairman of the governing body signing the Memorial on its behalf. The fees payable on grants of arms are laid down by the Earl Marshal from time to time. In 1825 the fee on a personal grant was fixed at £76 10s : and was not raised until 1936 when it went up to £81 10s. It has since been revised several times to keep pace with mounting inflation, the last occasion being with effect from 1st January 1981. For details of the principal fees at present pertaining see page 295.

Although arms cannot be granted to foreign nationals the Kings of Arms may grant honorary armorial bearings to them on the same conditions as they grant to a British subject, except that the grantee must be descended in the direct, legitimate male line from a subject of the Crown and must enter in the records of the College of Arms a pedigree proving this descent. In the case of United States citizens, this usually means establishing a descent from someone, no matter of what racial origin, who was living in America before the War of Independence. Naturally, such arms cannot be protected in America, unless the grantee has recourse to the protection afforded by the federal copyright laws, but the grantee can be certain that a similar coat has never been granted before and never will be granted in future to any person or institution over whom the English Kings of Arms have armorial jurisdiction.

DEVISALS OF ARMS

Some years ago, an American town wanted to be granted arms by the English Kings of Arms, but, as the Queen's Writ did not run in the United States, such a grant could not be made. However, an arrangement was reached whereby the Kings of Arms were empowered, by an Earl Marshal's Warrant dated 25th July 1960, to devise, that is design and record, arms for towns in the United States. By another Warrant dated 2nd October 1961, the Kings of Arms were further authorized to devise arms for bodies corporate in the Republic of South Africa (South Africa became an independent republic and seceded from the Commonwealth on 31st May 1961). Then, by another Warrant dated 1st February 1962, the permission to devise arms in the United States was extended to include corporate bodies other than towns. Before a devisal is made in the United States, the consent and approval of the Governor of the sovereign state in which the devisal is to be made is always obtained.

Such devisals are made on the same terms as grants of arms. Like all other new coats, they must be unique and, after they have been devised, they are recorded and thereafter are never again devised nor granted.

The document by which arms are devised is similar in appearance to an ordinary grant, but the wording is, of course, quite different. The arms of the Sovereign, the Earl Marshal and the College of Arms do not appear at the head of the patent, but they may be replaced by either the arms, or just the crowns of the Kings of Arms. The wording simply states that the Kings of Arms, having been requested by a certain body corporate, in a certain state, to devise its arms, and the Governor of the said state having signified his approval, they are pleased to devise certain arms, which are then blazoned in the usual way. The arms are painted in the margin and the document is signed and sealed by all three Kings of Arms.

Since devisals were instituted they have increased in popularity in the United States. Between 1960 and 1970 only seven devisals were made but in the first six years of the seventies there were fourteen devisals. Of these, many had beautifully decorated borders and one was written in Latin. In 1976, history was made when the Queen handed over a devisal to the Commonwealth of Virginia, of the arms used by the Company of Virginia Merchants, to the Governor of

424 a.

Virginia at Charlottesville. The arms (424 a) were designed for the Company of Virginia Merchants (there is a trick of the arms in the British Museum) but they appear never to have been granted. Later they were used by the Colony of Virginia. As will be seen the arms contain elements of the royal arms as well as four royal crowns. For this reason the devisal was only made after the Queen had signified that she was happy with this use of royal insignia.

GENEALOGIES

The tracing and recording of pedigrees form an important part of the heralds' duties, but genealogical research is too large a subject to be dealt with adequately in a book devoted primarily to heraldic insignia. We must be content with general observations.

To the student of armory, genealogy is sure to be a matter of interest, and he needs no persuasion of its value. The converse processes of tracing the ancestry or the descendants of some person in whom he is interested both yield much of historical interest. Indeed, some knowledge of genealogy is necessary to an understanding of various constitutional and historical matters.

Genealogy is not, however, entirely a matter of the ancestry, descents and alliances of royalty and the nobility. Much of the work of the present-day heralds in this field is in connection with families of humble background and associations. Here let me make the point I have already made about armorial bearings : genealogy is not a matter of snobbery. It should be entered into not with some preconception, or hope of a noble background, but in a spirit of scientific enquiry that aims at ascertaining the facts, and will accept the facts ascertained. Research may lead you into the sphere of court and castle, where family history has contacts with great men and great events ; or it may, with no less real interest, lead you by farm and forge, where you may find it touching on those deep social and economic or perhaps religious movements which form the true history of the people. One can have as much pride of ancestry in a village Hampden as in a baron of Magna Carta. Indeed, most people in Great Britain are descended from both, and therein lies the unity and strength of our society.

It is not within the scope of this book to deal in detail with the procedure of the heralds regarding the tracing and recording of pedigrees, or the fees payable in connection therewith. Those who require such information with a view to personal enquiries and applications should approach the appropriate Officers of Arms. They can be confident of a courteous and helpful reception.

The meetings and literature of The Heraldry Society are valuable to those who are interested (but not necessarily expert) in the subject. The headquarters of the Society are at 28 Museum Street, London, W.C.1.

425. Counter-seal of THOMAS DE BEAUCHAMP,
3rd EARL OF WARWICK, 1344 (see no. 6)

CHAPTER XXIV

HERALDIC AUTHORITIES AND SOURCES

ROLLS OF ARMS AND MANUSCRIPTS

A number of vellum rolls or manuscript books containing a record of armorial bearings, blazoned, painted or tricked, have come down to us. The oldest was compiled about 1264. Some of them record the arms of those present at a particular battle or tournament, such as the Siege of Caerlaverock, 1300, and the Battle of Boroughbridge, 1322 ; others are a more ambitious compilation of the arms of Sovereigns, Princes, Nobles, Knights and Esquires of which the recorder had knowledge; others again relate to the arms of persons connected with a particular locality.

271

There are also heraldic records known as ordinaries of arms in which various coats are grouped together according to the principal charges, e.g. all those bearing lions in one section, all with crosses in another, and so on. These were presumably compiled to enable a particular coat to be found and identified.

Another class of document is that which is not primarily heraldic, but is an historical or other record decorated with shields of arms in the margin, such as Matthew Paris's *Chronica Maiora*, in which the shields were done between 1217 and 1259.

A further important documentary source of information is the record made by the heralds on the occasion of their Visitations.

A list of Rolls of Arms and other important sources in this class appears in Sir Anthony Wagner's *Catalogue of English Mediaeval Rolls of Arms*, 1950. Some of them have been printed in *Archaeologia*, *The Genealogist*, and other publications. *Some Feudal Coats of Arms*, by J. Foster (1902), is a compilation from the principal Rolls.

ARCHITECTURE AND MONUMENTS

The heraldry and Gothic architecture of England arose and flourished together. We learn much of early heraldry from the sculptured and painted work in the Cathedrals, especially the Cloisters at Canterbury, Westminster Abbey and Hall, St. Albans Abbey, King's College Chapel at Cambridge, St. George's Chapel at Windsor, many of the college buildings at Oxford and Cambridge, and parish churches such as those of Great Yarmouth and Fotheringhay.

Of especial importance is the noble collection of more than 800 shields of arms, dating from the 15th century onwards, in the vaulting of the Cloisters at Canterbury. These have been cleaned and re-emblazoned in recent years, and a record has been published by the Friends of the Cathedral.

Equally important are the stall-plates of the Knights of the Garter in their Chapel at Windsor, to which several references have been made in earlier chapters.

Many monuments in stone and brass are rich in armory, and give innumerable examples of heraldic practice at different periods including the various ways of marshalling arms, the employment of badges, the design and treatment of accessories, and the use of heraldry on armour and costume. Funeral hatchments (referred to in detail in Chapter XII)

426. Seal of
HUMPHREY DE BOHUN,
EARL OF HEREFORD, 1320

427. Seal of
WILLIAM DE BOHUN,
EARL OF NORTHAMPTON,
1350

428. Seal of
JOHN, LORD BARDOLF

are important sources of information regarding the particular period when they were used. There is scarcely an ancient church in this country which does not contain some tomb, tablet, hatchment or window which deserves the attention of the student of heraldry.

SEALS

The art of seal engraving attained a high standard in England in the reign of Edward III. Figures of every kind, architectural, heraldic and other devices, with many varieties of accessory and legend, were introduced into early seals, and in particular they are a valuable source of information with regard to the heraldry of their period. From the reign of Edward the Confessor, the Royal Seals of England form a series of surpassing interest and value.

The use of seals in England became general within a few years of the Norman Conquest, and early in the 12th century they were universally adopted for the purpose of authenticating documents.

Signet rings were made either by engraving the design on gems, agates or other hard stones, or by cutting it on the metal of the ring. The larger seals (and many are of considerable size) were engraved on gold, silver, latten or brass, or steel. Jet and some other materials were sometimes used.

In form, seals were either circular, or pointed ovals, the latter being generally adopted by ecclesiastics, but not restricted to them. The Royal Seals are round. In rare instances seals are lozenge-shaped, triangular, or cut to the form of a shield.

The impressions were made in wax of various colours—green, red, different shades of brown, a dull yellow, or white. The more important seals were commonly impressed on both sides, the wax impressions being appended to documents, and not stamped upon them. Consequently two dies or matrices, each having its own device and legend, were employed, and these were termed the seal and counter-seal; but the double impression constituted the single seal, its two sides being distinguished as the obverse and the reverse.

In the 15th century it became customary to cover the wax with a layer of paper to preserve it, or to encircle the impression with a "fender" formed of rushes, leaves or plaited paper. Fenders have been found attached to seals as early as 1380.

Sovereigns, and other persons of high rank, had in addition to their official seal a personal or private one, termed *secretum*. The same person sometimes used more than one secretum, and where he held several offices he used a separate seal for each office.

Seals were evidently the delight of the early heralds, and seal-heraldry is accordingly heraldry thoroughly in earnest. Such achievements of arms as abound in seals, so complete, so spirited, so full of heraldic life and energy, rarely occur elsewhere. The history of heraldry is written in seals with accuracy and copious richness of illustration.

The Great Seals of England constitute an important chapter in historical heraldry. Every seal has two distinct designs. In one the Sovereign is represented on horseback, and in the other as enthroned. The mounted figures appear always to have been regarded as the obverse or seal, and those enthroned as the reverse or counter-seal. Until the time of John, the throne in these seals is a stool or chair with certain ornamental accessories. In the second seal of Henry III the royal seat becomes an elaborate Gothic throne, and the King rests each foot on a lion. Edward I copied his father's seal, but the design is better executed. The same seal was used by Edward II, with a castle of Castile added on each side of the throne.

Great improvements in design, including elaborate architectural enrichments, with peculiarly interesting heraldry, were introduced into the series of Great Seals made for Edward III. He began by placing two fleurs-de-lis (his mother being Isabella of France) above the castles in the seal of his father and grandfather. Then in October, 1327, he substituted for the old seal a new one of improved general design, with the fleurs-de-lis much more emphatic. In 1340 a seal appeared charged with two shields of *France Ancient and England quarterly* and with a lion seated on either side of the throne. After this, two Great Seals of Edward III were in use, sometimes concurrently—one by the King himself in which the legend runs, REX FRANCIE ET ANGLIE ; and the other, used in England when the King was absent in France, with the legend, REX ANGLIE ET FRANCIE. Another seal made in accordance with the Peace of Bretigny, 1360, omits the FRANCIE from the legend, but retains the quartered fleurs-de-lis in the shield as before. FRANCIE, however, resumes its original place before the close of the reign, and figures of the Madonna and Child, and St. George, were introduced in niches, with armed men, as though on guard, in the flanks of the seal.

Richard II and Henry IV merely substituted their own names for " Edvardus," and used the same seal as Edward III. In or about 1408, Henry IV added another seal, the largest and richest of all the medieval seals of England, in which the fleurs-de-lis are reduced to three in each quarter of the shield. Edward IV alternated the words of the legend with roses and fleurs-de-lis and diapered the ground of the obverse with roses and suns. Henry VII introduced a rose on a branch, and Henry VIII separated the words of his legend by alternate roses and fleurs-de-lis ; he added a fleur-de-lis and a lion to the obverse of his seal, and eventually he adopted a seal designed after the manner of the Renaissance, in which the Royal Arms appear encircled by the Garter.

The equestrian figures on the obverse of the Great Seals afford illustrations of arms and armour, and also of horse equipments. In the second seal of Richard I, the three lions of England for the first time make their appearance on the royal shield. Edward I places them on the bardings of his horse as well as upon his shield, but not on his surcoat ; and Edward III appears with a full display of royal blazonry on the appointments of his horse and his own person, including the royal crest on his helm. Subsequent seals reflect changes in armour and accoutrements. Henry VIII makes interesting use of one of his badges in the form of a greyhound running beside his horse. He also used a golden *bulla* which is notable because it displays on the reverse the Royal Arms encircled by the Collar of the Garter, five garter-encircled roses being shown, with the George pendant in the border.

Following her marriage with Philip of Spain, Mary adopted a seal showing on the obverse herself and her husband riding side by side, with her Royal Arms impaled by those of Spain, the ground being diapered with roses, fleurs-de-lis, castles and pomegranates. On the reverse, Philip and Mary are shown seated side by side on a throne with their impaled arms between them. Elizabeth I's seal is rich in badges, including a crowned rose, fleurs-de-lis and harp.

The Great Seals of subsequent monarchs show the changes in the Royal Arms already noticed (Chapter XIX). Charles I introduced a lion and unicorn to support banners of St. George and St. Andrew. On the third seal of Charles II the first Union Flag appears, and on the reverse the background to the equestrian figure consists of a view of London. The seal of William III and Mary generally resembles that of Philip and Mary, except the arms of the monarchs are not impaled. In Queen Anne's reign, symbolical figures of Piety and Justice were introduced supporting the Queen enthroned, and on the other side of the shield a departure was made by a representation of Britannia instead of the traditional equestrian figure.

The Hanoverian kings reverted to the equestrian tradition, while retaining the innovation of allegorical figures on the other side, e.g. in the case of George III they represent Justice, Peace, Learning, Strength, Victory and Plenty. Victoria and Edward VII introduced a representation of an ancient and a modern warship in the background to the equestrian figure, and George V was shown standing on the deck of a battleship. In the reign of George VI the Sovereign was represented on horseback on one side of the seal and enthroned on the other; this practice has been followed in the present reign.

The Great Seal of England adopted for the Commonwealth in 1649 showed on the obverse a map of England and Ireland with a fleet in the Channel, in chief the shield of St. George and in base the shield of Ireland. The reverse showed the House of Commons in session. The seal during the Protectorate contained the arms described in Chapter XIX.

From the detailed chapter devoted to seals in the early editions of this book, only a few further points can be selected for mention.

It has already been stated that supporters partly originated in the practice of early seal-engravers to introduce figures of animals (which were without doubt badges) on each side of either the shield or the crest.

Some of the most effective seals display the armorial insignia charged upon banners, instead of shields; thus the seal of Sir Henry Percy, eldest son of Henry, Earl of Northumberland, 1445, bears a lion holding a quartered banner of Percy and Lucy differenced with a label. One of the seals of Walter, Lord Hungerford, attached to a deed dated 1432, bears a helm and crest-coronet with a garb between two sickles for the crest, and below the helm a couché shield is charged with *Sable, two bars argent, in chief three plates,* for Hungerford; on either side of the shield is a large sickle, the well-known Hungerford badge, and above these sickles rise two banners, the dexter one bearing Heytesbury, *Per pale indented gules and vert, a chevron or,* and the sinister Hussey, *Barry of six ermine and gules* (336).

An interesting secretum is that of William Longespée, Earl of Salisbury (d. 1226), which is charged with his long sword and its belt. His seal bears the mounted figure of the Earl with his shield of six lioncels. Henry de Laci, Earl of Lincoln, 1272, has both seal and secretum charged with his lion rampant. The secretum of Henry, second son of Edmond, first Earl of Lancaster, bears *England differenced with an azure bendlet.* This adoption of a bendlet for cadency by a younger son shows a disinclination to multiply the differencing charges on labels.

Seals of the 13th, 14th and 15th centuries are particularly interesting when they bear mounted effigies of the princes, nobles and knights of the Middle Ages, with their surcoats, jupons or tabards or arms, their armorial shields and crested helms, and the bardings of their chargers also rich with heraldic devices (6).

Another very interesting class of seal is that which shows representations of the shipping of the time. In many of these there is little regard to proportion in the comparative sizes of the crews and of the ships that carry them, and also of these ships and the fish shown swimming beneath the keels. In some cases these vessels have arms displayed on the sails (418). The arms cover the entire area of the sails, making them " sails of arms," until in the 16th century shields of ample dimensions were charged upon the sails, as in the seal of Charles, Lord Howard of Effingham, Lord High Admiral of England, who encountered the Armada. In the seal of Thomas Beaufort, Duke of Exeter, an earlier High Admiral, c. 1416, the sail of the ship is charged over its entire surface with the arms of Beaufort; at the stern there is a banner of

France and England, and forward a banner bearing a cross. The seals of the Cinque Ports exhibit several curious ships, which display the Ports' banner of lions and ships dimidiated.

Among early Scottish heraldic seals of great interest must be noted the secretum of James I of Scotland, 1429, which bears the Royal Shield of Scotland ensigned with a crown of beautiful design, and supported by two lions rampant guardant, the earliest Scottish Royal Supporters. James V substituted for the lions *two unicorns argent royally gorged and chained or*. On his Garter-plate the crest is *a lion passant gules upon a coronet or, holding in his dexter paw a naked sword erect proper*, with the motto, *In my defence*. On his Great Seal, James V showed the lion in the crest passant guardant, as it was borne by James IV and his three immediate predecessors. The present crest of Scotland (Chapter XIX) was first adopted by James VI and I.

429. Seal of BEATRICE OF PORTUGAL, COUNTESS OF ARUNDEL AND SURREY, temp. Henry V

COINS

The heraldry of the coinage gives authoritative examples of the Royal Arms and Badges, and the form of the Crown, at various periods. In some coins the design has considerable interest apart from insignia.

Edward III's noble shows the figure of the King crowned and armed, his shield bearing *France Ancient and England quarterly*; he is standing in a ship which carries at its mast-head the pennon of St. George (430). This gave rise to the couplet:

Four things our Noble showeth unto me—
King, Ship, and Sword, and Power of the Sea.

The type was slightly modified in succeeding reigns. The rose noble had one or more roses added.

The angel bears on the obverse a figure of the Archangel Michael thrusting down the serpent, and on the reverse a ship with a cross for a mast, with the Royal Shield, a rose and an initial.

The George noble has a mounted St. George with the dragon. The sovereign has a figure of the reigning prince, generally enthroned, the reverse bearing the Royal Arms. Henry VIII's gold crown has a crowned rose and a crowned shield of arms with the Royal Cypher. The silver crown of Edward VI has the King on horseback and the Royal Shield, and that of Elizabeth substitutes a crowned bust for the equestrian figure. In both these silver coins the Royal Shield is surmounted by a floriated cross extending beyond the shield and dividing the legend into four parts. This arrangement of the cross was a prevailing type of the earlier coins; it first appears with the shield of arms on the shilling of Henry VII, and it was discontinued by James I. The crown of Charles II has four crowned shields of England, Scotland, France and Ireland arranged cross-wise, and this continued in the florin until the reign of George V, a second shield of England being substituted for France when the French coat was dropped from the Royal Arms.

In earlier editions of this book, unfavourable comment was made on modern coinage designs as compared with those of the past, the sovereign and the crown bearing Pistrucci's St. George being excepted; and Boutell expressed the hope that numismatic art might revive in this country. That hope has been realized in the issue of George V, 1927, and the coins of the later reigns. The "Scottish shilling," bearing the Royal Crest of Scotland, is particularly noteworthy from the heraldic standpoint.

430. Ship noble of Edward III

TILES

In the ornamentation of early encaustic or inlaid pavement tiles, shields of arms and various heraldic devices frequently occur; and in many examples they form decorative compositions in combination with foliage and traceries. Interesting heraldic tiles remain in the Cathedrals of Worcester, Gloucester, Exeter and St. Albans, and in many churches in various parts of the country.

CHAPTER XXV
HOW TO USE ARMS

THERE is much uncertainty as to how, when and where armorial bearings should be used, an uncertainty often arising from the fear of being considered ostentatious or vulgar. This nervousness sometimes inhibits people from ever using their arms, which is a pity as there is little point in having something that is meant to be used, but yet never, as it were, letting it see the light of day. In the use of arms, as in many other aspects of life, moderation, taste and custom combine to dictate the unwritten canons of acceptable behaviour. In committing these conventions to print I have no intention of laying down the law, for one man's meat may well be another's poison. I am simply attempting a resumé of what I believe to be a consensus of informed opinion.

WHAT MAY BE USED

Obviously the full achievement may be used, but there will be occasions when it will need to be simplified. This may be done in the following ways:

The helm and mantling can be omitted and the crest and wreath brought down to rest on the top of the shield.

The shield and supporters may be shown on their own, sans helm and crest.

The shield or crest may be shown on their own.

In all the above depictions the motto may be included or omitted. If the crest or arms are used on their own the motto may be shown either in a scroll beneath, or in a circlet environing the shield. The same is true of the badge, although badges are infrequently used in conjunction with the motto.

ARTISTIC DEPICTION

On the grant of arms the achievement will be painted in whatever way the artist considers apt and attractive; but, provided the blazon is correctly followed, there is nothing definitive about this representation. The only limit on the artist is the requirement for the heraldic objects to be recognisable, disposed and coloured in the manner detailed in the blazon; and the helm muſt be of ſteel with a closed visor. Apart from these reſtriċtions, the artiſt has considerable freedom. The shield itself may be of a variety of shapes—a heater (see page 19), a Tudor tilting shield, or some roccoco extravaganza—any version will do, so long as it is clearly a shield, however fanciful in design. A red lion rampant must be a lion, it muſt ramp and it muſt be red. But, providing it meets these specifications, its other features may vary widely: it may be fierce or docile, fat and contented or lean and hungry, smooth skinned or hirsute, and endowed with three, four or five claws on its paws. The helm, although it muſt be of ſteel with closed visor, may be a tilting helm, a pot helm, or of some elaborate Renaissance ſtyle. Similar licence is allowed in painting the mantling. This was originally a short cloak and it may be so depicted. On the other hand, it may be rendered quite fancifully in order to make a good design (which is why the ignorant often imagine it to be seaweed or foliage). In other words, one coat of arms may be drawn in a myriad different ways. It is in the versatility

431. The above representations of the arms of OXFORD UNIVERSITY are reproduced by kind permission of the Oxford University Press. They illuſtrate how the same coat of arms can be drawn in a variety of ways, yet each representation is heraldically accurate.

Stemming from this latitude in depiction that much of the charm of heraldry resides. By it an emblazonment can be subtly altered to suit the style of the object on which it is displayed. If arms are depicted on a piece of severely modern and functional architecture, they can be rendered in a suitably contemporary way; if shown in the centre of a highly ornamented plate they can be drawn to complement its design and balance its shape. I hope I have made this point clear without seeming to have over-laboured it; it is of prime importance if arms are to be displayed to the very best advantage.

Ways of Using Personal Arms

I list below some unexceptionable ways in which a man may use his arms. Obviously, what I write applies equally to a woman, subject only to the restrictions as to the way in which a woman may marshall her arms (p. 147):

On Stationery

At one time it was considered better to use any rather than printed stationery; but the cost of embossed stationery has now sent even the most aristocratic round the corner to a local jobbing printer. This decline of standards, patent in so many of the niceties of life, must be accepted and so, I suppose, must the printing rather than embossing of heraldic emblems. The full achievment is not used on private stationery, nor is it shown in colour. It is customary to use either arms, crest or badge with or without the motto. The representation is not normally depicted more than half an inch deep, although the nature of the device or complexity of the design may argue a slightly larger or smaller representation. The crest or badge may also be used on the flap of an envelope; arms are not normally used here. Generally speaking, printed postcards are not embellished with arms.

On Rings

There are basically two types of ring; one is scratch engraved with the arms or crest, the other has the arms cut into it in reverse so that it may be used for sealing. Scratch engraved rings are not much used and are invariably gold. Signet rings are popular and are equally acceptable with stones or in plain gold. It has long been traditional to have the crest engraved on the ring. But, if the arms are not too complicated, it is far more logical that they should be used, as the seal ring is the successor to the formal seal once used to authenticate documents, and this latter featured the arms. The only reason crests became fashionable was because they were usually easier to engrave on a small surface. My own experience has been that there is seldom any difficulty in having a shield or lozenge of arms engraved.

On Flags

"For a man's House is his castle" wrote Sir Edward Coke in his *Institutes*. On that basis there can be no objection to an armiger flying a banner of his arms, whether it be over his semi-detached house or his mansion. In some cases such a display of arms may seem a trifle comic but I cannot see that to demonstrate "here I am, this is me and my safest refuge" is ostentatious. But it would be absurd and would appear ridiculous to fly a standard which is too long and requires a high mast, over a small residence.

On Book Plates

This is a time-honoured and universally accepted use of armorial bearings. As with stationery, there was a time when embossed book-plates, printed from an engraved copper-plate, were de rigeur. This method of reproduction has a quality that ordinary printing cannot capture but which has now become so expensive that a person who sports an engraved book-plate is by many considered ostentatiously rich. So the printed book-plate has become respectable, although it is still frowned upon if printed in colour. Presumably, this is because at one time colour printing was vastly expensive and thus ostentatious. With the invention of colour lithography this is no longer the case, but I suspect that the old prejudice will remain for many years to come.

On Personal Property

Traditional and accepted uses of armorial insignia are on china, silver and pewter, etc; they may adorn portraits, hall chairs, the outside of the house, mantle-pieces, plaster work and wood carving, and be depicted in stained glass. What elements of the achievement are used is really a matter of personal choice. Generally speaking, the size of the representation will dictate whether arms, crest, badge or a combination of two or more, are suitable. To these time-honoured uses of arms I can add many now seen displayed in the most noble houses in the land. These include armorial screens and fire-screens, table mats, tapestries, chair-covers, cushions, rugs, place-setting cards, menus, and butter-stamps. Arms are also displayed on the doors of motor cars (usually on the two forward ones, but certainly not on all four doors).

When not to Display Arms

It is equally important to know where not to display one's arms. There are certain uses of arms that are still generally considered unacceptable. I will not comment as to whether I think the consensus of opinion is right or wrong; that would be invidious. I believe we are in a transitional stage and people must follow their own inclinations which time may or may not sanction.

At present (and these observations are in no order of importance) one should not: use arms on visiting cards; fly a car banner unless one is very grand, or on official business; send armorial Christmas cards or put arms on invitation cards, unless official, or quasi-official. Personal arms should certainly not be used in connection with any business enterprise, although in certain circumstances the badge may be employed.

WAYS OF USING CORPORATE ARMS

Although modesty in individuals is a virtue and ostentation a vice, this is not so with corporations. Their armorial bearings are, to some extent, their trade mark, to be used broadcast in order to advertise the body corporate. Because some corporations are either hesitant to use their arms in case they commit an heraldic solecism or else cannot think of ways in which they can be used, I make some suggestions as to usage, all of which I believe to be quite acceptable.

On Stationery

It is proper to use the full achievement, either in line or in full colour on writing paper, envelopes, invitations, circulars, pro formas, certificates and the like. It is also proper to make distinctions as to what parts of an achievement are used if such discrimination is required. By this I mean that the Chairman's stationery might be emblazoned with the full achievement, while circulars might simply be marked with arms and motto. It is preferable to use the badge either on the back flap of an envelope or at the top or bottom left on the front. If a corporation has no badge, then the crest, without helm, may be used.

On the seal

This is one of the most ancient uses of arms, indeed arms are still granted for use "on seals or otherwise according to the Laws of Arms".

Ideally, the full achievement should appear on a seal but unless a fairly large representation is used it will lose much detail when impressed. Of course, a large heavy press can be employed, but these are expensive and if economy is a consideration it is best to have a smaller seal containing just the arms, arms with crest above or arms with supporters. The circumference of the seal contains the legend, and it is sometimes possible to include the badge in the circumference beneath the shield or motto scroll.

On Flags

The usual and proper house flag is a rectangular banner (the size and proportions will be dictated by the height of the mast and weather conditions) on which the arms on the shield will be shown throughout. It is wrong to show the achievement on a plain rectangular flag. If shown in this way it should be pendent from the top seam and used simply as a decorative hanging, never as a flag flown from a mast. If a corporation has a standard (this will be painted on the Patent granting the arms and badge) it may use this in lieu of a banner. However, the standard, being a long tapering flag, will suffer in strong winds and is probably best kept for high days and holidays. There is no reason why a banner should not be flown every day, either from sunrise to sunset or during working hours. However, if economy has to be observed, it can be reserved for National Flag Days and such other occasions as are of significance to the corporation.

On uniforms

This use will have to be considered in the context of the nature of the corporation. If livery is worn, then the badge can be used on buttons and the achievement, arms, crest or badge on cap badges. The badge can be used on blazer pockets, blazer buttons, ties and overalls. Sometimes the arms are used on blazers and overalls and while such use is, strictly speaking, incorrect, it has been hallowed by custom and only a pedant would seriously object.

On book-plates

Most corporations have libraries and a good book deserves an attractive book-plate. Usually the full achievement is shown but there are no hard and fast rules.

On property

Some part of the achievement or the badge can adorn almost any piece of corporate property from motor cars to canteen crockery. It is really a question of deciding what is suitable. The answer will be dictated partly by the size of the object to be marked (it would be ridiculous to put the full achievement on a teaspoon) and partly by the nature of its use. For example, the badge would not be a sufficiently grand adornment for the directors' dinner service; this calls for either the achievement or perhaps the arms environed by a belt containing the motto. There are no particular rules; common sense and sensitivity are by far the best guides. In order to stimulate the imagination let me detail a few ways in which arms can be used to advantage, in most cases decoratively rather than purely functionally. They may be carved in wood, sculptured in stone or moulded in some man-made medium such as fibreglass; used in stained glass; worked in flowers as is sometimes done on the promenades of sea-side resorts; moulded in plaster for internal decoration such as on ceilings; gold blocked and stamped on leather chair-backs; on diaries, calendars, brief cases, Christmas cards and the like; on car badges and car-stickers; on butter stamps; on table napkins and cloths, drip-mats and table mats, and on bed linen, towels and blankets. Armorial emblems can also be woven into carpets and other materials, and printed on wall-paper.

On souvenirs

It is an old and accepted custom that arms, other than the royal arms, may be used on souvenirs. In the late 19th and early 20th centuries armorial porcelain souvenirs were enormously popular. The firm of W. H. Goss, which had many imitators but no peers, led the field and today artefacts made by this Company, which shut down in 1919, are avidly collected. As a corporation cannot stop anyone else producing souvenirs emblazoned with its arms, it should think of doing this itself. Ash trays, book marks, T-shirts and hold-alls are items suitable for such decoration.

In fine, the only real limit to the ways in which a corporation can use its arms is man's imagination; but in the case of personal arms it is that unquantifiable quality known as "good taste".

CHAPTER XXVI

RECENT TRENDS AND DEVELOPMENTS

GRANTEES

LESS than a hundred years ago, the vast majority of grants of arms was to individuals. Today, the position has altered and, although fractionally more grants of arms are still personal, there are often upwards of a hundred grants a year to corporate bodies. Grantees are far more widespread geographically than formerly. Many grants are made to individuals and corporations in Australia, New Zealand and Canada and, to a lesser extent, in other parts of the Commonwealth. As a country becomes established and prosperous, so people's minds turn to considering those things that make life more civilized and decorative, amongst which heraldry features. Also, it must be remembered, coats of arms stem ultimately from the Crown, so that a grant of arms provides a direct link between the Crown and the grantee. In the far-flung Commonwealth, such a link must seem particularly valuable.

Recently, too, more corporations have been considered eligible for a grant of arms than heretofore. Bentall's, a department store in Kingston-upon-Thames, was recently granted arms and, in 1966, the Savoy Hotel Ltd. was granted the following coat, redolent of royal associations : *gules on a cross argent, an ostrich feather ermine, between in pale two mill rinds gules and in fess two fleurs-de-lis azure, on a chief argent a paschal lamb couchant proper, between two roses gules, barbed and seeded proper.* It was also granted for a badge, *on a mount vert in front of a triple-towered castle a falcon rising proper.*

On 1st April 1965, the government of London was reorganized. 32 London Borough Councils replaced 70 County, Metropolitan and non-County Borough Councils and 15 Urban District Councils. The result was 32 prospective grantees and, at the time of writing, most of these new authorities have been granted arms, supporters and badges. Inevitably, many of the new arms are amalgams of the arms of the previous authorities from which they were composed. However, in some cases, the opportunity has been taken to produce a new and simple coat. For example, the new arms of the Royal Borough of Kensington and Chelsea, previously two metropolitan boroughs, are : *gules a mitre or, on a chief ermine, three crowns also or.* Had the old arms of Kensington, which contained fifteen charges, been jumbled up with the nine charges in those of Chelsea, one dare not imagine what the result would have been. Other fruitful sources of corporate arms are the new Police Authorities and the Universities, many of which have now been granted arms.

New knights, and High Sheriffs of Counties, who are entitled to armorial trumpet banners, frequently apply for arms, as do some of the new life peers. However, a glance at *Burke* or *Debrett* is sufficient to show that the peerage is less armigerous than of yore. Generally speaking, the recipient of a personal grant of arms is someone who has reached a certain status and position in life, who wants to pass to his descendants something which cannot be taxed, destroyed, or easily altered, and who has some knowledge and love of heraldry.

SALE OF ARMS

That there has been a great revival of popular interest in heraldry is undeniable. Never have so many books on the subject been published, nor has the Press paid so much attention to matters heraldic as during the post-war years.

This new interest has driven many to the College of Arms to sort out their armorial position and it has led to a wider and deeper interest in critical genealogy, but it has also given great impetus to the trade of the arms-monger.

The arms-monger may be defined as one who purports to sell representations of a person's arms, simply on the evidence of his surname. Thus, all Wrights, Thompsons, Browns and so forth, irrespective of whether related in blood, receive a picture of the same coat, usually culled at random from the pages of Burke's *General Armory*, or some other unreliable and unauthoritative book. Usually, but not invariably, the purveyors of these arms imply, but do not actually say, that the arms supplied are not really those of the purchaser. If they explicitly declare that the arms depicted are those of the purchaser, then an action taken against them in common law might well be successful, for they are describing their wares incorrectly and obtaining money by making a false representation.

Some of these firms operate in England, but the fullness of the harvest is to be reaped in the United States of America, where the interest in heraldry is in inverse ratio to the knowledge and understanding of it. Firms openly advertise to supply the "arms of your name" on everything from a door knocker to a bath robe. If it were not sad to see the ignorant deceived in this way, it would be funny, for the ways in which the arms are displayed are so appallingly vulgar, artistically meretricious and hopelessly inaccurate as to be a complete parody of true heraldry and heraldic usage.

DESIGN OF ARMS

Considering the number of grants of arms made annually, many of the coats granted today are still startlingly simple. Of course, Commonwealth interest in heraldry has resulted in a wide variety of new flora and fauna being introduced so that it is now no longer sufficient to blazon a duck simply as a duck, its blazon must be ornithologically correct. Although there is inevitably a number of representations of buildings and mechanical implements and instruments

432a. Ankh

432b. Shield of David

to be found, it is comfortingly small. The heralds try to steer their clients away from representational heraldry, I suspect far more conscientiously than ever their 19th or 20th century predecessors did.

The use of the stains murrey, tenné and sanguine is more popular, but they are not very satisfactory colours. It is often difficult to distinguish pale tenné from or, dark tenné from gules, and murrey from sanguine.

Certain charges, almost unknown in the last century, have recently become very popular. In the past seventeen years no less than fifty balances and pairs of scales have been granted, mostly to accountants, judges and magistrates.   A lot of accountants also favour the abacus, which was not known to heraldry until this century.   Books, both closed and open, inscribed and plain are widely used.   Mostly they appear in the arms of educational institutions, but many personal coats also contain books symbolizing learning.

The ankh (431), the Egyptian symbol of life and energy, has also become popular and makes a pleasing and symbolic charge.   As arms were rarely granted to Jews until this century, the Shield of David (*magen Dawid*) was not often used, although it is, in fact, a very ancient symbol (432).   Today, it occurs quite frequently and is usually blazoned

433. ORR-EWING OF
HENDON

434. PENNEY

as "two triangles interlaced," although more properly it should, I think, be described as a hexagram.

Strange, though by no means always unaesthetic, scientific symbols appear more and more frequently.   The University of Warwick has a double helix on a chief; Sir Ian Orr-Ewing matriculated arms containing *a representation of the path of two electrons rotating round a nucleus gules* (433), and Lord Penney, the noted atomic scientist, has arms which are blazoned *or a fess embattled and invected in base vert, between three representations of the symbol of the paramagnetic electron, those in chief being in the orbit of the third and that in base of the second harmonic azure* (434).   In fact, these symbols look like bows of ribbon tied in a stylized and attractive manner.

In recent years the device of dividing the shield per pall (40) or per pall reversed (the chief rather than the base being divided per pale) has become very popular. It is usually blazoned in a curious Anglo-French manner, namely : *tierced in pairle*, or *tierced in pairle reversed*. *Pairle* is simply the French word for pall and the French blazon for this method of dividing the shield is *tiercé en pairle*. In my opinion, there is a lot to be said for the basic English per pall. The pall itself (89) has also gained in popularity and palls drawn with some of the dividing lines (shown in 33 *a*) rather than straight lines are now occasionally found.

THE LAW AND HERALDRY

Recently the heralds have had to keep a sharp eye on the plethora of legislation that streams from the Mother of Parliaments, for some of it affects them closely. Invariably, such legislation, although it concerns the bearing of arms, ignores the problems which it creates. The new Legitimacy Act 1959 provides for the legitimization of an adulterine bastard, on the subsequent marriage of the parents, for all purposes other than the inheritance of honours. Whilst there is little doubt that arms are in the nature of an honour and may not, therefore, pass to a legitimized child, the Act made no definite provisions for the inheritance of arms. This is curious, inasmuch as the whole purpose of this type of permissive legislation would seem to be to enable a bastard child to conceal his true origin. Yet, if he wishes to bear arms, but at the same time pose as his father's legitimate child, he cannot do so. I hasten to add that I am certainly not saying that he should be able to do so, but simply that the law, bending over backwards to legislate for hard cases, appears to have been quite unaware of the heraldic problem created. As I see it, the only heraldic interpretation of the Act is that the legitimized bastard has no right to arms except by grant. The arms granted could, of course, be those of the father suitably distinguished, if a Royal Licence is first obtained, but there is certainly no right to arms by the ordinary rules of inheritance.

But, if some legislation has created heraldic problems by ignoring the existence of armory, the Trade Descriptions Act 1968 has shown at least some awareness of heraldry. Under Section 1 of this Act it is an offence for a person acting in the course of trade or business to apply a false trade description to goods or to supply or offer to supply goods to which a false trade description is applied. Armorial bearings may amount to a trade description if used in relation to particular goods in such a way as to amount to an indication as to any of the matters specified in section 2 (1) of the Act. These matters include indications as to the approval of goods by any person, or their conformity with a type approved by any person, or as to the person by whom they were manufactured, produced, processed or reconditioned, or as to any other history of them. For an offence to be committed the description must be false to a material degree.

Section 13 of the Act makes it an offence for a person acting in the course of a trade or business to give a false indication that goods or services supplied by him are of a kind supplied to any person. The use of armorial bearings to give a false indication of this kind may therefore also give rise to an offence.

It is open to any person to institute proceedings for an offence under this Act. A person aggrieved by the use of armorial bearings in one of the ways described may therefore prosecute the offender. It is also open to any person who wishes to do so to bring a possible infringement of the Act to the notice of the appropriate local weights and measures authority since the Act places a duty on these authorities to enforce its provisions.

Section 15 of the Theft Act 1968 makes it an offence to obtain money by deception. Accordingly, if a trader sells a representation of a coat of arms by representing to the purchaser that his purchase entitles him to use the arms in question, when it does not, then an offence under the Act is committed.

One of the two memoranda on the subject of these new Acts, published by the College of Arms, and from which I have, with permission, quoted from in the preceeding paragraphs, ends as follows :

" To sum up, every kind of misuse of arms is in principle actionable in the Court of Chivalry. However, such action can be initiated only by leave of the Court and Lord Goddard advised that such leave should only be given where there is some really substantial reason for it. In practice a demand for the legal protection of armorial bearings seems at present to arise mainly in cases of commercial misuse, and new and simplified protection against two forms which this may take has been provided by the Acts of Parliament mentioned above which became law in 1968. These may turn out to provide all that is in practice required. If not, Lord Goddard's recommendation will doubtless be considered further."

This allusion to Lord Goddard's recommendation refers to remarks he made in his Judgment when acting as Surrogate for the Earl Marshal in the case of The Mayor, Aldermen and Citizens of the City of Manchester versus The Manchester Palace of Varieties Ltd. before the Court of Chivalry in 1954 (briefly mentioned on page 261), Lord Goddard stated : " If therefore it is laid down as a rule of this Court ... that leave must be obtained before any proceedings are instituted, it would, I think, prevent frivolous actions ; and, if this Court is to sit again it should be convened only where there is some really substantial reason for the exercise of its jurisdiction. Moreover should there be any indication of a considerable desire to institute proceedings now that this Court has been revived, I am firmly of the opinion that it should be put on a statutory basis, defining its jurisdiction and the sanctions it can impose."

Fortunately, perhaps, there has been no rush to institute proceedings before the Court, as it seems unlikely that Parliamentary time would readily be given to legislation designed to place this particular Court on a statutory basis.

DISPLAY OF ARMS

Although there is still much ignorance concerning the ways in which arms can be displayed, there are encouraging signs that more liberal and informed ideas are taking root. The principal problem is to wean people and, more particularly, corporations from the view that arms can only be depicted in the exact manner in which they are shown on the Letters Patent granting them. This is an old and very sacred cow, but if heraldry is to be a living and vital art, this particular cow must be slaughtered. Somehow it must be brought home to armigers that all that is sacred about the design of a coat of arms is the nature of the charges (not their exact delineation), their colour (not precise shade) and their disposition on the shield or in the crest. Thus the blazon *or a lion rampant gules* is capable of many artistic interpretations. The lion may be large or small, have three, four or five claws on each paw and may be thin, fat, smooth, hairy, angry, placid, highly symbolic or alarmingly zoological, but he *must* be a lion and he *must* ramp and he *must* be clearly visible. The field may be either painted in gold, imitation gold, or any shade of yellow which clearly represents gold. Likewise, the red of the lion, as long as it is unmistakably red, does not have to conform to a British Standard colour and whether or not the lion is shaded is a matter for the artist to decide. The actual shape and type of shield, provided it looks like some sort of possible or impossible shield, is also a matter of design. In late Victorian grants of arms the shield was often an impossible, curvaceous thing with a heavy gilt frame, but as the heralds of the day were happy with it who are we to condemn it on any grounds other than aesthetic?

In the summer of 1968, The Heraldry Society mounted an exhibition of the work of living heraldic artists at the premises of the Reed Paper Group Ltd., in Piccadilly, London. It was called *Heraldic Design Today* and, to the best of my knowledge, was the first exhibition of its kind ever to be staged. It demonstrated not only the growing freedom with which modern artists interpret blazons, but showed some of the ways in which arms are currently used.

So often, the question is asked, " How can I use my arms without being ostracized as an ostentatious vulgarian ?" The simple answer is that they can be used wherever arms can, discreetly and tastefully, ornament or identify. Obvious places for the use of arms are book plates, or book stamps, seal rings, silver, porcelain (what could be more dignified than an armorial dinner service), stained glass (a free-hanging panel can be most attractive), stationery, motor-car doors and small articles of personal property such as brushes, combs, card cases, wallets, luggage, paper, cutlery, watches, cuff links and so forth. There is really no end to the ways in which arms, or the appropriate part of a full achievement can be used. Heraldry is, or should be, fun and not to use it is to take one's pleasures very sadly. As a considerable interest has been evinced in this aspect of heraldry, it has been dealt with more fully in Chapter XXV.

Fees on Grants of Arms

Reference is made on page 268 to the increase in fees, which were authorized by the Earl Marshal, to take effect from 1st January 1981. The Schedule of Fees is fairly extensive, but the principal fees are laid down as follows: £840 for a personal grant to a man and his descendants —if the limitation of the inheritance of the arms is extended to include all the other descendants of the grantee's father, an extra £210 is payable but, should a wider limitation be required, as it might be to include the descendants of the grantee's great-grandfather, the fee is *ad hoc*, depending greatly on the number of beneficiaries; £2000 for an impersonal grant (i.e. to a corporate body) with an extra £450 if supporters are included. If a badge is granted in the same patent as the arms, be it to an individual or to a corporation, the extra fee is £250. The fee for a grant of a badge in a separate patent is £350. As no hereditary peers have been created for nearly twenty years, there have been no grants of hereditary supporters. However, it is as well that the schedule of fees still allows for the possibility, for such creations may occur, and such a grant was made to Captain Mark Phillips after his marriage to Princess Anne. The fee laid down is £400, or £300 if granted in the same patent as the arms. The fee for life supporters, to which life peers are entitled, is £310, or £200 if granted in the same patent as the arms. The fee on a grant of a crest to existing arms is £350. In Northern Ireland the fees used to be less than in England, but since 1981 they are the same.

The grant fee includes the cost of the actual vellum document, decorated with the royal arms, the arms of the Earl Marshal and those of the College of Arms. The arms, and, if a badge is also granted, the badge are painted on the patent, which is engrossed by one of the scriveners at the College of Arms. However, there is no reason why, if a badge is granted, a standard should not be painted on the patent; the patent itself can also be decorated in any way which meets with the approval of the Kings of Arms. Such a patent is illustrated in Plate XXVIII. Not unnaturally, the cost of these embellishments, which, if very elaborate, can be considerable, must be borne by the grantee. Some very remarkable examples of finely illuminated patents have recently come from the studios of the herald painters.

ARMS OF A FEMALE GRANTEE

There have always been two schools of thought as to whether a woman, not an heir, or co-heir of her father and who is granted arms, should be regarded as an heraldic heiress. In a sense she is an heir, by grant, to arms. On the other hand, as male heirs in blood, though not in arms, to her father exist, she cannot be regarded as heir in blood to her father. If she is an heir, or co-heir in blood to her father, there is no problem. She is a truly armorial heiress and can transmit her arms as a quartering to her issue in the usual way. But what if male heirs exist?

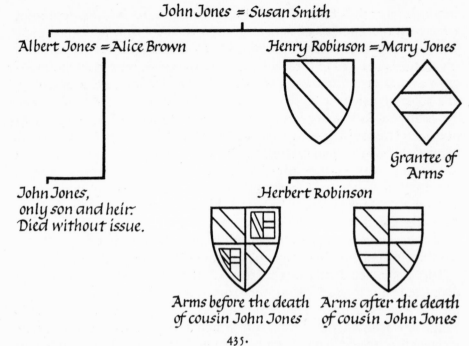

John Jones = Susan Smith

Albert Jones = Alice Brown   Henry Robinson = Mary Jones

Grantee of
Arms

John Jones,   Herbert Robinson
only son and heir.
Died without issue.

Arms before the death   Arms after the death
of cousin John Jones   of cousin John Jones

435.

The Kings of Arms have now ruled on this vexed question and have declared as follows : if arms are granted to a woman, with limitation to her and her descendants " according to the laws of arms," then, if she is not an heir or co-heir in blood to her father, her legitimate issue may, on her death, quarter her arms impaled with their paternal arms, all within a bordure of a suitable tincture. The illustration above (435) indicates how this shall be done. If the male issue of Albert Jones should eventually become extinct, then Mary Robinson would become an heiress in her issue and her descendants could assume her undifferenced arms as a quartering in lieu of the impaled coat within a bordure.

This ruling would not seem to apply to a bastard daughter, even if she had male brethren of the whole blood, for a bastard is *nullius filius* and in law has no father, no kin and no heirs save of its own body. However, it is curious to note that when King William IV assigned arms to his four illegitimate sons and five illegitimate daughters in 1831, although each was granted an individual mark of distinction, the arms of the married daughters were *impaled* with those of their husbands and not, as might have been expected, placed in pretence over them. As they were bastards, the fact that they were all the children of Mrs. Jordan and William IV, both of whom were alive, is not really significant. It certainly seems that there is a strong case for the descendants of the daughters to quarter their arms.

The Legitimacy Act 1959, to which reference is made on pages 124 and 291, poses yet another problem. Are legitimated brethren to be regarded, as far as the new ruling is concerned, as legitimate children, or bastards? In other words, are female children, having brothers, to be treated as bastards and so capable of transmitting any arms assigned to them, or as legitimate and so only able to transmit their arms in the new manner described above? So far, no test case has moved anyone to consider this slightly peripheral problem, but it does at least serve to highlight the fact that the 1959 Act was drafted without proper consideration being given to the wider implications of the clause touching on the inheritance and transmission of honours.

PEERAGE ACT 1963

Another comparatively recent Act of Parliament which leaves a number of questions unanswered is the Peerage Act 1963. This Act provides for the disclaiming of peerages under certain stated conditions. Clause 3 of the Act details the effects of a disclaimer. It states that it divests the person who disclaims (and if married, his wife) " of all right or interest to or in the peerage and precedence attaching thereto."

Does this mean that a disclaimed peer may not use supporters? It is a privilege of peers to be granted supporters, but, thereafter, the descent of the supporters is controlled by the actual grant. This states that they shall be inherited by those upon whom the peerage shall descend. Thus, as soon as the holder of the peerage dies, the new heir inherits the supporters. If he later disclaims, there is nothing in the Act to provide for the disclaiming of the supporters, nor is there any legal form by which a man can disclaim part of his arms. It may be argued that the use of supporters is one of the " rights " of a peer, but it is only an argument. Nothing has been laid down and until it is, it would seem that a disclaimed peer can suit himself until challenged.

The Life Peerages Act 1958 made no reference to arms, but this did not create any problems as the new Life Peers were treated in the same way as Lords of Appeal in Ordinary, created under the terms of the

Appellate Jurisdiction Act 1876, as amended by the Act of 1887. That is, they bore arms in the same way as other peers, but, if they were granted supporters, these were for life only. The only hereditary armorial privilege of Life Peers is that they may, if they wish, have chapeaux rather than torses beneath their crests.

MURREY, SANGUINE AND BLEU CÉLESTE

It will be noticed that I have drawn a distinction between the " stains " called murrey and sanguine which in earlier editions of *Boutell*, as in most text books on heraldry, have been equated (see page 27).

I did this because I found that murrey was used in the 15th century as one of King Edward IV's livery colours and also in one or two 16th century grants of arms. I also found one example of the use of sanguine in the 16th century. Thereafter, both colours seem to disappear from official heraldry until they were revived in this century, where artists have made a distinction between the two. Apart from the statements in the text books which, presumably, went unchallenged because the matter had been reduced to purely academic proportions by the disappearance of the tinctures from the Grant Books, there seems to be no reason why armory should not follow the dictionary in distinguishing between blood-red and mulberry colour.

Recently a new tincture has been borrowed from French armory, termed *bleu céleste* (pale sky-blue). This, like the Astral Crown (page 188), is normally only granted to institutions and distinguished persons connected with aviation.

NEW OFFICERS OF ARMS

The appointment of a Wales Herald Extraordinary has been noted (page 263). Since this appointment a totally new title has been added to the list of Heralds Extraordinary. In 1979 Mr. Phillip O'Shea was appointed New Zealand Herald Extraordinary. He is a civil servant in New Zealand and is especially concerned in assisting the English Officers of Arms in their concerns in New Zealand, that farthest outpost of the Commonwealth. As Wales Herald has no jurisdiction in Wales, so New Zealand has none in his part of the Antipodes, this is still reserved to the Kings of Arms, but there naturally is and there is intended to be an empathy between these newer officers and the countries whose names they bear. New Zealand's badge (435 *a*) is blazoned: *A complex Maori*

435a.

435b.

435c.   435d.

koru coloured in the traditional manner proper, ensigned by a representation of the Royal Crown also proper.

Another new title for a Herald Extraordinary is Beaumont. It was bestowed on Mr. F. S. Andrus when he resigned the office of Lancaster Herald in 1982. Traditionally the titles of the extraordinary officers usually reflect the titles of the Earl Marshal. The present Earl Marshal is, *jure matris*, Baron Beaumont, and it is fitting that this ancient barony should be commemorated by the creation of a herald of that name.

The Earl Marshal is also Earl of Surrey, so, when Sir Walter Verco resigned the office of Norroy and Ulster King of Arms in 1980, he was created Surrey Herald Extraordinary. This was not a new title, having been first used in 1856 for Mr. E. S. Dendy, later Chester Herald. However, since no badge was then assigned to the title, the Queen has now approved badges for Beaumont and Surrey Heralds Extraordinary (435 *b*; 435 *c*).

In Scotland a few noblemen appoint their own private officers of arms.

Thus, the Earl of Erroll has Slains Pursuivant; the Earl of Crawford and
Balcarres, Endure Pursuivant and a relative newcomer to the ranks of
these officers is Garioch Pursuivant, a private pursuivant to the Countess
of Mar. Mr. J. C. G. George was appointed to this office in 1976.

ARMS OF NORROY AND ULSTER

The arms of office of Norroy King of Arms and also those of Ulster
are blazoned on page 233. As has been mentioned, the two offices were
amalgamated and the first Norroy and Ulster King of Arms, with jurisdiction North of the River Trent and in that part of Ireland still remaining within the United Kingdom was appointed in 1943. He was created
as a single king, not by two separate Patents as two independent kings.
This position was slightly analogous to that of Queen Anne after the Act
of Union with Scotland, 1707. Thereafter she was not separately Queen
of Scotland and Queen of England, but Queen of Great Britain and
assumed arms to symbolise this union (page 214). Norroy and Ulster did
likewise. Some holders of the office have used the arms of one king or
the other, or else the two impaled. For this latter practice there was no
justification because, although it may be thought logical to combine
arms in this way, such a marshalling requires a Royal Licence. In any
case, it is not a satisfactory solution to the problem because, if the holder
of the office bore quartered arms, there would be three impalements, one
exhibiting quarterings, which would be over-complex and unaesthetic.
When the present editor of this book was appointed Norroy and Ulster
he sought to put matters right and in 1980 the Queen approved arms for
the joint office. The new coat is an amalgam of the two earlier coats,
namely: *Quarterly, argent and or, a cross gules, on a chief per pale azure and
gules a lion passant guardant crowned between a fleur-de-lis and a harp or*
(435 d).

IMPALEMENT OF ARMS OF OFFICE

On page 139 the impalement of arms of office with personal arms is
mentioned. That paragraph was written before the structure of local
government had been drastically altered by the Local Government Act,
1972, but the principle enunciated remains the same and has, in fact, been
extended by a ruling of the Kings of Arms, dated July 1980. The ruling
recites previous usage and quotes particularly the grant of arms to the

Norwich Union Life Assurance Society in 1938, in which the President of the Society and his successors are specifically authorised to use the Society's arms impaled with their personal arms. It also recites that in 1947 it was laid down that a lady Lord Mayor or Mayor might impale her marital arms with those of the Corporation of which she is head. The ruling then declares that it shall be suitable and fitting for the duly elected or appointed head of any armigerous body, whether corporate or not (for example, a Trust), to impale his or her family arms with those of the body in question, a married woman impaling her marital arms, a spinster her paternal coat.

CRITICAL BIBLIOGRAPHY

I have long felt that what the reader of *Boutell's Heraldry* really needs when he has come to the end of the book is a brief, critical and analytical guide to further reading, rather than the somewhat arid " Select Bibliography " which has heretofore occupied a couple of pages after the last chapter. I have, therefore, replaced the short list of books, which has appeared in previous editions, with a fuller bibliography, designed to be read as part of the book rather than used simply as a catalogue for reference.

I have tried to keep the number of titles mentioned within reasonable bounds ; consequently I have omitted mention of many excellent books, the contents of which do not really augment what is to be found in the pages of *Boutell*. Rather than list books in alphabetical order under authors' names, I have divided the bibliography into sections, each dealing with a different aspect of the subject. Also I have resisted giving full bibliographic details of each book. If I were to give such data it would almost certainly make the bibliography far less readable, thus defeating my object. I have simply given sufficient details for any good bookseller easily to locate the books.

HERALDRY IN GENERAL

Thomas Moule's *Bibliotheca Heraldica Magnae Britanniae* was published in 1822 and consists of a detailed bibliography of books on heraldry and closely allied subjects printed before that date. To this work I would refer the reader whose interest lies in the history of armorial literature. However, as Moule is essentially a scholarly bibliographer and not a critic I would, if I were sufficiently rich, try to acquire the following four works. Firstly I would have a copy of Gerard Leigh's *The Accidence of Armorie* (any edition from 1562–1612) as this was one of the first printed manuals of heraldry. I always feel that it is interesting to reflect that this book must have been read by many of the new men of the Tudor period, who added so much to the revenues of the heralds by their interest in arms and pedigrees. Leigh's book being but a brief treatise, I would also like to have a copy of *A Display of Heraldry* by John Guillim. This is the first really comprehensive book on heraldry and the 6th edition, edited and greatly augmented by James Coats in 1724, is by far the best, running to 460 folio pages. The first edition of this classic work was published in 1611. The next two editions were similar to the first but the 4th edition published in 1660 and the 5th in 1679 contain much extra material. The next great classic is

Joseph Edmondson's *A Complete Body of Heraldry* published in two handsome folio volumes in 1780. The title aptly describes the book. Edmondson, who was Mowbray Herald Extraordinary, but was, in fact, a practising herald and coach-painter, covers every aspect of armory, and in the second volume there is an Alphabet of Arms containing upwards of 50,000 entries, the precursor of Burke's *General Armory* (see page 296).

Finally I would get a copy of W. Berry's *Encyclopaedia Heraldica* published in 1828 (3 volumes and a supplement) and which has recently been reprinted in America. Berry styled himself " Registering Clerk " to the College of Arms. In fact, he was merely a writing clerk but obviously much of the current practice of heraldry must have rubbed off on him and is reflected in his book. His work, though often inaccurate, is truly encyclopaedic (it owes much to Edmondson) and is written in a critical and intelligent way, thus earning it a place amongst the heraldic classics.

Later in the 19th century two short treatises on heraldry were published, which stand out head and shoulders above the general run of Victorian manuals ; they are *A Guide to the Study of Heraldry* by J. A. Montagu (1840) and *The Pursuivant of Arms* by J. R. Planché, Somerset Herald (3rd edition 1874). The curse of heraldic literature is plagiarization and it is the absence of this, combined with a good literary style that makes these two books not only eminently readable but of real academic value.

A Complete Guide to Heraldry by A. C. Fox-Davies is generally held to be a modern classic, although Fox-Davies's scholarship has been attacked, and sometimes with justification, by heraldic purists. This book was first published in 1909 and was essentially a detailed account of the official practice of heraldry at that time. Contrary to popular belief heraldry does not rest upon its laurels ; old conventions are abandoned and new practices adopted. For this reason the *Complete Guide* soon became out of date. A minor revision was made by C. A. Franklyn in 1949 and in 1969 a new edition was published containing 277 footnotes and some new illustrations, designed to bring the text right up to date. I had the privilege, and it was a privilege—Fox-Davies's book having been my own introduction to heraldry—of editing this edition.

An introduction to heraldry, seen through the eyes of that competent, critical scholar and medievalist, Oswald Barron, is to be found in the 11th and subsequent editions of the *Encyclopaedia Britannica*. It is a fine essay and well worth reading but sadly it will not be found in the post-World War II editions of the Encyclopaedia.

A useful little manual of medieval heraldry, with a bias towards artistic representation, is W. H. St. John Hope's *A Grammar of English Heraldry*, first published in 1913. An edition revised by A. R. Wagner, Richmond Herald, was published in 1953. A. R. Wagner, now Sir Anthony Wagner, is the author of many valuable and authoritative works on heraldry and particularly on the heralds themselves. One of his earlier books was *Historic Heraldry*, published in 1939. Here he details the arms of many historical characters, each coat being beautifully illustrated by Gerald Cobb. In 1976 a very lush book, *Heraldry, Sources, Symbols and Meanings*, by Ottfried Neubecker, with some contributions by myself, was published. The principal value of this book is that, quite apart from being beautifully and lavishly illustrated, it attempts to deal with heraldry in Europe and not just in the United Kingdom. It seeks to give and to a great extent succeeds in giving heraldry wider dimensions than do most heraldic text books.

Another book which gives an unusual but appealing slant to the study of heraldry is *The Romance of Heraldry*, written and illustrated by C. W. Scott-Giles, Fitzalan Pursuivant Extraordinary (1965, revised edition). Here heraldry is approached in a way which would have earned Planché's approval, namely from an historic standpoint. There are chapters on many aspects of heraldry and history from the pre-heraldry of Saxon times, through the Order of the Garter, the Wars of the Roses, Charles II in the oak tree right down to modern commercial heraldry. This book and *Simple Heraldry* by Iain Moncreiffe and Don Pottinger (1953, but constantly reprinted) are quite the most civilized introductions to heraldry that I have ever come across. *Simple Heraldry* combines Don Pottinger's splendid and spirited cartoons with a scholarly, albeit simple text by Iain Moncreiffe. It may be that there is little in this book which cannot be found in *Boutell*, but sometimes having what one knows already restated in a different way, can open up new avenues of thought and generally stimulate the imagination. This is the sort of book which does just that.

There are various glossaries and dictionaries of heraldry. Apart from very old volumes, which are hard to come by and beyond the purse of the average student, there is *A Glossary of Terms used in British Heraldry*, which is anonymous (although actually the work of H. Gough) but was published by A. H. Parker of Oxford and so has become known as *Parker's Glossary*. The 2nd edition was published in 1894 and has recently been republished. Unfortunately, the new edition is simply a lithographed reproduction and so has not been brought up to date. A good pictorial guide to the charges used in heraldry is Charles Norton Elvin's *A Dictionary of Heraldry* (1889). Two fairly recent publications have helped to bridge the gap between Parker and Elvin and the present day. One is a substantial and well illustrated volume, *An Encyclopaedic Dicionary of Heraldry* (1970) by the late Julian Franklyn and Dr. John Tanner. It is authoritative and very comprehensive in its coverage of heraldry, in the widest sense of the word. Another is my own *An Heraldic Alphabet* (1973), a slighter work aimed at those who wish to paddle in, rather than plunge into, the deep waters of heraldry.

THE ART OF HERALDRY

This aspect of heraldry was more or less neglected until G. W. Eve's *Decorative Heraldry* (1897) was published. This was followed by his *Heraldry as Art* (1907) and by W. H. St. John Hope's *Heraldry for Craftsmen and Designers* (1913). All three books are well worth having, although second-hand copies do not often come on the market. Eve was essentially an artist whereas Hope was a scholar, but between them they certainly revived interest in the art and design of heraldry.

That this interest is sustained today is evidenced by the publication of two further books on the subject. *Heraldic Design* by Heather Child (1966) is a handsome book covering many aspects of armorial design and is very fully illustrated, many of the pictures being by the author, herself an heraldic artist of some note. Miss Child's book is a statement of what exists rather than a search for something new in armorial design. This would have been a pity had not a gifted American, William Metzig, written and illustrated a most inspired and inspiring book *Heraldry for the Designer* (undated but about 1972). Some of his designs are ugly, some uninteresting, but there are others which, by trying to say something old in a new way, revitalize the ancient forms.

HERALDS

The first book devoted to the College of Arms and the heralds was The Reverend Mark Noble's *A History of the College of Arms and the Lives of all the Kings, Heralds, and Pursuivants, from the Reign of Richard the Third, Founder of the College, until the Present Time* (1805). Even this is not its full title but it serves to explain the principal contents of the book. The 449 quarto pages are packed with interest and, it must be admitted, with the author's prejudices with regard to the biographies of some of the officers of arms. It contains many engravings of seals, portraits and monuments of heralds as well as fourteen useful appendices. It is a lovely book to own but copies rarely come on the market.

In fact Noble has been superseded by two recent books which, taken together, present a really detailed, scholarly and well-documented history of the heralds, the corporation familiarly known as the College of Arms and the actual building now occupied by the heralds. The first of these monumental works is known by the short title *The College of Arms 1963* and is the sixteenth and final monograph of the London Survey Committee. It was prepared by Walter H. Godfrey assisted by Sir Anthony Wagner, Garter King of Arms, and H. S. London, Norfolk Herald Extraordinary, and contains a complete list of all known English officers of arms whether in Ordinary or Extraordinary. The arms of the officers are blazoned and illustrated by line drawings made by C. W. Scott-Giles, Fitzalan Pursuivant Extraordinary. The book is prefaced by a detailed account of the building which was erected after the Great Fire of

1666 and there are 44 monochrome plates referring to the College building. The biographies of the heralds contain little real meat, being mostly in *Who's Who* style ; but no matter, for Sir Anthony Wagner's *Heralds of England* (1967) adds meat in abundance. This work has rightly been described as definitive. It tells of all that the heralds used to do and what they do today. It details their quarrels, their ups and their downs. The diverse and often diverting history of the College of Arms as an institution is unravelled in compelling, elegant prose. The book is superlative but, as is the way with such things, it is superlatively expensive and will probably be borrowed rather than bought. However, for the bookshelf, Sir Anthony long ago wrote a curtain-raiser to his *magnum opus* entitled *Heralds and Heraldry in the Middle Ages* (1956, 2nd edition). The sub-title describes the book succinctly : " An Inquiry into the Growth of the Armorial Functions of Heralds." Sir Anthony traces this growth from the early duties of the heralds to their eventual emergence as the armorial authority, dwelling particularly on their activities in making visitations and granting arms in the early 16th century. The contents of this comparatively brief work are incorporated in *Heralds of England,* but it is a most useful essay to have easily to hand. Wagner is also responsible for a slim octavo volume on the more important contents of the College of Arms Library—*Records and Collections of the College of Arms* (1951). It is a brief but invaluable guide to the treasures of the College.

A book by Rodney Dennys, until recently Somerset Herald, was published in 1982: *Heraldry and the Heralds*. It is an elegant *pot-pourri* which, like Gaul, is divided into three parts. The first is entitled "Some Aspects of Armory", the second "Heraldry, Politics and the Law" and the third "The Heralds in the Modern World". It is all good reading, but the third part is perhaps the most innovative.

THE LAW OF ARMS

The great authority on the law of arms is G. D. Squibb, Norfolk Herald Extraordinary. It is not surprising that the literature on this subject is jejeune to the point of being almost non-existent, as the Court of Chivalry, the place where armorial causes were heard, lay dormant from 1737 until it was revived in 1954. In 1955 The Heraldry Society published *The Law of Arms in England* by G. D. Squibb (1967, 2nd edition). Although only a 15-page pamphlet, this little work is probably all a layman needs to read in order to understand the legal aspect of heraldry. But, if the appetite is whetted, Squibb's *Reports of Heraldic Cases in the Court of Chivalry 1623–1732* (Harleian Society vol. CVII, 1955) makes interesting reading, and his *The High Court of Chivalry* (1959) is a very well-documented, definitive history of the court and its procedure. There is a chapter on the law of arms, lists of officers of the court and twenty-seven useful appendices.

REFERENCE BOOKS

The most quoted armorial reference book is *The General Armory of England, Scotland, Ireland and Wales* by Sir Bernard Burke, Ulster King of Arms (1884, 2nd edition). That this book was edited by a herald has given rise to the belief that it is an authoritative work of reference. Unfortunately such is not the case; it is but a collection of the blazons of arms, crests and supporters arranged alphabetically under the names of those who are supposed to have borne them. Many of the coats given are inaccurately blazoned, wrongly attributed, borne without authority or just plain bogus. Burke augmented Berry (see page 303) and Thomas Robson's *The British Herald* (1830), another alphabetical armory, who in turn based their works on Edmondson (see page 303). Although Burke's work is unreliable, nonetheless it is valuable if used critically. Where the date of a grant or visitation is mentioned as authority for the arms given, the coat is usually genuine; also, as so much 18th- and 19th-century heraldry was unauthoritative, Burke can be useful in identifying such bogus armorial displays. In other words, Burke must be used with caution. An extension of *The General Armory* was published in 1973. This consists of additions and corrections to the original publication, by Alfred Morant. It is edited by Cecil Humphery-Smith under the title *General Armory Two*. It should be used in conjunction with *The General Armory*, which has been reproduced recently by lithography.

The *General Armory* is complemented by Papworth's *Ordinary of British Armorials*, which was published after his death in 1874 and was reproduced by lithography in 1961. Papworth based his work on the coats listed in the 1847 edition of the *General Armory*, added coats he found detailed in twenty-five manuscripts, in one printed book and in " heraldic works of repute and trustworthy other sources." He simply rearranged the coats in the form of an ordinary, thus making it possible to identify a coat from its blazon. This means that it is necessary to be able to blazon coats with reasonable proficiency in order to use Papworth.

Although Burke details arms, crests, supporters and mottoes, Papworth is simply an ordinary of arms. The best ordinary of crests is Fairbairn's *Crests of the Families of Great Britain and Ireland* (1905, 3rd edition edited by A. C. Fox-Davies). This work is in two volumes. The first contains an alphabetical list of names with details of crests and mottoes; an alphabetical list of mottoes; and a key to the plates which form the second volume. In Fox-Davies's edition the pictures are grouped under charges, although not indexed, in a reasonably intelligent way. Thus all lions will be found together, followed by demi-lions and lions' heads but the order in which the various charges have been placed appears to be capricious. In the earlier editions of Fairbairn the pictures are in no sort of order and so identifying a crest can be a considerable labour. The small advantage which the earlier editions have over Fox-Davies's edition is that Fox-Davies excluded some crests which he knew to be bogus. This does not mean, however, that all the crests listed by him are genuine. They are not.

The simplest way of identifying arms is often through the motto. As mentioned, there is a list in Fairbairn and there is also one at the end of Burke's *General Armory*. A useful book devoted to the subject of mottoes is Elvin's *Book of Mottoes* (1860), which has recently been reprinted with a small supplement. The advantage of this book is that the meaning of mottoes in foreign tongues is given and sometimes also their provenance. The disadvantage of all published lists of mottoes is that they are hopelessly jejeune. I have myself been working on a book of mottoes for nearly three years and have already discovered well over 1,000 mottoes not given in Elvin.

Scottish arms are listed in Burke and Papworth but there is a separate ordinary of Scottish arms entered in the *Public Register of all Arms and Bearings in Scotland*, which record was instituted to fulfil the requirements of an Act of the Scottish Parliament of 1672 (Chapter 47) whereby no person of Scottish descent has a right to arms unless they are entered in this Register. The book is generally known as Balfour Paul's *Ordinary of Scottish Arms* (1903, 2nd edition), although it does boast a longer title. The arms are detailed in much the same way as in Papworth but there is also a useful index effectually making the book both an ordinary and an alphabet. Volume II of this book, covering the period 1902–1973, was compiled by the late David Reid of Robertland and Miss Vivien Wilson and was published by Lyon office in 1977.

In England we have no Balfour Paul but there are good reference books to grantees of arms, all published by the Harleian Society. The first, *Grantees of Arms to the end of the Seventeenth Century* (1915) gives references to College of Arms and also to Harleian and other manuscripts. The next, in two volumes, *Grantees of Arms 1687–1898* (1916 and 1917) only gives references to College of Arms grant books. This series, which simply gives the grantee's name, brief geographical description and the date on the grant, is the work of Joseph Foster. It was edited for the Harleian Society by W. Harry Rylands, Foster's manuscripts having been purchased by the British Museum in 1905. Foster was also the compiler of *Some Feudal Coats of Arms* (1902). This is a very lush book, admirably and fully illustrated, but unfortunately Foster's scholarship was not up to the difficult task of compiling an armory from the old rolls of arms, many of which simply consist of blazons. This book, therefore, must be treated with considerable caution.

The most useful current reference books to the arms of the nobility and gentry are Burke's *Peerage, Baronetage and Knightage*, at one time published annually but currently at irregular intervals (the last edition is dated 1976) and Burke's

Landed Gentry, the latest edition was published in three volumes (1965, 1969 and 1972). The former work has narrative pedigrees of peers and baronets (not knights) and the latter of landed, or now frequently not-so-landed gentry. Recent editions of both these books are more reliable than earlier editions as the pedigrees entered have now been critically examined and the arms have been checked by an officer of arms. Debrett's *Peerage, Baronetage, Knightage and Companionage* used to appear annually and gave the arms and living collaterals in the male line of peers and baronets and the biographies of Knights and Companions or Commanders of Orders of Chivalry. Of recent years the Knights, Companions and Commanders have been dropped and the book appears only occasionally, the last edition being dated 1980.

The best reference books to the bibliography of heraldry are Thomas Moule's *Bibliotheca Heraldica Magnae Britanniae* (1822), which has already been mentioned and which has recently been reprinted. It is brought up to date by G. Gatfield's *Guide to Printed Books and Manuscripts relating to English and Foreign Heraldry and Genealogy* (1892) and S. T. Cope's *Heraldry, Flags and Seals : A select Bibliography* (ASLIB, 1948) ; also there is a new edition in preparation of the *Class Catalogue of Books in the Library of the Victoria and Albert Museum and the National Art Library, South Kensington, Heraldry*, which was last published in 1910.

PERIODICALS

The only heraldic magazine regularly published in Great Britain today is *The Coat of Arms*. It is published quarterly by the Heraldry Society, 28 Museum Street, London WC1. It was first published in 1950 and it contains both popular and scholarly articles on heraldry and allied subjects, both book reviews and occasional articles on aspects of foreign heraldry. It is well illustrated and is noted for its lively correspondence columns. The Heraldry Society also publishes a quarterly news sheet called *The Heraldry Gazette*. This contains up-to-date details of the doings of the Society and of heraldry in general. The Institute of Heraldic and Genealogical Studies publishes an interesting quarterly, *Family History*. Although this publication is slanted more towards genealogy than heraldry, from time to time it contains useful heraldic material. There is a number of magazines published in the Commonwealth and by local Societies which are devoted to heraldry. Of these the most professional is *Heraldry in Canada*, published by The Heraldry Society of Canada, 125 Lakeway Drive, Ottawa.

Over the years there has been a number of publications either entirely or principally devoted to armory, and bound volumes are often to be found on the second-hand market. If the price is not too high they are always worth buying. Perhaps the best of these periodicals was *The Ancestor*. Its twelve volumes, edited and to a great extent written by Oswald Barron, appeared between 1902 and 1905. Barron was one of the *enfants terribles* of the heraldic world of his day. Like Horace Round, a frequent contributor to *The Ancestor*, he questioned accepted truths, destroyed myths, ridiculed the absurd and shook established institutions. But his criticism was not entirely destructive; his articles are full of sound scholarship and his periodical is as readable today as when it was published. Even the editorial notes and correspondence are still fresh. There is a valuable index to the twelve volumes but it is rare, and if discovered, should be snapped up at once.

Two more pedestrian periodicals, but still full of good, sound material were *The Herald and Genealogist* and *Miscellanea Genealogica et Heraldica*. The former, edited by J. G. Nichols, appeared in eight volumes between 1863 and 1874. The latter ran, under various editors, for seventy years from 1868 until 1938.

SCOTTISH HERALDRY

The bearing of arms is essentially a matter of law and as English and Scottish law remained distinct and distinctive after the Act of Union in 1707, so did the heraldry of the two kingdoms. There are, of course, many similarities between the heraldic systems of Scotland and England but there are also many and important differences. So, while most books on heraldry contain references to Scottish armory none deals with it in depth. This has been left to the Scots themselves and they have done it admirably. *Scots Heraldry* by Sir Thomas Innes of Learney, Lyon King of Arms, clearly sets forth current Scottish practice. The last edition of this book was edited by the author's second son, Malcolm Innes of Edingight, now Lord Lyon King of Arms, and was published in 1978.

George Seton wrote a book similar to Innes's, *The Law and Practice of Heraldry in Scotland* (1863). The only reason why this excellent work is not quite as useful as *Scots Heraldry* is simply because of its age. Heraldry has developed remarkably during the last hundred years, and while I would advise anyone to buy a second-hand copy of Seton, it must be in addition to and not in place of Innes.

J. H. Stevenson, Marchmont Herald's splendid *Heraldry in Scotland* (1914, 2 volumes) is a much weightier book than either Seton's or Innes's and, although the law of arms is carefully expounded, it has a more historical and antiquarian slant than its rivals. I use this word in a purely amiable context for all three books are valuable in their own right and for their own reasons. A far less legalistic work than any of those so far mentioned is *Heraldry in Relation to Scottish History and Art* (1899) by Sir J. Balfour Paul, Lyon King of Arms. This book nicely complements the others and is well worth having.

The most compendious work on early Scottish armory is Alexander Nisbet's *System of Heraldry* (1816 edition; 2 volumes). This is a sort of Scottish

Guillim (see page 302) but later writers have cautioned readers to treat some of the statements expressed with circumspection, while readily admitting that, in the words of Sir Thomas Innes, Nisbet is "a positive mine of information" and "indispensable to the serious student." Another early work to be treated with equal care but which contains much of value is *Science of Herauldrie* (1680) by Sir George Mackenzie of Rosehaugh.

SPECIAL SUBJECTS

There are so many facets to heraldry that this section of the bibliography could go on for ever. I have had, therefore, to be both selective and brief. The books I have detailed I believe to be either the only or the best authorities on their subjects.

FLAGS. *Heraldric Standards and Other Ensigns* (1959) by Lt.-Col. R. Gayre of Gayre and Nigg. This is a good guide to armorial, as distinct from national, flags. These latter are comprehensively covered by Captain E. M. C. Barra-clough, R.N. in his latest (1978) edition of *Flags of the World*. An excellent "coffee-table" book, but in using this expression I in no way denigrate the value of the work, *Flags through the Ages and Across the World* (1975), has added a new dimension to the study of flags, or vexillology as it is now called. It is by Dr. Whitney Smith, Executive Director of the Flag Research Centre, Winchester, Massachusetts. This book is a companion volume to Dr. O. Neubecker's book noted above.

CORPORATE HERALDRY. *Civic and Corporate Heraldry* (1971) by G. Briggs. This details all corporate arms in England and Northern Ireland and is fully illustrated. It supersedes to a great extent *The Book of Public Arms* (1915, 2nd edition) by A. C. Fox-Davies although this book still has a value as it contains Scottish and a number of European corporate coats and contains various editorial notes of interest. Another book which is partially superseded by Briggs's is *Civic Heraldry of England and Wales* (1953, revised edition) by C. W. Scott-Giles, although this too is still worth having as Scott-Giles gives the rationale behind many of the coats. Also he blazons them in a simplified manner, which some will find helpful, and includes details of devices used by municipal bodies, which are either unheraldic or not officially recorded.

The Armorial Bearings of the Guilds of London (1960) by John Bromley is the last word in the arms of the extant guilds. Each coat and its component parts are examined in the greatest detail and there is a coloured illustration by Heather Child of the complete achievement of each company. There are also photographs of many patents and innumerable line drawings. This is a truly splendid, scholarly and definitive work.

ECCLESIASTICAL HERALDRY. The classic works on this subject are *A Treatise on Ecclesiastical Heraldry* (1849) by John Woodward and *The Blazon of Episcopacy* (1897, 2nd edition) by W. K. P. Bedford. The former book is a fairly lengthy treatise on the subject and although valuable is often uncritical. Bedford lists the arms, under the various sees, of every bishop of every diocese and quotes his sources; his book also contains a useful ordinary. The subject of the heraldry of the Popes is admirably covered by D. L. Galbreath's comprehensive study *Papal Heraldry* (revised 1972 by Geoffrey Briggs).

ARMS OF WOMEN. There is only one book on this topic *The Bearing of Coat-Armour by Ladies* (1923) by Charles A. H. Franklin, so it is fortunate that, although rather out of date, this work is both authoritative and definitive.

BADGES. *Heraldic Badges* (1907) by A. C. Fox-Davies is an alphabet of medieval badges. Unfortunately its value lies principally in its being the only book solely devoted to badges. There is some good material on royal badges in *Royal Beasts* (1956) by H. S. London and many badges and standards are illustrated in *Banners, Standards and Badges from a Tudor Manuscript* (1904). This manuscript was a copy in line of College of Arms manuscript I 2, made by Thomas Willement between 1829 and 1831 and was reproduced in the De Walden Library series, with an introduction by Lord Howard de Walden. The granting of badges was introduced at the time that Fox-Davies wrote his book but there is still no list of the many badges granted since that time.

MEDIEVAL HERALDRY. Various authors over the past hundred years have made sorties into the rather neglected study of early armory. Round, Barron, St. John Hope and London all published books or articles on special aspects of pre-Tudor heraldry. As the principal evidences for the original development of arms are seals and rolls of arms, what was really needed was a catalogue of seals (Birch's catalogue of seals in the British Museum only scratches the surface) and a catalogue of medieval rolls. The latter need was ably supplied by Sir Anthony Wagner in the first volume of *Aspilogia* (*Being Materials of Heraldry*) entitled *A Catalogue of Mediaeval Rolls of Arms* (1950). This is a very full, detailed and scholarly catalogue of all known rolls and books of arms from the dawn of heraldry until 1500. The second volume *Rolls of Arms Henry III* (1967) contains detailed analyses of the Matthew Paris Shields *circa* 1244–59 by T. D. Tremlett, and of Glover's Roll *circa* 1258 and Walford's Roll *circa* 1273 by H. S. London. It also includes additions and corrections by Sir Anthony Wagner to *Aspilogia I*. Heraldic terminology in the 12th and 13th centuries has been dealt with most expertly by Prof. G. Brault in *Early Blazon* (1972). This book not only contains a glossary of terms used in blazon but also sixteen valuable introductory chapters. *History and Heraldry 1254–1310* (1965) by N. Denholm-Young studies another aspect of early heraldry: the historical and sociological value of those rolls of arms made before 1310. The book is far more concerned with history and heralds than with actual arms but it is a critical and interesting work of scholarship on a neglected aspect of heraldry.

Beryl Platts has flown an interesting kite in *Origins of Heraldry* (1980) in which she claims to trace connection between early Norman arms and devices previously used on the continent. Any armorist interested in this naissant period of heraldry will need to consider Mrs. Platt's arguments.

PICTURE BOOKS

The history, grammar and law of heraldry are all very well but what attracts most people is the colour of heraldry. So here are a few books whose greatest, but not sole appeal lies in their splendid illustrations.

The Stall Plates of the Knights of the Order of the Garter 1348–1485 (1904) by W. H. St. John Hope is a rare, vastly expensive but quite wonderful book, containing 91 full-sized colour facsimilies of the arms of the early Garter Knights. The Catalogue of the *Heralds' Commemorative Exhibition 1484–1934* (1934) contains 55 plates, several of which are in colour. Once rare, this book was reprinted in 1970 and consequently is available at a fairly modest price. An enlarged and far more profusely illustrated version of Fox-Davies's *Complete Guide to Heraldry* is his *Art of Heraldry* (1904). If a copy of this book ever comes on the second-hand market it fetches a vastly inflated price but it is a very magnificent tome. Although not strictly an heraldic work, H. Trivick's *The Craft and Design of Monumental Brasses* (1969) is beautifully illustrated, a great many of the brasses being armorial.

The Great Tournament Roll of Westminster (1968, 2 volumes), with an introduction (occupying one volume) by Sydney Anglo, contains a collotype reproduction of the complete roll, all 59½ feet of it. Although this is a magnificent and magnificently expensive book it is sad that not all the roll has been reproduced in colour. In contradistinction, *Lines of Succession* by Jiří Louda and Michael Maclagan, Richmond Herald, is remarkably reasonably priced. It gives the arms (in colour) and descents of the royal families of Europe, containing 150 genealogical tables bedight with arms. There are also monochrome illustrations and maps which help the reader find his way through the dynastic maze of European royalty.

GLOSSARY AND INDEX

Abaissé, Abased—lowered.

Abatement—a difference for illegitimacy, 123.

Abbot, insignia, 228.

Abbots Nullius Dioceseos, insignia of, 228

Abeyance—the state of a peerage when it is vested in two or more coheirs, both or all of whom have precisely the same claim. When there are several equal claimants, e.g. descendants of the daughters and co-heiresses of a deceased peer, none can maintain a claim against the others, and the peerage remains abeyant, and is not held by any of them, until by the death of other claimants only one remains, and he has a right to claim the peerage.

Abisme, Abyss—the centre of the escutcheon ; applied to a minor charge occupying the middle point to indicate that it should be drawn small in relation to other charges (obsolete).

à bouche—said of a shield with a notch for the lance to rest in.

Abouté—placed or connected end to end.

Accessories—the heraldic accompaniments to a shield of arms, e.g. helm, crest, wreath, mantling, supporters, motto, badges, coronet, etc.

Accollé—side by side, especially of two shields so placed ; also entwined about the neck.

Accompagné, Accompanied by—alternative to "between" when denoting the position of a charge in relation to others.

Accosted—side by side.

Accrued—of trees when grown to maturity (rare).

Achievement, Achievement of arms—a complete display of armorial bearings, 13.

Acorné—having horns or attires.

Acorned—of an oaktree when bearing acorns, 85 ; "fructed" is more usual.

Addorsed, Adossé—back to back ; said of beasts, etc., and of wings so placed ; also Endorsed.

Administrators Apostolic, insignia of, 228.

Admiral, Lord High, 253, 277.

Admiralty flag, 89, fig. no. 436.

Adoption, differencing for, 124.

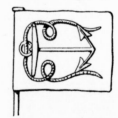

436. Admiralty Flag

Adorned—decorated.

Adumbrated—shadowed; of a charge shown only in outline, or *in umbra* (rare). Adumbration also means the shading used to throw charges into apparent relief.

Aeroplane, as a charge, 236.

Affronté, Affronted, Affrontant—of a beast or object so placed as to show its full front to the observer; sometimes wrongly used as a synonym for guardant (q.v.).

Agnus Dei—the Holy Lamb, emblem of St. John the Baptist, 73.

Aguilated, Aigulated, see Aquilated.

Aiguisé—pointed; the more usual term is urdé.

AIKENHEAD arms, 85.

AIKMAN arms, 85.

Ailettes—square appendages blazoned with the wearer's arms, and fastened upright on the shoulders, found in some early 14th-century effigies; see fig. no. 13.

Air Force Badges, 172, Plate XIV.

Aislé—winged.

ALABAMA flag, 249.

à la cuisse—at the thigh; indicating the point at which a leg is couped or erased, 77.

Aland, Alant—a mastiff with short ears.

Albany Herald—a Scottish Officer of Arms, 264.

Albert Medal, 202.

ALBERT, Prince-Consort, 216.

ALCOCK arms, 78.

ALDAM arms, 83.

Alerion, Allerion—an old term for an eagle, which, when so blazoned, was often depicted without legs or beak, 76.

ALEXANDRA of Kent, Princess, Hon. Mrs. A. Ogilvy, 222.

ALEXANDRA, Queen, 249.

ALICE, Princess, daughter of Queen Victoria, arms, 219.

Alisé—globular.

Allumé—of beasts' eyes when flecked with colour.

Allusive arms—arms allusive to the name, title, office or property of the bearer, 100.

ALLWRIGHT arms, 45.

Altar—shown as a square pedestal with a fire on it.

ALWELL arms, 45.

Ambulant—walking.

AMERICA, UNITED STATES OF, arms, 248.

Amethyst—purple (obsolete).

AMHERST, Earl, supporters, 181.

Amphiptère—a winged serpent.

Amphisien cockatrice—a basilisk (q.v.).

AMPLEFORTH COLLEGE arms, 231, Plate XXIII.

Anchor, 89.

Anchored, Anchory, Ancré, Ancred—a cross so termed has each limb ending in the flukes of an anchor (rare), 50.

Ancient, Anshient—a small flag on the stern of a ship, or on a tent.

ANDREW, Prince, 221.

Angels, 61, 177.

Angenne—a six-leaved flower, or sexfoil.

Angled, 31.

Angles—a pair of rods each bent in a right-angle, interlinked saltirewise, having rings at each end.

Animé—having fire issuing from the mouth and ears.

Ankh, 283, fig. no. 432*a*.

ANNE, Princess, 221.

ANNE, Queen, 194, 214.

ANNE of Denmark, Queen of James I, 249.

ANNESLEY, Earl, supporters, 181.

Annodated—embowed in the form of the letter S.

Annulet—a ring, 58, fig. no. 437; mark of the fifth son, 116.

Annuletté, Annulated, Annuly—ringed at the ends.

Ant, 81.

ANTARCTIC TERRITORY, British, arms, 246, fig. no. 407.

Antelope, 69 (the natural animal; to be distinguished from the Heraldic Antelope—q.v.).

437. Annulets interlaced

ANTHONY arms, St. Anthony's cross, 50.

Antique crown, 189.

Anvil, found as a charge, depicted normally.

Apaumé, Appaumé, Appalmed—of a hand or gauntlet when showing the palm.

APPLEGARTH arms, 85.

Apre, Apree—an heraldic beast drawn like an ox with a short tail (rare).

Aquilated—scattered with eagles' heads (rare).

Arbalest, Arblast—the cross-bow, 90.

ARBLASTER arms, 90.

Archbishop—marshalling of arms, 139, 145, 224, 227; mitre and staff, 224.

ARCHBOLD arms, Plate XI.

ARCHDEACON (L'ERCEDEKNE) arms, 104.

Arched, Archy—in the form of an arch; also Enarched; 31.

Argent—silver, usually represented as white; see Tinctures, 27; contraction: *arg.*

ARGYLL, Duke of, 94.

Arm (limb), 62.

Armed—of beasts, monsters and birds in reference to teeth, talons, horns and claws; when applied to men or human limbs it is synonymous with armoured; also applied to arrows, 89.

Armed at all points, Armed cap-à-pie—of a man completely encased in armour.

Armes parlantes—alternative for allusive arms (q.v.), 100.

Armiger—strictly, an esquire; also applied to any man possessing heraldic arms.

Armigerous—having a right to bear heraldic arms.

Arming buckle, 91.

Armorial bearings—definition, 13; origin, Chapter I; see Arms.

Armory—that branch of heraldry which deals with armorial insignia ; also a book recording the arms of persons, families, etc.

Armour, 61.

Arms (heraldic)—definition, 13 ; right to bear, 264; grants of, 265.

Arms of adoption—an armigerous person may by will adopt a stranger in blood to possess and continue his name and arms ; the arms so borne are arms of adoption, and require the authority of the Sovereign's Special Warrant.

Arms of alliance—arms denoting the union of families by marriage.

Arms of assumption—arms assumed in former times with the approbation of the Sovereign, e.g. when a man took the arms of a person he had captured or overthrown in battle.

Arms of community—borne by corporate and other bodies and communities, e.g. cities, universities, societies, etc.

Arms of concession—arms including part of the Sovereign's insignia, conceded as an augmentation of honour (see Augmentations).

Arms of descent, or paternal arms—those borne by hereditary right.

Arms of dominion—borne by Sovereigns, not as personal arms, but as those of the realms over which they rule, 222.

Arms of office—borne in addition to personal arms by holders of certain offices, e.g. Bishops, Kings of Arms, etc., 139, 145, 224.

Arms of pretension—borne to denote a claim or supposed right to a sovereignty or other rank without the actual possession of it.

Arms of succession—arms taken on inheritance to certain estates, manors or dignities to which insignia appertain.

ARMSTRONG arms and crest, 62.

Arraché—erased (q.v.).

Arrondie—rounded or curved.

Arrow, 89.

ARTHUR, Prince, son of Henry VII, 166.

ARUNDEL (family), arms, 78, 101, 122; badge, 168.

—, FitzAlan, Earls of, 158, 161, 178.

—, Herald Extraordinary, badge, 263.

Ascendant—issuing upwards, as a flower.

ASHCOMBE, Lord, supporters, 181.

ASHFIELD, Lord, supporters, 181.

ASHTON rebus, 101.

ASKEW badge, 168.

Aspectant—respecting (looking at) one another.

Aspersed—semé (q.v.).

Assis—sitting ; sejant is the more usual word.

Astral crown, 189.

At gaze—of a stag when standing with the head turned to face the observer, 69.

Attires—the antlers of a stag ; the beast is said to be attired, 70.

AUCTIONEERS AND ESTATE AGENTS' INSTITUTE arms, 234, Plate XXIV.

AUDLEY arms, 114.

Augmentations—honourable additions to heraldic insignia, Chapter XI.

Aulned—bearded, of barley.

AUSTRALIA, COMMONWEALTH OF, badge, 85, arms, 241, Plate XXVI, grants of arms in, 287.

Avellane cross—formed of four filberts (*aveline*) placed crosswise; they tend to be fined down into sceptre-like figures, 52.

Aversant—showing the back part.

Axe, 89.

Aylets, or sea-swallows, resemble Cornish choughs.

Ayrant—of birds when in their nests (rare).

Azure—blue (from Arabic *lazura*); see Tinctures, 27; contraction, *az.*, sometimes *b*.

BABYNGTON badge, 168.

BACON arms, 72.

Badger, also Brock, or Gray, 74.

Badges, Chapter XIV, 10, 146, Plate XII.

—, Royal, 163 ff., 209 ff.

Bagwyn—a monster consisting of the head and horns of an heraldic antelope and the body of a horse (rare).

Bailloné—gagged; said of an animal, especially a lion, when holding a staff in its mouth.

Balance—a pair of scales.

Bale-fire—a beacon.

BALLIOL COLLEGE, OXFORD, arms, 230.

BALTIMORE, Lord, 249.

Bande—the bend in French heraldry.

Banded—encircled with a band or ribbon.

Banner—a square or oblong armorial flag, 252, Plate XXVII.

Banneret, Knight Banneret, 252.

Bannockburn, Battle of, 92, 236.

Bar, 40.

Barb—applied to the leaf-like sepals appearing between the petals of the heraldic rose; also to the head of an arrow, 89.

Barbed—having barbs (q.v.); also bearded.

Barbel, 79.

BARBER-SURGEONS' COMPANY, 81.

Barded—furnished with bardings, i.e. the caparison of a horse, frequently charged with armorial insignia.

BARDOLF arms, 109, 133, Plate II.

BARHAM arms, 71.

BARLEY arms, 85.

Barnacles, or Breys—a curb used on a horse's nose when breaking the animal; fig. no. 438. The water-fowl named barnacle is also found in heraldry.

438. Barnacles

439. Barry-pily

440. EARL BEATTY

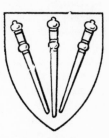

441. BOURDON

442. Chapeau

Crane (the bird), 77.

CRANSTON arms, 78.

Crenellated, Crenellé—embattled; the apertures are the cren-
elles or embrasures, and the pieces of wall which rise
between them are merlons.

Crescent, 83, 93; mark distinctive of the second son, 116.

Cresset—a fire basket.

Crest-coronet, 155; fig. no. 444.

Crested—combed as of a cock.

Crests, Chapter XIII, 146.

443. SAXONY

Crests, Royal, 155, 161, 209 ff.

Crest-wreath, 155.

CREVEQUER arms, 48.

Cricket, 81.

Crined—of hair or mane, 62, 72.

CROMWELL, OLIVER, arms, 215.

Cronel—the crown-shaped head of a tournament spear.

444. Crest-coronet

Crosier, 93, 223 *et seq.*

Cross, Chapter VI.

Cross crosslet, 51.

Cross-bow, 90.

Crow, 78.

Crowns—Chapter XVII, Plate XVI.

—, Royal, 183.

Crozier—the pastoral staff of a Bishop, 93, 223 *et seq.*

Crusades, influence on heraldry, 4.

Crusilé, Crusily—scattered with crosslets, 35, 52.

Crwth—sometimes applied to a violin; strictly, the ancient Welsh fiddle.

Cubit arm—a hand and arm couped below the elbow.

Cuff—the tincture must be stated if different from the sleeve.

Cuirass—the breast-plate.

Cuisse, see *à la cuisse.*

Cuisses—armour covering the thighs.

CULCHETH arms, 76.

CUNLIFFE, 74.

CUNNINGHAM, Earl of Glencairn, supporters, 179.

CUNYNGHAM, Bart., supporters, 181.

Cup, 94.

Cushion, 94.

Cyclas, 22.

Cypher, a monogram, e.g. the Royal Cypher ER ensigned with a crown.

D'ABERNOUN brass, 252.

DACRE, arms, 80; knot and badges, 170.

Dagger—distinguished in heraldry from a sword in having a shorter and more pointed blade.

DALZELL, Earl of Carnwath, arms, 61.

Damasked—diapered (q.v.).

D'AMORY arms, 133.

Dancette, Danse, Daunce—a fess dancetty. Dancetté, Dancetty, 30. Dancetty floretty, 31.

Danish axe, 90.

Danish Kings of the English, 206.

Dannebrog—a Danish order of chivalry. The cross paty argent fimbriated gules in the arms of Denmark is the Cross of the Dannebrog, 249.

Dantellé—dancetté.

D'ARCY arms, 110.

D'AUBIGNY arms, 136.

DAUBYGNÉ arms, 111, 157.

DAUPHIN of France, 79; his crown was set with fleurs-de-lis and arched with dolphins.

David, Shield of, 290, fig. no. 432b.

Deans of cathedrals, marshalling of arms, 139.

Debruised—of a charge overlaid by an ordinary, 68.

Dechaussé—dismembered, 68.

Decked—adorned.

Decollated, Decollé—having the head cut off at the neck.

Decorations, 202.

Decrescent—of a crescent when the horns are to the sinister, 83, 93.

Deer, 69.

Defamed—having no tail; also Infamed.

Degrees—steps, as of a Calvary cross, 49; a structure placed on steps is said to be degreed or degraded.

DEIRA, Kingdom of, attributed arms, 206.

DE LA RIVER arms, 9, Plate II.

— — VACHA arms, 115.

— — WARR badge, 168.

de l'un en l'autre—counterchanged, in medieval blazon, 35.

De-membered—dismembered (q.v.).

Demi—halved, e.g. demi-lion; the upper or front half is always understood, unless the contrary is stated; fig. no. 445.

DENMARK arms, 64, 249.

DERBY, Stanley Earl of, crest, 161.

D'ERNFORD arms, 75.

Design of arms, 289.

DESPENSER, LE, arms, 58, 138; motto, 175.

Developed—fully displayed, as a flag.

Devisals of Arms, 268.

DEVORGUILLA arms, 230.

Dexter, the right-hand side of the shield from the standpoint of the man behind it.

445. Demi-lion rampant

447. Fleam

Genet—a spotted animal resembling a martin.
Genouillières—armour protecting the knees.
GENTLE arms, 48.
Gentleman—in heraldry, the lowest rank of armigerous persons.
GEOFFREY OF ANJOU, 4, 163, 206.
George Cross, 202.
George, Lesser George—badges of the Order of the Garter, 194, Plate XVII.
GEORGE I, 196, 215.
GEORGE II, arms, 215, Plate V.
GEORGE III, 194, 215.
GEORGE IV, 215.
GEORGE V, 201, 279.
Gerattyng—powdering fields for difference.
GERVAYS arms, 90.
Gimball, or Gimmel ring, see Gemel ring.
Giraffe—termed camelopard (q.v.).
GIRTON COLLEGE, CAMBRIDGE, Plate XI.
GLANELY, 1ST LORD, 189.
GLENCAIRN, Earl of, supporters, 179.
Gliding, glissant—the movement of snakes.
Globe, Terrestrial, 95.
Glory, see Halo.
GLOUCESTER, City of, 236.
—, De Clare Earl of, 133, Plate XXVII.
—, Despencer Earl of, 138.
—, Duke of, 220.
—, Eleanor de Bohun, Duchess of, 137.
—, Thomas (Plantagenet), Duke of, 37, 166.
Glove, 95.
Goat, 73.
Gobony—alternative to compony (q.v.), 33.
GODFREY, Cardinal, arms, 226, Plate XXII.
Gold, see Or.
GOLDEAR arms, 52.
Golpe—a purple roundel (rare), 57.
Gonfanon—a flag suspended from a transverse bar attached to a staff, and commonly
    swallow-tailed at the fly.
GORDON arms, Plate III.
Gorge, see Gurges, 95.
Gorged—encircled round the neck or throat.
GORGES, DE, arms, 95.
Gorget—armour protecting the throat.
Goutte, Goutté, Gutté—a drop, scattered with drops, 35.
Gradient—walking slowly, as a tortoise.
Grafted—inserted and fixed in.

448. Hemp-bracke

449. Leopard's face
jessant-de-lis

Key, 96.

King of Arms, King of Heralds, 139, 145, 202, 229, 261; crown, 187. In addition to the Herald Kings, there are Kings of Arms associated with the Orders of the Bath, St. Michael and St. George, and the British Empire. Their duties are not armorial.

KING'S COLLEGE, CAMBRIDGE, arms, 230.

KINTORE, Earl of, 88, 126, 187.

KIRKPATRICK arms, 105.

Knight, Knighthood, Chapter XVIII, 146.

— Banneret, 252.

Knights Bachelor, 201 ; badge, Plate XX.

KNIGHTS OF ST. JOHN, 52, 191.

Knife, 96.

Knots, 169.

KYRIELL arms, 106.

KYRKEBY, DE, arms, 111.

Label, or Lambel, 57, 114, 118, 218 ff. ; mark of the eldest son, 116.

LACY—arms, 64, knot, 169.

Ladies, bearing of arms by, 147, Plate XI.

Lamb, 73 ; see also Agnus Dei.

LAMBERT, 73.

Lambrequin, 156.

Laminated—having scales.

LANCASTER, City, arms, 119.

—, Duchy of, arms, 119.

—, Dukes of, 23, 178.

—, Earls of, 119, 161, 277.

—, House of, 165.

—, John of Gaunt, Duke of, 119, 120, 122, 138, 166.

Lancaster Herald—an English Officer of Arms, 263.

LANE augmentation, 126, Plate VIII ; crest, 187.

LANGLEY, Edmund, Duke of York, 94, 120.

LANGTON rebus, 101.

Language of heraldry, Chapter II.

Langued—used when referring to the tongue of a creature, 67, 70.

Larmes, Goutté de—sprinkled with blue drops, 36.

Latin cross, 49.

Latticed, see Treille.

LAVEALE arms, 73.

Leaves, 85.

LEEDS (City) arms, 40, 73, 236.

— UNIVERSITY, arms, 231.

LEESON arms, 84.

Leg as a charge, 62.

450. A cross
lozengy

451. Lozenges
in cross

Monogram, usually termed Cypher (q.v.).

Monsters, 81.

MONTAGU arms, 81, 115, 137, Plate II; crest, 161.

MONTEAGLE, motto, 174.

MONTFORT, Simon de, Earl of Leicester, 252.

MONTGOMERY Earls of Eglintoun, arms, 163.

MONTHERMER arms, 75, 115.

Moon, 83.

MOONEY arms, Plate IV.

Moorcock, 78.

Moor's head, 62.

Morion—a steel cap.

Morse—a clasp or band fastening a robe, often ornamented.

MORTIMER arms, 58, 109, 136; panache, 158.

— Earl of March, 165, 178.

Mort's head—a skull.

Mottoes, Chapter XV.

—, Royal, 212 ff.

Mound—the orb, emblem of sovereignty, consisting of a ball surmounted by a cross; it forms the highest ornament on the Royal Crown.

MOUNPYNZON arms, 78.

Mount—a hillock, usually in the base of the shield.

Mountain cat, 71.

Mounted—applied to a horse when carrying a rider.

MOUNTENEY, DE, arms, 105.

MOWBRAY badge, 169.

— Duke of Norfolk, 125, 160, 166.

MOYNE family, 160.

Mullet, see Molet.

MUNDEGUMBRI, seal, 163.

MUNSTER arms, 248.

—, Earl of, 123.

Muraillé—masoned.

Mural crown, 188, 236.

Murrey—purple red (mulberry colour); see Tinctures, 27.

Musimon—a hybrid of the ram and goat with four horns.

Mutilé—dismembered, 68.

Naiant, or Natant—swimming.

Naissant—applied to a living creature issuant from the middle of a fess or other ordinary, 68.

NASSAU arms, 213.

Naval badges, 171, Plate XIV; naval crown, 156, 188.

Navel point, 21.

Nebulé, Nebuly, 30.

Pierced—perforated and showing the field or some other tincture through the hole.

Pigg arms, 72.

Pigot arms, 101.

Pike (fish), 79.

Pile, 43.

Pillow, 94.

Pily, 43.

Pily-bendy—a field divided into a number of pile-shaped pieces bendwise, fig. no. 452.

Pinioned—having wings.

Pinson—a chaffinch, 78.

Pius IX, Pope, 229.

Planta genista, 85, 163.

Plantagenet, House of, 85, 207.

Plants as charges, 84.

Plate—a silver roundel, 57; platy, or platté, scattered with plates.

Plenitude—of the moon when full, 83.

Plume, 158.

Plumetty—a field of overlapping feathers (rare).

Plymouth, City of, 188.

Point of the shield, 21.

Pointed, Cross, 50.

Poitiers, Battle of, 126.

Poix, Goutté de—sprinkled with black drops (pitch), 36.

Pole crest, 161.

Pole-axe, 90.

Pommé, Cross—having each limb ending in a ball, 51.

Pomme, Pomeis—a green roundel, 57.

Pommel—the ball at the end of a sword hilt, fig. no. 453.

Popinjay—the parrot; when proper, depicted as green with red legs and beak, 78.

Port—the gateway to a castle.

Port of London Authority, 82.

Portate, Cross—a cross in bend, as though carried on a man's shoulder.

Portcullis—a defence for a gateway; Royal Badge of the Tudors, 97, 212, Plate XII.

— Pursuivant—an English Officer of Arms, 263.

Porter arms, 90.

Portsmouth, Duchess of, Plate XI.

Potent—a fur; see Tinctures, 27.

—, Cross, 51.

— rebated, Cross, 51.

Potenté, Potenty, 30.

452. Pily-bendy

453. Pommel

454. Scaling ladder

455. Cross urdy

Vambrace—armour for the forearm ; vambraced—applied to an arm in armour, 62.
Vamplate—a guard for the hand on the tilting-spear.
Varied fields, 33.
VAUX OF HARROWDEN, Rev. Lord, 229.
Venus—green (obsolete).
Verdé, or Verdoy—semé of leaves or plants.
VERE, DE, Earl of Oxford—arms, 36 ; augmentation, 125 ; badge, 165.
Verolles, Verules, Virolles—rings encircling hunting horns.
Vert—green ; see Tinctures, 27.
Verted, or Reverted—the same as flexed or reflexed.
Vervels, Varvels, 77.
VESEY arms, 50.
Vested—clothed.
Vicars—insignia, 228.
VICKERS LTD., badge 173.
Victoria Cross, 202.
VICTORIA, Queen, 197, 198, 216 ; crown, 185.
—, State of, 241.
VIRGIN ISLANDS, British, arms, 246.
Virolles, see Verolles.
Viscount, coronet, 187, Plate XVI ; see Mantle.
Visitations, Heralds', 11, 262.
Voided—of a charge with the middle removed, leaving little more than the outline ; cross voided, 48.
Voiders—flanches (rare).
Vol—two wings cojoined, tips upwards, 77.
Volant—flying, 75.
Vorant—devouring, 68.
Vulned, Vulning—wounded, wounding, so that the blood drips, 77.

WADSLEY, DE, arms, 105.
Wake knot, 169.
WAKEFIELD, City of, arms, 87.
WALDEGRAVE—arms, 8, 32 ; panache, 159.
WALES, Dragon badge of, 3, 81, 218, Plate XII.
— Herald Extraordinary, 263.
—, Princes of, 64, 166, 167, 218, 221, 258, Plates V and XV.
— — Edward, the Black Prince, 24, 77, 119, 121, 161, 165, 192.
—, Diana, Princess of, 222.
—, Royal Dynasties of, 218.
WALSH arms, Plate IV.
WAND, Dr. J. W., motto of, 224.
WARD (family) arms, 51.
WARENNE, DE, arms, 37, 111, 132, 137.

456. Yale